Understanding Your Child's Health

Susan K. Schulman, M.D.

Understanding Your Child's Health is adult informational reading material. It is intended as a guide for parents and other adults who help to raise children. The opinions expressed in this publication are one pediatrician's point of view. Always consult your child's physician in matters relating to child health.

Copyright © 2009 Hamodia Treasures

ISBN 13 978-0-9864394-2-1

Published by Hamodia Treasures
207 Foster Avenue, Brooklyn, NY 11230

Graphics and layout Mr. Benzion Roth
Cover design Ms. Etana Rachel Holowinko

Distributed by Israel Book Shop
501 Prospect Street #97, Lakewood, New Jersey 08701
Telephone 732-901-3009 Fax 732-901-4012
www.israelbookshoppublications.com
Printed in Canada

Abraham J. Twerski, M.D.
Founder and Medical Director Emeritus

W hile there are indeed many books on child care, *Understanding Your Child's Health,* by Dr. Susan Schulman, is an important addition. It is a book that should be read not only by new mothers and fathers, but by all parents.

The chapters on the proper way to nourish children are very useful. There is much confusion about what really is proper nutrition. Given the alarming increase in childhood obesity, it is important to have the most reliable information on this topic. Furthermore, there can be serious issues confronting weight control with the weekly Shabbos foods and the customary foods on Yamim Tovim, especially Pesach. Nowhere else can we find proper guidelines for these occasions.

In today's world, there is much more that parents must know about aspects of child health and safety that were not dealt with in the past. There have also been many changes in pediatrics regarding behavior and emotional problems. Many serious issues that were simply ignored in the past are now recognized. This comprehensive book deals with many of these topics.

Of course, Dr. Schulman also provides "state of the art" information about many childhood conditions, such as bedwetting, ear problems, allergies, and infant colic.

Bringing a child into this difficult world is an awesome responsibility. Parents must provide their children with the means to develop healthy bodies and healthy personalities. This is a formidable challenge, and parents should not rely on their own ideas of what constitutes optimum parenting. Dr. Schulman's book is an invaluable guide for today's parents.

To my Bobby,

You are my partner in:
- marriage
- raising a wonderful family
- grandparenting
- walking, hiking, biking, skiing, skating, and tennis.
- giving medical care to our community
- learning — Torah and medicine

May Hashem grant us many more vigorous years
of this multifaceted life partnership.

■ ■ ■

ACKNOWLEDGEMENTS

I want to thank the staff of *Hamodia, Binah Magazine* and Hamodia Treasures for making this publication possible. The cooperation, dedication and professionalism of this wonderful organization is truly remarkable. I am especially grateful to Mrs. Mimi Rosenberg and Mrs. Rivky Posner — production managers; Mrs. Rachel Hubner and Mrs. Ellen Appelbaum — editors; and Mr. Benzion Roth — graphic designer, and Ms. Raizel Shurpin, layout, who have all worked hard to see it to completion.

I also want to thank Etana Holowinko for her incredibly creative and professional cover design. She has truly devoted herself and her prodigious talent to this time-consuming project.

I would like to make special mention of Audrey Rosner, my Pediatric Nurse Practitioner. She has enhanced my own understanding as a pediatrician every day for over thirty years. Her patience, her wisdom and her expertise as a clinician are all unsurpassed in the world of pediatrics. The patients and I are truly fortunate to have her with us.

TABLE OF CONTENTS

TABLE OF CONTENTS

Author's Introduction to this revised and expanded edition

This new edition of Understanding Your Child's Health is much more complete than the original. It has revisions and updates of the original topics, and many new topics added. I truly hope that it will be on the shelf of every Jewish household to be used as a reference when issues arise with the health of children.

It has always been my purpose to educate parents and caregivers. With the publication of this edition I am also aiming to educate the entire community.

I sincerely hope that the chapter on Immunizations will reassure the community that giving vaccines is safe and the only reasonable choice. I have been particularly alarmed to hear that some of the parents are refusing all vaccines. This practice will immediately leave many infants unprotected from severe childhood bacterial meningitis caused by HIB and bacterial pneumonias caused by Pneumococcus which were common in the early days of my practice.

These germs are always around since they live in everyone's throats. The vaccine keeps the germs from invading. Not giving these vaccines will cause new and extremely devastating cases of these dreaded and totally preventable diseases, with permanent brain damage, deafness, and even death as the result.

Some of the new chapters are written to increase awareness of conditions that are worthy of the community's support and understanding. For example:

The chapter on Autism will give everyone a better understanding of how these children see the world.

The chapter on Prematurity will help the community acknowledge the challenges and problems faced by families of these little ones.

Continued

The chapter about Seizures and Seizure disorders will demystify these events and reduce the unfair prejudice which is inflicted on so many normal and healthy seizure patients.

The chapters on Breath Holding and Fainting, and the three chapters on Injuries will give everyone a better understanding of what is really an emergency. The discussion of MRSA will alert the whole community of the nature of this new and potentially serious infection.

The various new chapters on Coughs, Headaches, Lice, etc. will round out the information base needed by everyone who deals with children.

Finally, as in my first edition, I have devoted a significant portion of this book to educate the whole community about what we must do to prevent childhood obesity.

This critical job has become a true community health priority, since it is now known that obesity is actually a serious disease with multiple complications. All of the chapters on exercise and nutrition are geared to make the whole community more aware of the right choices we must make to enable our children to grow up without the risk of this vexing problem.

It is time we realize that the subtle changes that have occurred in the diet (packaged junk foods, processed foods, etc) and activity habits (none at all for many kids!) in the last 50 years, has created an epidemic of obesity.

The solution to this problem is the responsibility of the entire community, including the educators and community leaders. The changes in such things as school diets, snack policies, and exercise during the school day must be implemented by the whole community.

I sincerely hope the education I have provided will start many of my readers on a quest to improve the health habits of their families, students and neighbors.

Dr. Susan Schulman

The First Two Years

CHAPTER 1

Advice to New Mothers and Fathers

Key Points

- New mothers need help and rest.
- Short visits are best. The new mommy is tired.
- New babies can be acclimated to night and day.
- Only the first few weeks are this hard!

The birth of a new baby is a time of special joy for the new parents. It is also one of the most exhausting times in their lives.

Whether the new baby is a first or one of many, the first two weeks are particularly difficult. The words "sleep deprivation" take on new meaning after the birth of a baby. Here is a list of important things that will help you through this exhausting time.

Advice to the new mother – special considerations

- As the time for delivery gets closer, try to get as much sleep as possible. You will feel much better if you do not have a sleep deficit before the baby arrives. Most women lose at least one night's sleep the day of the birth. Afterwards, there will be very few uninterrupted nights. Try to get at least 8 hours a night in the last month before the birth.

- When you pack for the hospital take along earplugs (soft foam ones), your most comfortable pillow, and an eye mask. Hospital environments are not very conducive to sleep.

- If you are planning to nurse for the first time, have a lactation specialist check you in the beginning of your ninth month. If there are problems identified they can be easily corrected at that time.

■ Inform the family that you only want the closest relatives to come to the hospital after you give birth. Most important: these early visits should be very brief. You have only two or three days in the hospital. It is not a reasonable time to be entertaining anyone.

■ Do not take a cell phone to the hospital and do not connect your bedside phone. After you give birth, people tend to forget that you went through a very physically-tiring experience and that you might not be particularly comfortable. Make lists of important phone numbers before your baby is born. Give the lists to your helpful relatives who will make phone calls for you.

■ Have your husband bring his phone so that you can both call the most important people immediately after the birth.

■ The arrangements for the *shalom zachor, vacht nacht, bris,* or *kiddush* should not be the mother's responsibilities. Designate the people who will do this before you go to the hospital. If it is your family custom for the new mother to go to these events, just make a short appearance. You are not required to look your best, and you should not feel that you are the hostess.

■ During the first two weeks, allow yourself to recover and gather strength. Accept all the household help that is offered to you. Do not jump right in and assume your usual responsibilities. This is the right time to be pampered. When the baby is a little older, no one will expect you to need help with preparing meals and shopping and other tasks.

■ If this is your first baby, make sure that both you and your husband get used to handling the baby. Have someone show you how to bathe, swaddle, burp, hold, feed, and dress him, and then do these things yourselves, at least some of the time. It is a bit awkward at first, but you both can do it as well as anybody. It is fun!

■ If you are nursing, skipping feedings after the milk comes in might cause engorgement. If you have nighttime help, just feed the baby and let the helper settle him.

■ Take care of yourself for the first two weeks. Take naps. Try to sleep whenever possible. Eat healthy, nourishing meals and snacks. Drink extra fluids, take your vitamins, and go for gradually-increasing walks every day to build up strength. Do not try to diet right away. Do not worry about your weight until at least two months after the birth. Nobody looks slim at this time.

The new baby – the first two weeks

■ In the hospital the baby will wear hospital clothing. When preparing to leave the hospital, bring baby clothes that are right for the season. Use common sense.

■ Do not use thick, plush baby blankets even in the car seat or carriage. They are not safe at all. They are a real smothering hazard. In cold weather, use a snowsuit or bunting that can be zipped so the baby's face will not be hidden by it.

▪ Hospitals do not provide pacifiers. It is acceptable to bring a newborn pacifier to use in the hospital between feedings. It has been shown recently that babies seem to have a lower risk for "crib death" if they are pacifier users. Even brief periods of sucking seem to help.

▪ You will need a "swaddle" blanket. This can be a large, thin, stretchy receiving blanket that can be wrapped around the infant, or − a new invention − a blanket with Velcro tabs that is designed to do the job more easily. It has been shown that the age-old practice of swaddling babies actually makes them feel good and allows them to sleep more peacefully.

▪ You will need a rear-facing infant car seat to take the baby home.

▪ If you are nursing your baby, do not go home without a pump. When the milk first comes in you will have an oversupply. Pumping before and after feedings may be required to keep you comfortable and make the milk more accessible to the infant.

▪ Portable baby swings and bouncy seats that vibrate, have visual stimulation, and make soothing noises can be very useful in the first few weeks of life. They stimulate relaxing reflexes in the infant.

▪ Get the baby used to the difference between night and day. During the day, keep him in a bright sunny room and talk to him and play with him after a feeding. Wrap him loosely when he sleeps. Do not try to make the house quiet. At night, keep the room dark and quiet. Do not stimulate him too much after the feeding. Wrap him in a secure swaddle blanket when he goes to sleep. This will make the nighttime sleep deeper. It is not safe to fall asleep in bed or on a couch with your baby. Feed the baby sitting up in a glider chair or rocking chair or a pillow support in bed.

▪ Always put the baby in a crib, bassinet, infant seat or bouncy seat or swing for sleeping. Do not let the baby sleep with you in the bed. It is not safe! (See Chapter 3, The Facts About Infant Sleep Safety)

The most important thing to remember is that the newborn period passes very quickly, as do all the parties and excitement. (Remember the wedding?) Soon the relative calm of babyhood sets in. Things really do get easier with time. The joy and *simchah* of becoming parents evolves into the special satisfaction and joy of raising your child.

May we all enjoy much *nachas* from your special bundle of *simchah*!

▪ ▪ ▪

CHAPTER 2

When a Baby Is Born Too Soon
Understanding the Issues of Prematurity

Key Points

- The more premature the infant is, the higher the risk of complications.

- Most premature infants go on to lead healthy lives.

- Parents of preemies are going through a stressful time, and need support and help from family and friends.

The birth of a premature infant can be characterized by mixed emotions. There is joy at the beginning of a new life, and there is fear that the fragile infant will encounter major hurdles in his journey to become mature and well enough to go home. Here is an overview of prematurity and the challenges encountered during this difficult time.

Why too early?

Full-term gestation is defined as 38 to 42 weeks after the last menses. Although most babies are born during that time frame, occasionally the birth comes sooner. The most common cause for prematurity is infection in the mother. Even minor urinary tract infections or infections of the genital tract can set off premature labor. Sometimes there are factors in the mother such as imperfections in the cervix or placenta which lead to premature birth. Many times the cause is not known. There are some times when the obstetrician decides to deliver the baby early when the unborn infant is in danger and in need of medical treatment.

The NICU — Neonatal Intensive Care Unit

Premature infants and infants who have any problems soon after birth are admitted to the NICU. This specialized unit is run by pediatric specialists known as Neonatologists. In the NICU a team of specially-trained nurses care for the fragile infants. In most NICUs there is one nurse for 2 or 3 infants. The infants are attached to monitors and the nurses check on them frequently to make sure they are stable.

As the infants grow and improve, they advance from intravenous feeds to tube feeds and on to nipple feeds given carefully by the NICU nurses, until breastfeeding can be established and/or the parents are able to feed their own babies .Parents are encouraged to spend time with their infants even when they are very sick or immature. They are even asked to hold the infants very close against their skin in a special program called "kangaroo" care. This contact helps the preemie to develop neurologically and emotionally.

Prematurity — a matter of weeks

In general, the closer the baby is to term, the fewer the complications, and, conversely, the more immature an infant is, the more complications can be anticipated. The survival rate for infants born at 23 weeks' gestation is much lower than in those born at 35 weeks. Each week of maturation gives the baby a better chance. While it is generally true that bigger babies do better, the real deciding factor is the number of weeks of development.

Infants who are born under 1000 grams (2.2 pounds) are known as micropreemies. Although many micropreemies grow up healthy and neurologically intact, these tiny babies have a greater risk for all complications than larger infants.

Neurological complications of prematurity

Prematurity can cause immediate and long-term problems with the brain and nervous system.

One major problem is *Intraventricular hemorrhage* (bleeding in the brain). These bleeds can be small or large. The large hemorrhages often result in neurological problems such as cerebral palsy, stroke, seizures, and developmental disabilities. The smaller hemorrhages cause little or no damage.

Vision and hearing impairments can also occur in a small percentage of preemies.

The incidence of neurologic disabilities is increased in small preemies, but many of the tiniest micropreemies develop normally without disabilities. In some children, there are learning disabilities such as processing disorders, reading problems, or math problems which only become evident when the child is school aged. Any ex-preemie who is struggling in school should be evaluated for learning disabilities.

Eyes

There is a particular eye problem that can occur in preemies known as *retinopathy of prematurity (ROP)*. This condition can range from mild to severe. It usually occurs in infants born weighing 1500 grams (3 pound 5 ounces) or less. The infants are checked by an ophthalmologist starting at 4 to 5 weeks after birth and then periodically until the eyes have fully matured to full-term condition. If serious ROP is noted, it can be treated if necessary by laser surgery. ROP can lead to visual impairment or even blindness if not treated in a timely fashion.

Skin

The skin of a 23-week premie is extremely thin. The immature infant cannot stay warm without special care to the skin and a special warmed environment such as an overhead radiant heat open bed or closed incubator, which maintains a constant temperature for the infant. Extreme care must be taken when moving and handling a tiny preemie to prevent injury to the paper-thin skin.

Breathing problems

If there is warning that a baby might be born prematurely, the mother can be given injections for a day or two before the birth that help the baby's lungs mature in time for the birth. Right after the birth the baby is observed for distressed breathing. If the infant is having trouble breathing, a tube is placed in the trachea (windpipe) and the tube is attached to a respirator. Sometimes a nasal cannula is placed in the nose and attached to a machine known as a CPAP. These techniques assist the baby with breathing. The machines deliver oxygen and air under pressure until the infant is able to breathe on its own. One sign of improvement in the breathing problem is when the baby requires less and less oxygen added to the air in the machine.

When the baby continues to improve, the machines can be removed and the oxygen can be delivered nasally without high pressure. Eventually they can breathe room air without assistance.

RDS

Many premature infants have *respiratory distress syndrome (RDS)* – formerly called hyaline membrane disease — which is related to immaturity of the lungs and the lack of a substance called *surfactant.* This deficiency can be helped with the administration of an artificial *surfactant* through the breathing tube. RDS usually takes several days to resolve. Preemies are also prone to many other breathing problems like air leaks, collapsed lungs and, pneumonias. These problems can be life-threatening, but they are usually manageable in a NICU setting.

Feedings

When a small preemie is first born, he is usually not ready to be fed by mouth or by tube. At this time feeds are given through intravenous lines. The feedings, known as TPN, contain sugar, water, fats and proteins. When the baby is ready for small amounts of liquid food, the best milk is breast milk which is fed through a feeding tube. The milk can be fortified by adding a special packet of vitamins and calories to it.

As the baby gets more mature, bottle and breast feedings can be started. The baby usually must be able to eat on his own and gain weight properly before he is allowed to go home.

Infections

Premature infants have an immature immune system, which makes them prone to infections. Many of these infections can be life-threatening, so a full evaluation is needed every time the baby seems ill. This includes a lumbar puncture (spinal tap), urine and blood cultures and sometimes x-rays. These tests are not dangerous for the baby. Fortunately, most infections are treatable with antibiotics.

Necrotizing enterocolitis (NEC)

NEC is a very dangerous infection of the wall of the bowel in a premature or sick infant. NEC sometimes requires surgery to remove the injured segment of the intestine. It has been shown that infants who receive even small amounts of breast milk have a lower incidence of this devastating complication. For this reason the mothers are encouraged to pump their milk and bring it to the NICU in the early days and weeks after the birth of a preemie.

Apneas and bradycardias

Apnea is a long pause in the baby's breathing which can lead to *bradycardias.* *Bradycardia* is a slowing of the heartbeat. These episodes are due to the immaturity of the premature infant's brain, which sometimes "forgets" to trigger a breath. This problem goes away with time, but some infants require stimulant medications (like caffeine). Persistent apneas with bradycardias are often the cause for delay in the time of discharge. Apnea monitors are sometimes used at home to alert the parents of an episode so they can stimulate the infant to start to breathe. These monitors are very rarely used. Most NICUs do not let the baby go home until the problem resolves itself.

Jaundice (yellow color of the skin due to high bilirubin levels)

Most preemies become jaundiced (yellow) in the first week of life due to immaturity of their livers. Preemies are more susceptible to brain injury from the high bilirubin levels than full-term babies. This is why treatment is so important. Jaundice is treated by placing the baby under a phototherapy lamp. A mask is put on the baby's eyes to protect them from the light. Phototherapy usually continues for about 2 to 3 days.

Time of discharge

The preemie usually is ready to go home at about 36 to 37 weeks' gestation, or about 3 weeks before the due date. If there have been serious complications, the discharge might be delayed until the problems are resolved.

Final thought

When a small preemie is born, the parents need the love and support of family and friends. In the first few days, every hour can be critical. Even when the infant seems stable there is no way to know if things will continue to go well. The rollercoaster ride takes the parents up and down, day by day, until the day of discharge. Everyone should encourage the parents and pray for the wellbeing of the delicate little bundle of potential. We are truly fortunate to live in this day and age, when even tiny preemies have a good chance for normal survival.

CHAPTER 3

Understanding Breastfeeding

Everyone knows that the natural way to nourish an infant is to breastfeed. The English word *nursing* is from the same source as *nourishing*. It seems like it should be as natural as pregnancy, labor and delivery. The problem is, breastfeeding doesn't always work out well for the mother and the baby. There are many factors involved that can influence the success or failure of nursing. Here is an overview of the subject.

Key Points

- Have a lactation consultant check for potential problems before the birth.
- Breast-feeding can be difficult at first.
- Most women find it very rewarding.
- Support is critical to success.
- If it doesn't work out, formula works fine.

BENEFITS OF BREASTFEEDING

Advantages to the mother

The greatest advantage to the mother is the special pleasure of watching the baby grow and thrive on her milk. Once the mother and baby are adjusted to each other, nursing is fun. For many mothers, breastfeeding can be a very special bonding experience.

From the first few minutes of the baby's life, the mother gets special benefits from nursing. As she nurses the new infant, the uterine muscles contract vigorously from oxitocin that is released in response to the suckling. This helps shrink the uterine muscles to their proper size.

As they settle in to their life together, the mother enjoys quiet time with her baby as they bond with each other. Many women lose weight rapidly after the pregnancy from the metabolic changes caused by nursing. Nursing is convenient; the milk is always ready, with no bottles to wash after feedings. Since nursing mothers generally do not become pregnant when nursing it gives their bodies a chance to recover before their next birth.

Advantages to the baby

Colostrum, the transparent first milk produced, provides the baby with high levels of protection from many types of infection. As the colostrum changes to real milk, the level of protection decreases, but there is still a constant supply of substances and cells that protect the baby. The bonding experience, with skin-to-skin contact, has been shown to be beneficial to the baby's overall health.

It has been claimed that breastfeeding leads to higher intelligence, lower chances of allergy, lower chances of obesity, and fewer ear infections. We know it is very good for most, but not all, babies.

Unfortunately, some babies who breastfeed still get allergies, ear infections, and are sometimes obese in childhood. Regardless of all of these issues, breast milk is still the most perfect, naturally-designed, ideal food for a young baby.

PROBLEMS WITH BREASTFEEDING

Maternal issues

Some mothers have inverted nipples, which make it difficult for the baby to latch on. For first-time mothers, it is a good idea to have a lactation consultant check the nipples in the beginning of the ninth month so problems such as inverted nipples can be corrected before the birth. If the inverted nipples are not corrected before the birth, a lactation consultant should be brought in to help get the baby on to the nipple.

Sore nipples

Even when the baby is sucking well, many mothers experience sore nipples in the first few weeks of nursing. The key to avoiding this problem is to make sure that the infant is latched on to the nipple with a deep grasp, including the top and the bottom of the nipple and most of the aureola. If there is nipple pain it should only be during the first few sucks. If it continues to hurt, the nipple should be pushed deeper into the infant's mouth. If the pain is gone but it returns as the feeding progresses, the nipple should again be pushed in, since the baby is probably sliding off as he relaxes. Lanolin creams and breast shells, which air the nipple after feedings, are useful.

If the nipples have accommodated to the nursing and at a later time they become sore, it is almost certain that they are infected with yeast. Additionally, it is quite possible that the baby has thrush, a yeast infection in the mouth. If this happens, both the mother and the baby should be treated.

Engorgement

When the milk first comes in, on day 2 or 3 in young mothers, the breasts can get very swollen and painful. This condition, known as engorgement, requires careful management to prevent infection.

Most people know that the more the baby nurses, the more milk is produced. This does not apply to the problem of engorgement! When the milk first "comes in" there is often much more than the baby can consume. Most women produce at least enough for twins. The production stays on overdrive for about a week, no matter how much the baby nurses. There is also a very uncomfortable swelling of the breasts, which can block the milk flow and make the breasts painful and hard. Engorgement can sometimes flatten the nipple, making it difficult for the baby to latch on. This causes sore nipples and a frustrated infant.

Since the milk keeps coming in even if the breasts are not emptied, there is no advantage to trying to limit the emptying. Drainage is the most important task.

The best way to avoid the problem is to make sure the breasts are soft before and after each feeding. If they are too full to nurse, a pump should be used to drain out enough to make the latch-on easier. At the end of the feeding, if the breasts are still full, the pump should be used to drain out whatever is still there. The milk that is pumped out can be used for at least 6 months if it is stored in the back of the freezer in small baggies.

The amount of milk that can be stored from pumping during these few days is truly astounding. After the milk production adjusts itself to the needs of the baby the pumping is much less productive.

Hot showers and hot compresses can help soften the breasts to promote milk flow. It has also been shown in real studies that green cabbage leaves can be used to reduce the swelling. The leaves should be wrapped around the breasts.

Engorgement only lasts for a few days. When it subsides, the nursing becomes more comfortable.

Mastitis

When milk does not flow properly, a tender cord-like area in the breast forms. This blocked duct can develop into an infection, causing pain and fever. Whenever a painful area develops, every effort should be made to get the area to drain by changing the baby's feeding position, using hot compresses and pumping. If the condition worsens and the mother feels ill, antibiotics are usually necessary.

The mother's diet

Mothers who are nursing need a good, well-balanced diet that has adequate fat content. Low-fat maternal diets cause the milk to be less nutritious. The diet should include calcium-rich foods like milk or soy products. Nursing mothers should stay on the prenatal vitamins they were taking during pregnancy. If they are anemic, the mothers should continue taking iron.

If the baby is colicky, certain foods should be eliminated. These are: all juices, broccoli, cauliflower, cabbage, onion, and green pepper. It is occasionally necessary to eliminate milk from the mother's diet. When this happens, she should take calcium supplements.

All nursing mothers need adequate hydration to maintain good milk supply. In hot weather, a lot of water is needed just to keep the mother from losing her milk.

Infant issues

Premature infants often have to wait until they reach 36-week gestational age to have the energy and coordination to nurse. Many do well on pumped milk until that time. Some infants are born with poor muscle tone or other neuromuscular problems, which can make nursing difficult. Breast milk can be fed to the baby in tube feeding or a bottle.

Severe tongue-tie can interfere with nursing. This can be easily corrected surgically.

Breastfeeding can often protect against food allergies, but in some families it actually causes the problem. If the nursing baby develops eczema, a chronic runny nose or cough, or ear infections, food allergies can be the problem. Milk, eggs, soy, peanuts, tree nuts, and fish are the most common allergenic foods. When allergies are severe in breast-fed infants, these protein foods in the mother's diet could be causing the problems. In this rare situation, manipulating the mother's diet can help the baby until he outgrows the sensitivity.

Frequently asked questions

When should I start nursing my baby? To get off to a good start it is really a good idea to nurse in the delivery room. This first feeding familiarizes the baby with the mother's nipple. Even mothers who have had cesarean sections can and should nurse in the first few hours after delivery. When the first feeding is delayed and bottles are given, the baby will sometimes reject the mother's nipple when she tries to feed. The longer the delay in the first breastfeeding, the higher the chance of nipple confusion.

Do I have to nurse my baby? Nursing is really fun when you get used to it. I usually try to encourage the new mother to nurse, but if things do not work out, formula feeding is not bad for the baby at all. Babies do well with either type of nourishment.

Can I take medication when I nurse? Many medications, such as most painkillers, thyroid hormone, asthma medications, antihistamines and most antibiotics are okay for nursing mothers. Other medications should be checked out by the pediatrician or the pharmacist to make sure they are safe.

Can I give one bottle a day? One bottle a day is usually okay once the baby is accustomed to the nursing. During engorgement it is not a good idea to delay nursing, since it can cause more swelling. After the engorgement settles down, giving the baby one bottle a day works well for most babies.

How long is a feeding? Some babies are quick and finish in 10 minutes or less. Some babies are slow and need to stay on the breast for much longer. Some fall asleep and wake up a few minutes later and start again. In general, the feeding should not have to be more than 45 minutes.

How often should I feed the baby? Try to space the feedings to 2 ½ to 4-hour intervals from the beginning of one feeding to the beginning of the next. This will usually give 6 to 8 feeds a day. If the baby is demanding every hour, try to burp him, soothe him, rock him, and give a pacifier for him to suck on. When you let his stomach gradually empty for a couple of hours, the baby will have more room to fill up next time. Most babies need at least 6 feedings in a 24-hour day. If the baby is sleeping more than 4 hours during the day, he should be woken to feed. At night we allow them to go longer between feedings.

How do I know that the baby is getting enough? The baby must have several wet diapers a day and, in the beginning, at least one bowel movement a day. The best way to tell if the baby is getting enough nourishment is to weigh the baby. If the baby, after the initial weight loss of the first few days of life, is gaining well, he is getting enough.

When do I encourage self-settling? At about 4 months of age the baby can be fed before falling asleep. Putting him into the crib awake allows him to learn how to self-settle. (See Chapter 7, Sleep In Children)

When should I start solid foods? Introducing solids decreases the milk supply and may result in staining and other hormone changes in the mother. If the baby is thriving you can delay starting solids until 9 to 12 months. If you do not start solids, the 9- to 10-month baby should be given something big that he cannot really bite off, like a bagel, just for practice. If the baby is hungry and not gaining well, solids can be added to his diet any time after 5 to 6 months.

What happens if the baby sleeps long hours at night? When the feedings are more than 6 hours apart, the hormone changes can, in some mothers, restore pre-pregnancy cycles. One feeding in the middle of the night keeps the hormones in balance for nursing.

What happens if I have to go to work? The more hours you are away from the baby, the more chances you have of losing the nursing. Some babies reject the breast when they get used to bottles.

Most working moms pump at work. Pumping works well for most women up to about 4-6 months. For many mothers, the pumping is not the same as nursing, and the milk supply decreases. Shorter workdays, closer jobs, and having the baby brought for feedings are the best options.

What happens if I become pregnant? Breast milk decreases in volume during early pregnancy. It is not usually necessary to stop nursing right away unless there is staining or threat of miscarriage. Most mothers can go to 3 feedings a day and then drop one feeding each week until the baby is weaned

Babies need either breast milk or formula until 1 year of age. Depending on the age of the baby, each feeding can be exchanged for formula or milk or solid feedings as the breast-feeding is weaned.

What is the right age to wean? The answer is; whenever the mother and the baby are ready. I have babies being nursed past three years of age, and some who wean themselves during infancy. Most are weaned when the mother becomes pregnant or at about 15 to 18 months.

"I have always tried to put my nursing babies on a feeding schedule from the first weeks of life. It makes me feel more in control of my time and my routine. My mother-in-law feels that I am being cruel to the babies. She prided herself on always nursing her babies on demand so

they never felt neglected. Am I doing the right thing?"

The best two presents you can give a baby are enough milk and a happy, well-adjusted family. As long as the baby is thriving, you know that you are giving enough milk. Most healthy and non-colicky babies are really flexible and can learn the rhythm of the day. The feedings can be on a relatively loose schedule.

It may take a couple of weeks and some adjustment. A little crying until he settles down, or using a pacifier to delay the feeding, is not harmful until the baby gets the idea.

Here is the routine:

- He gets fed, held, and burped.
- He gets played with and stimulated.
- He gets put down, whether asleep or awake.
- He sleeps until he wakes up, to the next cycle of the routine.

If doing this makes your life and the life of your husband and family more manageable, there is nothing wrong with it.

On the other hand, many mothers find that they would rather follow the baby's cues and not try to maintain any schedule. If this makes the family and the mother happy, the baby will do well, too. If the baby is cared for with love and affection, any baby care style that works for the family is the right one.

Keeping it all in perspective

It is important to remember that even though there are often problems with initiating breastfeeding, most of these subside in a couple of weeks. New mothers need a lot of reassurance and encouragement when nursing does not come easily. Lactation consultants can be very helpful when problems arise. The attitude of the husband and family is important when it comes to dealing with nursing issues. The more positive feedback she gets, the more a young mother will want to try.

If, however, the baby cannot be nursed, the mother should be reassured that the baby will be fine on formula. There is no need to feel guilty. The baby will not remember what he is fed during infancy!

CHAPTER 4

The Facts About Infant Sleep Safety

Key Points

- Infants should sleep on their backs.
- Natural bedding adds to the risk.
- No smother hazards in the crib.
- Co-sleeping is dangerous.

Since 1994 the American Academy of Pediatrics has advocated that infants should sleep on their backs to prevent "crib death." The campaign, called "Back to Sleep," was undertaken in response to research published first in New Zealand, then Australia, England, and many other countries, which showed that infants who sleep on their tummies had a statistically significant greater risk of crib death than infants who sleep on their backs. It has been speculated that the reason for this is that infants, who cannot roll over, will sometimes breathe in their own exhaled carbon dioxide when they are sleeping on their faces. This causes a deeper sleep, in which their muscle tone becomes so relaxed that they allow themselves to smother.

Since 1994 the percentage of babies who are placed prone (on their tummies) to sleep decreased by about 80 percent, and the number of infant crib deaths decreased by more than 50 percent.

Additional risk factors

In addition to the position of sleep, the research also showed that **the nature of the**

bedding and the environment in the crib had effects on the infant's safety. In New Zealand, where babies sleep on sheepskin, the prone position was found to be particularly dangerous. All natural bedding such as fur, straw, and beanbags were also found to add to the risk. Overdressing was also found to be a risk factor. Quilts, quilted bumpers, and plush toys in the crib were found to add to the danger.

It was suggested from this research that infants should sleep on a firm surface covered by a flat, well-fitted sheet; they should be dressed as warmly as needed, and should be covered or swaddled only with loosely-woven or thin cotton blankets.

It was also recommended that no stuffed animals, plushy or quilted toys, or bumpers or blankets be placed in the crib with an infant, to avoid the risk of accidental asphyxiation.

Obviously these recommendations also apply to baby strollers and carriages.

Co-sleeping

In a study out of Scotland, published in the prestigious journal *Pediatrics,* a number of unexplained infant deaths were reviewed, and one additional inquiry was requested of the families. That is, "Was the infant sleeping with anyone at the time of death?" The results of the inquiry showed that a very high percentage of these unexplained deaths occurred in a bed or couch with an adult sleeping nearby. There were infants sleeping with nursing mothers, infants sleeping with siblings, and infants sleeping with grandparents.

The risks were particularly high if there was any use of alcohol or any smoking in the environment.

This is not so surprising if you think of what is in an adult bed besides the unconscious adult. (All sleep is a form of unconsciousness.) There are pillows, blankets and quilts – all of the bedding we are so careful to avoid in the crib. Couches were particularly singled out in the study as dangerous for the baby when sleeping with an adult.

What does all of this mean? In the United States, where the crib death rate is pretty low, it means that any one baby is probably not at great risk. If an infant simply cannot adjust to sleeping on its back, prone sleeping – in a proper crib environment – is probably not going to cause any serious harm. As we know, many nursing mothers are accustomed to sleeping with their infants. How often do we hear of an infant's death from this habit?

Rarely – but it does happen. The community doesn't always know about it, since the accident is called a crib death …

Many times parents are awakened by the thump and cry of an infant falling out of their bed. In my own practice, a four-month-old baby had to be resuscitated after the mother awoke suddenly and found her baby blue and lifeless under her quilt. Another mother found her infant trapped by the neck, dangling between the bed and the wall. These infants, *baruch Hashem*, survived.

What do we expect from totally exhausted mothers who drift off to sleep with their nursing infants? All mothers of newborns are sleep-deprived. It is not their fault when they lose their awareness of the baby as they sleep.

There really is no way around the danger. The infant must be put down in an infant seat, bassinet, crib, or even the floor, before the adult falls asleep. Even if the risk is very small, it should not be assumed that any baby is safe in an adult bed. The statistics against co-sleeping with infants have been gathering over the last ten years. **There is a danger in this habit.**

I know that some people advocate sleeping with children, but in my 30 years of practice I have not found a parent who enjoys a good night's sleep while sleeping with an infant or child. Sleeping with an infant is not only uncomfortable, it is not safe.

We must always do our best to ensure the health and safety of our babies. It is our end of the special bargain we make with babies when they are born. We agree to do **everything** for them. We have to feed them, burp them, change them, dress them, soothe them, hug them, kiss them, love them, tickle them, and keep them safe. What do the babies have to do to keep their end of the bargain? The babies do not have to be good, or quiet, or easy to care for. They only have to be cute!

They all seem to hold up their end of the bargain. So the rest is up to us.

CHAPTER 5

The Truth About Immunizations

I am often asked about the advisability and safety of giving immunizations to a child. Many mothers are afraid that the shots could cause autism, mercury poisoning, or serious illness. I know that claims of these consequences have appeared in magazines and other sources of information. As convincing and emotional as they are, these claims are spurious and based on unfounded science. The tragic truth is that there are children in our own community suffering and dying from preventable diseases such as whooping cough, measles, and meningitis because of their parents' misguided decisions not to vaccinate.

Key Points

- Newer vaccines are safer than the ones given 20 years ago.
- There is no evidence that any vaccine causes autism.
- The risk of not giving vaccines is much higher than the risk of giving them.
- We protect the community by having all of our children vaccinated.

I give my own grandchildren all of their immunizations on schedule. The newest vaccines, which we now administer to children, are the safest and most effective in medical history. If I feel confident doing this for my own family, you should also feel that it is right for your children.

Modern vaccines are the marvels of our time. Frequent epidemics of diphtheria swept through every city in the world and left thousands of children dead until the development of the diphtheria vaccine in the 1940s. Since that time, one by one, many more devastating diseases have been conquered through the development of specific vaccines. These vaccines have enabled people to develop immunity without suffering from the actual disease.

There are two types of infectious diseases for which we immunize children: viral and bacterial.

Viral illnesses

Viruses cause *Influenza, Polio, Smallpox, Varicella (Chicken Pox), Measles, Mumps, Rubella, Hepatitis A, Hepatitis B,* and *Rotavirus Gastroenteritis.* These diseases are only spread by people. If the whole world's population were immunized against these viruses, they would be eradicated. This has already been achieved with smallpox, so immunization is no longer needed. There is a possibility that measles and polio may be eradicated in the next twenty years. The incidence of chicken pox has decreased dramatically over the last ten years since the vaccine was approved.

The vaccine against hepatitis A has been extremely effective in our community. After over ten years of seeing more than 50 cases per year in my practice, there have been *none* since one year after the vaccine was approved. We no longer receive letters from schools warning of exposure to hepatitis, requiring gamma globulin shots. Yet this virus is still present in our community, and anyone who has not yet been immunized is susceptible. Israel, which has a high incidence of this disease, has only just started immunizing children with this vaccine.

The oral vaccine against Rotavirus will have a big impact on the yearly incidence of this winter gastroenteritis. This virus causes severe vomiting and diarrhea and dehydration in young infants and toddlers. Children who have received this vaccine have 90% protection from this illness.

Most of these viruses remain the same over time, so once immunity is achieved, it lasts for a lifetime. The flu viruses, unfortunately, change their proteins very often, so immunity to one strain is not useful the next year when a new flu comes along.

Bacterial diseases

Bacteria cause *Diphtheria, Pertussis, Tetanus, Hemophilus Influenza B (HIB) Meningitis, Pneumococcal Pneumonia,* and *Meningococcal Meningitis.* The vaccine for HIB decreased the number of cases of bacterial meningitis by 90 percent within two years of its incorporation into the regular vaccine schedule. This completely changed my life as a pediatrician, since I averaged 6-8 cases a year of this devastating, life-threatening infection before the vaccine became available.

Similarly, the new vaccine against Pneumococcus released just a few years ago has decreased the number of young children admitted to the hospital with bacterial pneumonia by 85 percent. These germs, which can live harmlessly in a healthy child's throat, can become invasive and cause disease. They are not always obviously contagious from one person to another, since a contact can pick up the germ and not get sick from it. There is little chance of eradicating these diseases.

SIDE EFFECTS

DPT and DaPT

Diphtheria, a fatal throat infection, and *Tetanus,* a fatal infection of the nervous system, have been well-controlled since this vaccine has been given. *Pertussis,* which is a coughing illness that lasts about three months, is often severe and even fatal when contracted by a baby.

Despite the fact that millions of lives have been saved by these miraculous vaccines, there has always been a small incidence of serious side effects. The original DPT vaccine often caused fever and, rarely, convulsions and a shock-like reaction. There was a time in the 1970s when the health service in England stopped giving the vaccine, due to an increase in the number of crib deaths. Within one year, there were epidemics of pertussis, causing 30 deaths in small children. During that time – when no child was immunized – the incidence of crib deaths did not change at all. The Health Service realized the mistake, and the vaccine was reinstituted – but there were many cases of pertussis over the next few years until they gave catch-up doses to the children who had not been immunized.

In the former Soviet Union, where the bankrupt governments have not been able to maintain their vaccine programs, there are currently epidemics of diphtheria and pertussis.

For fifty years we gave DPT vaccine to everyone, knowing that the benefits outweighed the risk. About ten years ago, a newer vaccine, DaPT, was approved. This change tamed down the pertussis component that was causing the worst side effects. Now the incidence of severe reactions has been reduced to nearly zero. We no longer have to advise parents to give Tylenol on the day of the shots to avert high fever.

A new form of DaPT is being given as booster doses to adolescents and adults. They were previously only immunized with DT. By adding the new pertussis vaccine back into the tetanus booster the incidence of pertussis will decrease in the whole community.

MMR

The Measles-Mumps-Rubella vaccine, approved in the 1970s, has greatly reduced the number of cases of all three of these viruses. Measles is a vicious 10-day illness that comes with a severe cough, high fever, and a significant risk of brain damage and death. Mumps, which is characterized by painfully enlarged salivary glands, is milder, but can affect fertility in boys and can also cause a serious brain infection. Rubella, also called German Measles, has caused the most devastating problems. Unborn babies, infected through their mothers, are often born blind, deaf, and brain-damaged.

This vaccine has saved millions of lives. The children who receive the MMR will sometimes run a fever, occasionally with a flat rash, about 10 days after the injection. Doses are given at age one and five.

Several years ago, an article was published in England claiming a relationship between autism and the MMR vaccine. Since that time, the researchers who were quoted by the author have issued a retraction, claiming that their statistics were not valid for the conclusions that were made. Several large studies, costing millions of dollars, were conducted in Europe, Asia and the United States, trying to find a relationship between the vaccine and the incidence of autism. There was no evidence to confirm the claim in any of the studies.

Meanwhile, many parents were so frightened that they stopped immunizing their children. In England and Israel, where certain Orthodox Jewish groups are refraining from immunizing their children, there was recently an outbreak of measles; at least one measles-related death of a child who was not immunized was reported.

When you stop and think, you will realize that the risk of not giving this vaccine is far greater than the risk of giving it. Also, anyone who doesn't immunize is relying on the rest of the population to protect their child. This is really not fair at all. In order to keep these diseases under control, we must all accept the tiny risk involved. (See appendix for information on *Autism's False Prophets: Bad Science, Risky Medicine, and the Search for a Cure,* by Paul A. Offit, M.D.)

Mercury

The fear that the trace amounts of mercury in some of the vaccines could cause trouble was based on a mistake. The mercury that causes damage to the nervous system is a totally different compound than the one used to preserve the vaccine. Despite the fact that there was no evidence that there ever was any damage caused by the mercury, it was removed from all vaccines, and there are no vaccines being produced today with mercury in them, except some of the flu vaccines.

Varicella – chicken pox

The big question about the varicella (chicken pox) vaccine is: Why is it necessary? The answer is that there is a small but significant incidence of death, and there are a large number of children admitted to the hospital with serious bone and skin infections complicating chicken pox.

Since the recommendation was issued to give the vaccine to all children, the number of children suffering these severe infections has dropped dramatically. The vaccine is only about 85% effective against chicken pox, but it is 100% effective against severe chicken pox. The children who do get the disease after receiving the vaccine have mild cases.

Does the vaccine give permanent immunity? In Japan, where the vaccine was given for thirty years, people immunized 30 years before had the same immunity as those who had chicken pox during the same period. The incidence of shingles (a painful recrudescence of the virus in a region of the skin) seems to be somewhat lower in vaccine recipients. To ensure the durability of the vaccine, a booster dose is being given at around age 4.

Polio

Polio is a devastating viral infection of the nervous system, and used to cause thousands of cases of paralysis every year as epidemics swept through cities. OPV, Oral Polio Vaccine, which was developed in the 1960s, completely stopped the epidemics. This live vaccine had a small incidence of causing the disease itself. There were three cases of polio in the United States per year that were caused by the vaccine. In the year 2000, the decision was made to change to the killed vaccine, injectable IPV, which has no incidence of complications.

Flu vaccine

Flu vaccine is now recommended for babies 6 months old to kids 18 years old, as well as children with chronic illnesses. This is because there are often secondary infections such as ear infections and pneumonia after the flu. There is a nasal spray vaccine, Flumist, that is approved for children over five years old. It is probably a better vaccine, and it is now covered by insurances. I have always advised my patients to immunize the whole family to prevent flu. Anyone who has experienced this miserable disease and watched it spread to the entire household knows how important it is to try to avoid the flu.

Multiple injections

Because of the number of vaccines now being given to each child, the current practice is to give multiple shots at one time. Many parents (and grandparents) have expressed their concerns about this practice. This has been clearly shown to be safe, and does not increase the incidence of side effects at all when compared to giving only one shot at a time.

The newer vaccines are safer than the ones used in the past, because each one only contains a few antigens. The old DPT contained at least 3,000 antigens, many of which caused side effects and did not add to the protection. The refined DaPT, IPV, pneumococcal vaccine, Hepatitis B and the HIB, when combined, have only about 25 antigens. This is due to better identification of the antigens required to provide maximum protection.

Understanding risks and benefits

There is always some risk in everything we do with our children. We put them on school buses, we cross streets, we drive with them in the car. All of these activities have risks. We don't think about these risks because we have faith that G-d conducts the world. We have one obligation to our children – to do the best we can to protect them.

We know that **the risk of illness is far worse than the risk of immunization.** Immunizing children is the right thing for everybody. For a tiny amount of risk, we gain tremendous benefits to the health of our children. We have been blessed in this generation with wondrous medical advances. It is our job and privilege as parents to make the most of these gifts and to be grateful to the One Who made them available to us.

■ ■ ■

CHAPTER 6

GERD and Colic in Infants

Key Points

- Excessive crying in young infants is often caused by gastrointestinal distress.

- GERD and colic are different, but they can occur in the same infant.

- These conditions are treatable by a variety of methods.

- The best way to judge a treatment is by watching the baby for improvement.

Most young infants eat and sleep, pass normal regular bowel movements, and cry only when they are hungry or need a fresh diaper. There are, however, many infants who cry for a large part of the day and night. They scream in pain after feedings, before bowel movements, or even right in the middle of a good sleep. These babies can be thriving and healthy, but the crying is a real problem. The infant is tired and miserable, the parents are frustrated and exhausted, and the siblings are annoyed and resent the amount of attention they lose to this screamer. Over the years this problem was called *infant colic*. The general impression was that it had no cause, no treatment, and it went away by about three months of age.

An incredible amount of nonsense has been published in pediatric journals trying to prove that the babies are only crying to relieve tension and that it is just neurological immaturity. Parents have been blamed for being too tense around the baby, not holding or feeding the baby properly, and many other unfounded improprieties. The most ridiculous premise was that there was no physical basis for the crying, and that the infants were not in pain.

About ten years ago, physicians started to look more carefully at the problem and found that some of these infants actually have digestive difficulties. A small percentage of the babies seemed to have true colic. This consists of pain in the abdomen from cramping and gaseous ballooning of the bowel. Uncoordinated contractions of the intestinal muscles were noted. The condition seems to be an infant form of Irritable Bowel Syndrome.

At the same time, it was noted that the majority of "colicky" infants actually had acid reflux that caused the crying. Since that time, pediatricians have been analyzing the behavior of these screaming babies to prescribe specific treatments that alleviate the pain. Although these problems sometimes both occur in the same baby, there is a difference between colicky behavior and reflux behavior. Here is a discussion of the two entities.

COLIC

An infant who has pure colicky pains can scream for hours, often even when held in his parents' arms. He often folds forward, draws up his legs, and kicks while he is crying. His belly feels tense like a basketball and tapping on it produces a hollow sound. Burping or passing stool and gas sometimes stops the crying. Warm baths, swaddling, rocking, or being walked in the stroller sometimes help.

Some colicky babies seem to improve when riding around in a car. To take advantage of this, a device was even invented to simulate a car ride by vibrating the crib and having the sound of a car motor and the wind noises of an open car window.

There are several specific problems that can be addressed before we give up and start driving all night.

All babies swallow air while feeding

Sometimes excess air is swallowed by a nursing baby if the mother's milk is flowing too fast and the baby has to gulp to keep from choking. Bottle nipples can also be a source of excess air swallowing. It is important to remember that any air that is swallowed and not burped up will have to travel all the way through the intestines until it gets passed from below.

We often recommend that nursing babies who are gulping should be stopped after every 2 or 3 minutes and burped. Bottle-fed infants often benefit from bottles that are designed to minimize air swallowing. The Dr. Brown's bottle is a good example.

Infrequent bowel movements

Most babies pass stools with every feeding in the first couple of weeks of life. As time goes by, the frequency of stools decreases. If a baby is uncomfortable, it is important to note how often he passes stools. If days are going by without a bowel movement, and the baby is colicky, it is wise to induce bowel movements at least once a day.

This can be done by using a glycerine suppository or a Pedia-Lax. Giving small amounts of prune juice sometimes helps. If the baby is really straining and not passing stools easily, he should be brought to the doctor. Sometimes the anal opening is too tight and needs to be stretched. (Infrequent bowel movements in a happy, comfortable, not colicky, nursing baby are not a matter of concern.)

The foods a nursing mother eats can cause problems in some babies

If the infant is colicky, eliminating all juices, caffeine, chocolate, and a few vegetables can help. These are onions (cooked, fried, and raw), broccoli, cauliflower, cabbage (including cole slaw), and green pepper. Fruits and all other vegetables, including yellow and red peppers, are okay. If eliminating these offending foods does not help, it might be worthwhile to try eliminating cow's milk and all milk products from the mother's diet.

Infant formulas can be a source of the problem

They are made of either milk or soy protein. Some babies who are colicky improve by switching from one to the other. Hydrolyzed formulas, Nutramigen and Alimentum, are "predigested." This means that the basic proteins are broken up into small components. Elemental formulas, Neocate and Ellecare, are artificial. They are made of amino acids, which are the smallest building blocks of proteins. Some babies who are colicky on regular formula or who cannot tolerate any of the foods in the mother's diet, might benefit from a hydrolyzed formula or an elemental one.

Probiotics can help infants with colic

Probiotics are germs that are known to be beneficial, which are added to the digestive tract. Culturelle (*lactobacillus GG*), or Biogaia Infant Drops (beneficial bacteria) and Florastor (a beneficial yeast) help relieve the colic in some babies. The dose is half a capsule of Culturelle once a day, and half a packet of Florastor twice a day. The formula companies are starting to add probiotics to the formulas in the

United States. These newer formulas might be helpful in preventing colic. (See Chapter 34, Probiotics)

Herbal colic remedies sometimes help

"Gripe Water," kimmel tea, chamomile tea, and other herbal remedies sometimes help the cramping.

GASTRO ESOPHAGEAL REFLUX DISEASE (GERD)

This condition occurs when the acidic contents of the stomach travel back up the esophagus, causing damage to the lining of the esophagus. This causes a pain known as "heartburn." Not all reflux babies spit up. The reflux may back up only to the lower part of the esophagus.

GER without the D

It is common for babies to spit up all the time and not have GERD. Even though the food comes back up through the esophagus, it does not cause pain. This is GEReflux, but it does not become GERDisease until it actually causes a problem. When the reflux causes erosion of the wall of the esophagus, the baby will show painful signs of heartburn.

GERD babies cry intensely after or during feedings. They often gulp during and between feedings. They sometimes wake up screaming after falling sleep contentedly after a feeding. The refluxing baby will often stiffen his legs and body and arch his back, throwing his head back. The upright position seems more comfortable, and many GERD babies are difficult to put down. Here are a few points about the management of this acid reflux:

Sleep position can be important in reflux disease

A slight upward angle at the head of the mattress can be helpful. This is done by putting a folded towel under the head of the mattress, creating a 20-degree angle.

These infants often sleep better sitting up. It has been noted, however, that infant seats are not the best sleep chairs for reflux infants. This is because the baby is folded in the middle, creating upward pressure on the belly. A bouncy seat or swing, which allows the baby to keep his abdomen stretched out while seated, is better.

Some infants with reflux need to sleep on their tummies. This is reasonable if all precautions are taken. This means no soft quilts or bumpers, a firm, flat mattress, no toys or stuffed animals in the crib.

Thickening feeds can help sometimes

If the baby is bottle fed, it sometimes helps to add rice cereal to the formula (1 tablespoon to every 4 ounces). Thickened feeds seem to satisfy the baby with fewer ounces, so the stomach is less full. The hole in the nipple has to be opened to accommodate the thicker formula. (I have never found that giving cereal after a feeding helps a breastfed infant.)

Burping is very important

The acid-full milk sometimes comes up with a delayed burp.

Constipation can add to the problem

Constipation can delay the emptying of the stomach contents into the small intestine. The longer the milk stays in the stomach, the greater the chance for reflux. Some babies are still spitting up the last feeding when they start the next feeding. Making sure the GERD baby empties his bowels regularly is important.

Antacids can help, and are often necessary in order to stop the problem

There are three types of antacids:

▪ *Acid neutralizers* like Mylanta or Maalox. These only work for the time they are in the stomach. They can give quick temporary relief from the burning pain. The usual dose is ½ cc per 2 pounds of body weight, given up to 7 times a day.

▪ *H2 blockers* like Zantac, Axid, and Pepcid. These are acid blockers that actually prevent the acid from being secreted in the stomach. The usual dose is 1ml per 5 kg of body weight, every 8 hours (7 a.m., 3 p.m., and 11 p.m.). These medications give a lot of relief and can be used for as long as needed (usually a few weeks or months). A recent report in a major pediatric journal showed no side effects, even after years of use.

▪ *Proton Pump Inhibitors (PPIs)* These are proton pump inhibitors such as Nexium, Prilosec, and Prevacid. The PPIs are even more potent in blocking acid production than the H2 blockers. The usual baby dose is 7.5 to 15 mg, 2 times a day. Sometimes even more is needed. This is actually the same as an adult dose, but babies need that much in order to get benefit. The only group that has shown side effects is small, premature infants. All the other babies do very well with these medications.

The best way to judge the effectiveness of these treatments is to watch the baby. If there is much less crying, the treatment is working. The spitting up might still persist, but it will not cause pain, since there is no acid.

Silent GERD

It is possible to have the acid contents of the stomach come up to the throat and be swallowed again with no symptoms of GI distress. This silent reflux has recently been linked to problems in the throat. *Chronic hoarseness* is one symptom that often responds to antacid treatment. The ENT specialists can look deep into the throat and find signs of acid burns that lead to this diagnosis.

Reflux has also been implicated in **apnea in newborn infants, chronic cough**, and even **sinus disease** and **ear infections**. The research is still being done to determine the validity of these observations.

The medical test for acid reflux is performed in an overnight stay in a hospital. A probe is placed in the baby's esophagus, and acid levels are recorded over a period of time. This test is not very popular, since the reflux can be intermittent and be missed by the probe. Most physicians diagnose reflux by observing the baby's behavior and by observing the response to medications.

Final thoughts

We have always known that babies with colic and reflux usually thrive. While it is not necessary to treat them, it is also no longer necessary to leave them in pain until they outgrow the problems. With current medical understanding and the availability of medications, it is possible to relieve many of these infants and their families so they all can enjoy the first few months of their lives.

CHAPTER 7

Skin Care for Infants

Key Points

- Babies have thin, delicate skin.
- Birthmarks are caused by little blood vessels (blue or red) or extra pigment (tan or brown).
- Sunscreens are not effective — use shade and clothing in the sun.
- Eczema is often caused by a food allergy.
- Yeast often invades the irritated diaper area.

The skin is a very remarkable organ in the human body. Although it often goes unnoticed, it performs a variety of jobs for us. It is the vital protective wrapping for all of the body's structures. As it covers bones, muscles, blood vessels, and internal organs, it helps maintain body temperature and hydration. Through the sweat mechanism, it also plays a role in the maintenance of the salt balance in the body. Pigment production helps defend the body from harmful sunburn. The intact skin barrier prevents infection by bacteria, parasites, fungi, and some viruses. The sensitive nerve endings on the skin give essential signals to the brain about the environment, such as temperature, humidity, and texture.

Proper care of the skin is essential to everyone's health and comfort. Immature skin is very thin and vulnerable, so infants and babies need the most careful skin care.

Newborn infants

Very young infants have very delicate skin. Preemies have paper-thin skin that breaks down from the slightest friction. Full-term newborns have skin that is less than one-third the thickness of that of an adult. This means it is more prone to sunburn, irritation in the diaper area, and other rashes.

There are different skin types, which are determined by the types of skin that the parents have. Babies with darker hair and complexions are less delicate than blond- or red-haired infants, who have fair complexions.

Sun protection

All newborns must be kept in the shade on sunny days. This means long sleeves, covered legs and feet, or a good umbrella. Sunscreens are not effective on such thin skin.

Birthmarks

In the newborn period, birthmarks often appear on the skin. If these birthmarks are blue or red, they are caused by clusters of blood vessels in the skin. The most common red ones are on the eyelids, nose, lips, and the back of the head. These are called *flame nevi*. They are usually gone by the first birthday.

The ones identified as *strawberry hemangiomas* often grow thicker and larger with time. Massaging the mark several times a day will often prevent the hemangioma from growing thicker. If these are very large, or if they cover the eyes, they need medical attention. Laser treatment is often therapeutic.

Brown or tan marks are caused by pigments in the skin. These do not always appear at birth, but once they appear they are usually permanent. Light ones never need to be removed. Very dark ones that are also large must be monitored as the baby grows. Some of them will have to be removed in adolescence.

NEWBORN SKIN PROBLEMS

The most common skin problems in newborns are diaper rashes, baby acne, and cradle cap.

Diaper rash

Newborns have frequent and loose bowel movements, which can easily irritate their skin. Soiled diapers should be changed as soon as they are detected. Urine alone is rarely irritating because of the new gel technology in disposable diapers.

If a baby soils his diaper during sleep or is inadvertently left in a soiled diaper too long, the skin can become red. This contact rash can be both prevented and treated by using a barrier to keep the skin from being further irritated while it is healing. After a bowel movement, the skin should always be cleaned with either a little water, lotion on a tissue, or baby wipes. Very sensitive skin can be irritated by the chemicals in the wipes or even the chemicals in the diaper. When this happens, changing brands often helps. I have found that the Seventh Generation brand sold in Babies"R"Us is very helpful.

In baby boys, a cornstarch-based powder applied to the area before closing the diaper works very well. In baby girls, using powder is not a good idea. The powder gets inside the genital area and can cause a problem. A cream is needed. Most barrier creams have either a white zinc oxide base or a clear petroleum jelly base. All of these provide protection, but some seem to work better than others. Do not use Desitin on baby girls because powder is mixed into the cream.

If the treatment is not effective and the diaper rash develops pimples or dots, or if the skin breaks down, a doctor should be consulted. Sometimes a medicated cream is needed.

Baby acne

Baby acne appears on the baby's face at around one month of age. This pimply red rash usually goes away on its own over time. The use of an antifungal cream such as Spectazole will sometimes be needed in very severe cases to get rid of the yeast (not the one that causes thrush) that causes this common problem.

Cradle cap

Cradle cap is the accumulation of a greasy, scaly substance on the scalp and forehead. The old-fashioned method of applying oil or Vaseline to the scales and scrubbing the scalp an hour later with a washcloth and baby shampoo works well. A comb can be used to scrape the oiled scales off gently. If the problem is persistent, dandruff shampoos can be used. The scales are sometimes invaded by the same yeast that causes baby acne, and using antifungal shampoo can help. Occasionally, application of 1-percent hydrocortisone cream is needed.

Bathing

The question of how often to bathe a newborn and what to use for soap often comes up. It is generally felt that too much bathing can dry the skin and cause cracking and peeling. Most of the time, 2-3 baths a week are enough for a newborn. The soap used should be fatty, like unscented Dove. The "baby bath" liquids are not really good for the skin.

After bathing and wrapping and patting (not rubbing) the skin with a towel, a lotion could be applied while the skin is still a little damp. This traps the water back into the outer layers of skin. Sensitive skin needs unscented and uncolored lotion. Applying oil all over the skin is not a good idea, since many babies break out from the occlusion of the pores.

Heat rash

This rash of tiny raised papules occurs on the neck, chest, and upper back when the baby has been sweating. Gently spreading cornstarch on the rash is helpful. To prevent this problem, do not overdress the infant and keep him in a cool, shady environment.

OLDER BABIES

After the first three months of life the baby's skin is less delicate, but there are certain problems that become more evident. The most common ones are eczema and chronic diaper rashes.

Eczema

Eczema is an itchy rash that appears as patches of reddened skin that is dry and breaks down. The cause is not always known, but 70 percent of the time it is an allergy to a particular food in the child's diet. The most common foods that can cause eczema are cow's milk, egg whites, soy, peanuts, tree nuts, and fish. Infant formulas are based on either milk or soy. In formula-fed infant the offending food is milk or soy. The mother's milk sometimes exposes babies to all of the foods in the mother's diet.

Changing the type of formula or altering the diet of the baby or the nursing mother to remove all or some of the problem foods often clears up the eczema. Once a problem food is identified, it should be stopped for about six months and then tried again. Most food allergies disappear by that time.

Treating eczema

There are differing opinions as to how to treat eczema. The "dry" method advises little or no contact with water and the application of Cetaphyl lotion to clean the skin. The "wet" method is to use water to soften the skin and then to apply moisturizer.

One of the most effective "wet" methods of treating dry skin with eczema is to give daily 20-minute baths followed by the application of lotion while the skin is still damp. An area that is particularly red or itchy is rubbed with 1-percent hydrocortisone ointment two to three times a day until it improves. If the eczema starts to weep and crust, an antibiotic ointment may be needed. Adding two tablespoons of bleach to the bath water and soaking for 20 minutes can help remove the invasive bacteria and prevent infection. Eczema that is more severe needs to be treated by a physician.

Chronic diaper rashes

Most diaper rashes are caused by contact sensitivities. The more persistent rashes that do not clear up with barrier creams and powders are probably invaded by the yeast called *Monilia.* Yeasts love to grow in moist skin, so the most vulnerable areas are the diaper area and the places where skin folds on skin, such as the chubby creases in the groin and under the chin.

Monilial rashes usually have solid red areas with satellite dots in the periphery. Powder helps to keep the creases dry, but often a medicated cream is needed. Clotrimazole is very effective in most cases. If the baby's stools are very loose and the diaper area is red, sometimes a probiotic such as Culturelle, ½ capsule once a day, or Florastor, one packet two times a day, will improve the stools and help to clear up the rash. (See Chapter 34, Probiotics)

Any rash that does not improve with these basic measures should be checked by a physician.

CHAPTER 8

Sleep in Children

Key Points

- Sleep is as vital as food and water.
- Sleep can be prevented by hidden caffeine in foods.
- Fears can interfere with sleep.
- Lack of exercise can add to sleep problems.
- Melatonin is safe and sometimes effective.
- Lack of sleep affects behavior and learning.

Sleep is as necessary as eating and drinking! We cannot function without sleep. Besides resting the body, sleep helps the brain process memories and experiences. When childhood sleep problems arise, everybody suffers – the sleepless child, as well as the sleepless parents and siblings. To understand sleep problems, we need to know the basic facts about sleep.

Quantity of sleep

On average, these are the quantities of sleep required.

- **Newborn - 4 months:** 16-17 hours a day in about seven equal blocks
- **4 - 9 months:** 15 hours a day in four or five longer blocks, two thirds of the sleep being at night
- **10 months - 3 years:** 12 hours in one block at night, plus two 1-hour daytime naps.
- **3 - 10 years:** 12 hours at night, no naps
- **Teens:** 9 hours (if they get less, they make it up by sleeping long blocks on weekends)
- **Adults:** 8 to 8 ¼ hours (now you know why you are chronically tired!)

Quality of sleep

Sleep is characterized by two different types of brainwaves: *non-REM* sleep, which is divided into four stages, and *Rapid Eye Movement (REM)* sleep, which is dream sleep.

Non-REM sleep

- **Stage I:** Drowsy, but still able to respond to voices, noises, and other stimuli.
- **Stage II:** Dozing, falling asleep, but easily aroused. This is the sleep you see at a lecture when people close their eyes and let their heads fall and suddenly wake up as they fight to stay awake.
- **Stage III:** Asleep. All muscles are relaxed and breathing begins to slow.
- **Stage IV:** Deep sleep. In this stage, outside noises would not be noticed, and the person is hard to wake up. At the end of Stage IV there is a brief awakening before going on to the next phase, REM sleep.

REM sleep

REM sleep is the special sleep when dreams occur. During this phase, the brain is very active, but the *body is extremely still*. Only the breathing muscles and the eye muscles are really working. We only enter REM sleep at the end of a non-REM cycle, which consists of 2-4 stages.

These stages of sleep occur in cycles throughout the night. The early part of the night, Stages I and II, occur repeatedly until the first REM sleep occurs, about two hours after falling asleep. The early REM cycles are very short, and last only a few minutes. They are followed by progressive periods of Stage II-IV sleep. As the night goes on, the REMS get longer and longer. REMS can be over 90 minutes in length. Dreams are the most long and intense in the early hours of the morning, just before arising.

SLEEP PROBLEMS

There are many different aspects of sleep that can be disturbed in childhood. The following is a discussion of the most common sleep problems.

Self-settling

Self-settling is the ability to get oneself to sleep. Since there are cycles of lighter and deeper sleep all night long, everyone wakes a little, several times a night – to roll over, fix the blanket, or even look around to see that everything is okay. *If a child is always helped to fall asleep, he will want that help several times a night,* whenever he has his natural awakenings at the end of each sleep cycle. If he knows how to fall asleep without assistance, he will do it right away and go back to sleep without crying.

Newborns almost always fall asleep while feeding. After about four months of age, it is best to try to feed the baby before bedtime and put him in the crib while still awake. He then will find some way of helping himself to fall asleep. A cloth diaper or thin blanket, or a small soft toy, can be introduced as a transitional object that will help him fall asleep. Many people find themselves rocking, shaking, rolling the carriage, or allowing the baby to pull on the mother's *sheitel,* ear or finger, or lying in bed with the baby to get the baby to sleep. These are all transitional methods. I really prefer not using these *adult-dependent* methods, since they do not allow the baby to learn to settle himself down.

It is not easy to break a habit, so if you are going to train a baby to settle himself, be prepared to tolerate crying for the first few tries. Self-settling is a skill. During the learning phase, the baby will cry from frustration when you do not give him the transitional method he is accustomed to. After about three nights, he will acquire the skill and he will stop crying when you put him to bed. Dr. Richard Ferber, in his book, *Solve Your Child's Sleep Problem*, describes a gentle, gradual method for weaning a baby or child off of settling methods that are not independent.

Sleep apnea

Sleep apnea means short cessations of breathing during sleep, causing the child to awaken briefly to start breathing again. This disrupts the sleep very much, so that **a child with sleep apnea will usually show symptoms of sleep deprivation.** This often happens when the child's airway is blocked during sleep and he must wake up briefly to breathe. A snoring child will have loud breathing that sometimes stops for a few seconds, followed by a louder snore that occurs when the block is cleared. These children often have severely enlarged tonsils and/or adenoids, chronic allergies, or chronic nasal infections with sinus problems. Very obese children (and adults) are prone to sleep apnea.

Sleep apnea is diagnosed by a sleep study, which is done in a special laboratory.

If the underlying cause cannot be treated medically, the surgical removal of the adenoids will often solve the problem in young children. In obese adults and adolescents, weight loss may be required to solve the problem. CPAP, a mechanical device that keeps the airway open can sometimes be prescribed.

Night terrors

During a night terror, a child will awaken and scream or thrash around. When the parent goes to him, the child is not really awake and does not respond to comforting, often pushing the parent away. This is not a nightmare. During dream sleep, the body is very still. *This is a partial wakening.* The child is between Stage IV sleep and the next phase, which might be Stage I or REM. His body seems awake, but he is not aware of his surroundings. In this state, the child could get up and walk around or start talking but not be aware. This is a benign condition, which stops by itself after five to fifty minutes. If you do nothing, it will be okay, as long the child is kept safe. The child never remembers the episodes. Despite all the screaming, he is not suffering at all. If you waken him, he will wonder why you are bothering him.

There is a way of stopping these night terrors if they happen repeatedly. In the beginning of the night, allow the child to fall asleep and sleep for about forty-five minutes. Wake him up fully, and then put him back to sleep. This method interrupts the disturbing cycle of brain-wave activity that has developed.

Nightmares

Nightmares are bad dreams that frighten the child. Unlike night terrors, the child remembers the dream. They happen infrequently and are usually not an ongoing problem. They reflect fears or problems going on in everyday life. Reassurance is all that is usually needed.

DIFFICULTY FALLING ASLEEP

Most kids will fall asleep as soon as their heads hit the pillow. There are some kids, however, who lie awake for a long time and sleep does not come. This is a miserable problem, which should be taken seriously.

Energy

Children are physiologically programmed to have a lot of energy. They are driven to move all of their muscles to ensure good development of strong muscles and straight bones, as well as strong hearts and efficient lungs. If the day goes by without exercise, there is a buildup of energy that creates a restless feeling. Children need to burn off their energy. If the child's school day is too sedentary, he will be too pent up to fall asleep. It is essential that children be allowed vigorous exercise as soon as possible at the end of the school day. This means running around, a trip to the park, jumping rope, or some indoor activity that burns energy, like dancing.

This should not be right before bedtime since the exercise makes them alert and mentally active.

Sleep routines

From an early age, it is advisable to develop a sleep routine to prepare the child for sleep. Brushing teeth, singing songs, reading stories, saying good night with a kiss, followed by *Shema* and *Hamalach Hagoel*, is a normal bedtime routine for a child even as early as one year of age. It takes a few minutes, but it is worth the time, since the parent and the child both benefit.

Caffeine

If your child is having difficulty falling asleep, make sure he is not getting any caffeine in his daily diet. Caffeine is a drug that can take up to 24 hours to wash out of the brain, so consuming it, even early in the morning, is not acceptable. Watch out for the hidden caffeine in food:

- All coffee-flavored foods, including yogurt, candies, and ice cream, contain caffeine. Some cakes (including chocolate cakes) have coffee in the recipe.
- Dark chocolates are very full of a caffeine-related compound, and eating them can be like drinking coffee.
- Soft drinks, such as certain orange sodas, Mountain Dew, and all colas (unless labeled caffeine-free) contain large amounts of caffeine.
- All non-herbal tea and all tea products have caffeine. Snapple, Tealicious, Nestea, and iced tea mixes all have caffeine, unless they specifically say otherwise.
- If you are sure there is no chemical reason for the child's difficulty falling asleep, there are other possibilities to be considered.

Naps

It is important that afternoon naps not be too late in the day. If the child falls asleep in the late afternoon, try to wake him up in about 20 to 30 minutes. He will be irritable for a few minutes, but he will soon come around, and then he can make it to bedtime without falling apart. A longer nap can disturb his night sleep.

Fears and anxieties

Nighttime brings darkness, and an anxious child might feel frightened to be alone. Mild fears might be exaggerated by the child to gain more time with the parents. If the fears do not seem as strong as the child claims (most parents can tell), firm but gentle reassurance will usually suffice. If the child is truly terrified, there may be something troubling him. It is very helpful to try to get the child to express what exactly he feels is so frightening. This will sometimes reveal that he heard about someone who died recently, or that someone has threatened him. He may not articulate these disturbing thoughts the first time you ask him. Keep the door of communication open by gently reminding him that he should always tell his mother or father when something is troubling him.

If the extreme fear of bedtime does not resolve after a few weeks, a professional child psychologist should be consulted.

Melatonin

If there are no fears, but the child simply cannot fall asleep, he may be lacking in a secretion of the pineal gland, which is found near the brain. This substance, called melatonin, is the signal to the brain that sleep is approaching. It sets the sleep clock in motion. This is why it is often used to treat the sleep disturbance that is associated with jet lag.

Melatonin is secreted mostly in response to darkness. An interesting observation has been made. Babies who are taken outside during the afternoon hours and are exposed to bright daylight seem to sleep better at night. Their brains are able to respond better to the onset of darkness. It is thought that melatonin is strongly suppressed during the daytime light exposure, and then it is secreted generously when darkness comes.

Many of us in the pediatric community recommend synthetic melatonin to be given as a supplement at bedtime for children who have difficulty falling asleep. A recently-published paper also showed that melatonin is very useful in children with brain damage who cannot sleep. Melatonin can be purchased in a health food store or drug store, and is safe to be used any time it is needed. There have been no toxicities reported, even in long-term use. The usual dose is 1/2 to 1 milligram at bedtime, to be given with a calcium-rich food like milk or cheese or a supplement like Tums. The dose can be as high as 6 milligrams, but most kids do well on doses between 1/2 to 3 milligrams.

Benadryl

Occasionally, the antihistamine Benadryl can be used to help a child fall asleep, if recommended by your pediatrician. Most kids get a little drowsy from Benadryl, but some get agitated instead. If this happens, do not try it again. It will wear off in four hours.

The consequences of lack of sleep

The important thing to note is that a child who does not sleep sufficiently can have problems during the day. Whether it is sleep apnea or other issues, a sleepless child is often irritable, intolerant, miserable, and restless. Rather than acting sleepy, he may be hyperactive and have difficulty concentrating. His whole personality is affected.

Sleep is a critical factor in overall good health. Always take the matter seriously if a child cannot sleep. Consult your doctor if you feel that there is a real problem.

■ ■ ■

CHAPTER 9

Understanding Development in the First Year of Life

A newborn infant can be looked upon as a genuine miracle. From its early beginnings as a microscopic cell, a whole human being has formed in only forty weeks! His skin, bones, digestive system, muscles, heart, liver, kidneys, and nervous system have all developed in a miraculously orderly fashion to make this new person possible.

The newborn is also an incredible bundle of potential. He will go on to grow in every parameter. His body will grow, and his brain and nervous system will grow more complex. His motor function, cognitive function, and emotional function will continue to develop.

As he grows from infant to baby to toddler to child, his personality will mature. His personal strengths and weaknesses will be revealed. He will become an individual. He will learn from every aspect of his life and grow in understanding and knowledge.

Key Points

- Normal development means continued progress.
- Lack of progress is a cause for concern and needs evaluation.
- Every experience creates new complexity in the developing brain.
- Motor control progresses from head to toe.
- Myelin sheaths enable nerves to control muscles.

Is my baby developing normally?

Parents often ask the question, "Is my baby developing normally?" They compare their child to a more advanced child of the same age and they worry that there is something wrong.

Some sensory functions, like hearing, smell, taste, and touch, are very well developed before birth. Others, like vision, are only partially developed at birth.

Milestones – signposts of developmental progress

There are certain motor developmental milestones that normal infants and toddlers must reach, such as smiling, head control, sitting, crawling, standing, and walking. The timing of these is so variable that some normal children walk at 8 months and other normal children walk at 18 months or older.

How do we know when to worry about a baby who is at the later end of the spectrum? In general, if the baby is showing good progress in his awareness of his surroundings, his social responsiveness, and – as he gets to be around 15 months old – his ability to understand words, I reassure the parents. Being a relatively late crawler or a late walker does not matter if his cognitive development is good.

We must all remember: **normal development means continued progress.** If there is no significant improvement in skills over a period of months, there is probably cause for concern.

BRAIN MATURATION –
THE PHYSICAL BASIS FOR DEVELOPMENT

The process of development is enabled by certain physical changes in the brain that occur in response to environment and genetic factors. The following is an overview of the process of cognitive and motor development.

Cognitive (the thinking functions of the brain)

The newborn brain is made up of millions of interlocking and branching complexes of nerve tissue. As the baby develops, the brain tissue continues to increase in complexity. New branches and connections are constantly being made. Every sight, sound, taste, smell, and touch creates a memory and a new connection in the brain. As the brain tissue continues to mature and increase in complexity in various areas of processing, the cognitive skills develop. It is these skills that govern the entire thinking function of the person.

Experience creates new connections

At birth, the first functions a baby will demonstrate are reflexive behaviors, such as crying, sucking, breathing, and eliminating. As the infant lies quietly while he is awake, he uses his eyes and ears, sense of smell, and sense of touch to gather information about his surroundings. As time goes by, the connections formed by these experiences create patterns. Recognition of parents' voices and smells comes early. At about 6 to 8 weeks, the infant will start responding to a smiling face with a smile. From that time on, he will develop a social personality. Even at this early age infants are individuals. The general nature of a child will be determined by a combination of genetic traits and environmental factors.

Language development comes with exposure to live human interactions, which include speech and communications. The more the caregivers and siblings of the infant *talk* to the child, the sooner he will develop receptive language. Warning! Tapes and audiovisual presentations are never a substitute for real human language contact. They can only be used as an adjunct. Reading picture books and pointing out the animals and objects encourages the growth of language.

Expressive language develops more slowly, and is very dependent upon how much the child is encouraged to speak a language. Multiple languages are easy for a young child to learn if he is given the chance to practice speaking each one.

With time, the child's brain becomes more able to process words. **If there is no understanding of words at all by one year of age, an evaluation, including hearing screening, should be done.** Speech can be delayed in some normal children, especially in families of "late talkers." Most of these children communicate very well by using gestures. By 18 months, the child should understand what is said to him and he should be able to follow simple commands.

Neuromotor development –
how the infant develops muscle control and motor skills

The physical basis for the development of the function of the nerves and muscles is a finishing process that takes place in the nervous system during the first year of life. This process produces the covering of each nerve with an insulating sheath called *myelin*. This insulation allows the impulses to travel directly to their target muscles, which enables the motor skills to develop. Without myelin sheaths, the impulses jump from one nerve to another. This explains why newborn infants move their whole bodies when they are startled.

Myelination, as the process is known, **starts in the head and progresses down the spinal cord over the first year of life.** The earliest nerves to get myelin sheaths are the ones that control the breathing muscles, the eating muscles, the eyelids, and the facial muscles involved in crying. The smile nerves come soon after, followed by the neck control nerves. Then the trunk control nerves get their myelin, allowing the baby to turn over and sit up. The nerves controlling the arm muscles get their myelin in turn so that at 4 months the baby can reach towards an object. At 5 months, he can hit the object. At 6 months, he can grasp the object in his hand. At 9 months, he can use two fingers to pick up a small object.

Eventually, the nerves at the bottom of the spinal cord get their myelin sheaths. These are the ones that allow walking and bowel and bladder control. In some normal children, this part of the process is slower than in others, explaining the discrepancy between early and late walkers.

Many agencies offer "Early Intervention" to children under three who are not reaching their milestones in the normal age range. If there is concern about lack of progress in developmental skills, a complete "Early Intervention" evaluation is indicated. Sometimes occupational therapy, speech therapy, physical therapy, and special education intervention is needed to maximize the progress of the child.

Final thought

When we watch a mischievous one-year-old toddle over to the cabinet and dump out all of the pots and pans and go on to crawl inside to hide, we should be awestruck. Just one short year ago he was a floppy, helpless little bundle of potential. Now he is a bundle of ingenuity, trouble, and energy. It is truly a miracle!

CHAPTER 10

Are Your Children Truly Bilingual?

Key Points

- Language ability develops *easily* in very young children.
- Bilingual means *understanding, speaking, and thinking* in both languages.
- *Speaking English* from an early age is the key to English language development.
- Poor English language development is a handicap in an American child.

All children learn to understand and speak a language from their caregivers and the people around them. In an effort to insulate their children from secular influences, some segments of the Orthodox Jewish community use only Yiddish as the language at home, in the community, and at school. In America, where English is the common language, this can create difficulties in English language acquisition.

The following is a discussion of this practical developmental issue.

Are your children really bilingual? The answer may surprise you. Although we take pride in the fluency our boys and girls have in speaking Yiddish, the truth is that only the girls are really bilingual. They are equally fluent in English and Yiddish. Most of the boys, however, have very poor command of English.

The girls are truly *bilingual,* which means that they can think and speak in whichever language they are using. The boys can only think in Yiddish and then translate the thoughts from Yiddish to English before they can speak in English. This is called *English as a Second Language.*

This is the reason that the boys have heavy European accents, awkward grammar, and very poor ability to express themselves. The boy will say, "Mine hand hurts me," and point to his elbow.

Embarrassing handicap

This lack of fluency is very embarrassing to the boys. They are aware that most people in America can speak and use English better than they can.

Besides their lack of English speaking ability, the boys also have trouble doing tasks that require English, such as reading documents, writing letters, and filling out forms and applications. They often ask their mothers and sisters – and eventually their wives – to do it for them.

The girls are able to speak and read clearly in both Yiddish and English. When they get married, they are often required to do all of the talking when there is a need to deal with the secular world. The call to the gas company to discuss a bill or the call to the phone company to change a service is usually made by the wife. If the Yiddish-speaking husband tries to interact with these people on the phone with his broken English, *he is looked upon as less than intelligent*. If he goes into the English-speaking work force, he is severely handicapped by his lack of language ability.

"Some of the boys are fluent in English"

We can always point to certain boys or men who can speak English beautifully even though they grew up in a Yiddish-speaking environment. They are fortunate. They have talent in languages. Very few people have this talent. Without innate talent, the acquisition of language is very difficult after early childhood.

Language potential

All normal babies are born with the ability to master several different languages. It is not at all unusual for a young child to hear different languages spoken by different caregivers and easily learn all of them. Even children who have a developmental handicap such as Down's syndrome are often multilingual.

Speech delay in multilingual children

The young child who learns more than one language might start talking fluently a little later than a monolingual child. There is often a delay as he sorts out the words in the different languages. This is not a sign of trouble, since the languages get sorted out within a few months. Even adding a third language is not a problem.

Knowing multiple languages is an advantage to any child

Every language that is developed in a child's brain will add to his ability to understand and express these languages later in life. I always encourage Israeli parents to speak Hebrew to the children and have them respond in kind. These children understand the *tefillos* and the *Chumash* much better than their peers who don't have this advantage.

What causes the problem?

What causes the great discrepancy between our Yiddish-speaking American-born boys and girls? They are raised in the same families. They have the same intellectual abilities. The schools are under the same auspices. They all have complete command of Yiddish. What gives the girls the ability to think in English and speak without accents? Why can't the boys do it as well?

Language development

Here is how children develop the ability to use the English language:

A child's brain has *two language processing centers for each language – the Receptive* and the *Expressive.*

When a baby hears English, an *English Receptive* region in the brain opens up. With continued exposure to English, the region will begin to develop, and the child will be able to discern and perceive the particular sounds that make up the language. This includes the specific English *phonemes* – the sound fragments that characterize language. The phonemes come together to make up words and are also the building blocks of *accents.*

As time goes by, the child learns and understands more and more new words and expressions. The English Receptive region grows as his receptive vocabulary increases.

Speaking is different from understanding

When this same child starts to speak and think in English, a new region – the *expressive region for English* – opens up. The more the language is spoken actively by the child, the bigger this new Expressive region grows, as it fills with new words and phrases that can be thought and spoken. Eventually it equals the Receptive center. Once both regions are fully developed, English becomes a natural part of the child's mind and can be used at will.

The girls' advantage

This happens at an early age in our girls, who are exposed to more English-speaking places and people in their lives outside of school. They are often required to speak

English from an early age. As a result, most girls are able to use both languages equally well. They are *bilingual.*

The boys' disadvantage

Because of their different learning environment, most boys in our community understand English adequately, but they **do not start speaking English until about age 7,** when it is introduced into the curriculum at school. **This is too late for most of them.** If the English Expressive region is not allowed to open by about age 4, it becomes much more difficult to open with each passing year. **Learning to speak proper English will become more and more difficult.**

English as a Second Lang+ge

The older child who tries to start speaking English will be forced to use his only fully developed Expressive center, the Yiddish one, to formulate the thoughts that he wants to express in English. English thus becomes a "second language." The accent, awkward grammar, and poor vocabulary are the results.

How do we solve this problem?

Have them speak English as youngsters. The solution is easy. It does not require that the schools add anything to their curriculum. The best way to give the boys real command of English is to have the mothers, who have the best English accents and vocabularies, speak English to them and have the boys respond in kind.

If doing this all the time is not acceptable, a lot can be gained by doing it only in the home, or even doing it only one day a week.

One suggestion: A family could make one day a week "English Day." On that day, at breakfast, dinner and after dinner, all of the children in the family will practice speaking only English. They might also read aloud from books written in English. The mother would speak only English, and listen and gently correct the children if they make errors in grammar or pronunciation when they respond. English Day could be made into a fun family time. Even this limited exposure, if begun early, will help the development of both the English Receptive and the English Expressive regions.

By maintaining the integrity of Yiddish as the primary language there would be little, if any, impact on the "flavor" of the home. If the boys are encouraged to speak English even part time, they will become truly bilingual. They will be much happier with themselves. Their poor command of English will no longer be a source of embarrassment, feelings of inadequacy, and dependency.

CHAPTER 11

The Timing of Toilet Training

The timing of toilet training has changed over the years. Most mothers have to work outside the home and the task of toilet training, which requires several days of careful monitoring, is pushed off until the child is older. I received this letter addressed to my advice column in the *Binah Magazine.*

Key Points

- Early training is the norm throughout the rest of the world.
- Training takes a few days of closely watching a child's body language.
- Later training often causes fear and impatience.
- All kids get trained eventually.

Dear Dr. Schulman,

My son is three-and-a-half years old, and he is still in diapers. He is terrified of using the toilet, especially for bowel movements. His teacher tells me that there are several other boys in his class with the same problem. Why are we having so much trouble toilet-training these kids?

Young Mom

Timing is the problem

We are seeing many kids with this exact problem since the trend has been to train them at an older age. They are simply too smart and resistant to change when they are older. Toilet-training is meant to develop an automatic habit that "making" is for toilets, not diapers. Children wearing the new gel type of disposable diapers do not feel wet when they urinate. They sometimes feel uncomfortable when they have a soiled diaper, but many do not complain. They just remain accustomed to ignoring the whole business as they go about the tasks of toddlerhood. Late training requires them to deal with it at a time when they are more likely to have other preferences. When kids are trained at younger ages, they simply incorporate using the toilet into their routine before they have a "mind of their own."

Your parents were trained before two years of age

The average age for toilet-training children has been rising steadily in the United States since the invention of the washing machine, and recently, the availability of disposable diapers. In 1950, the average American child was trained by 18 months. Now the average age is over 30 months.

In most places in the world today where mothers have to wash their own diapers, children are still being toilet-trained by 18 months of age.

Toilet-training requires time and effort, usually for a few focused days. Because most mothers work outside the home, it is simply much more convenient to let the child remain in diapers. Most kids will train themselves eventually, even if it takes until four years of age or older.

Many psychologists write that it is better for the parents to wait until the child is "ready." Some experts even claim that early training leads to psychological damage. I disagree. It has been my experience that waiting until the child is over 2 ½ to begin training is not a good idea. The older child is much more likely to feel afraid and become resistant to the whole concept. This leads to withholding bowel movements and painful experiences when he eventually does defecate.

When a baby is put on a potty seat at the age of one and a half whenever he shows body language indicating he is "pushing," he is not frightened at all. He just gets used to it and associates the activity with the potty. This kind of training requires watching the child and being aware of his body habits. Most kids defecate after a meal, since the natural reflex is to empty the bowels when the stomach is full. This requires the parent to become adept in observing the child before he is trained to go to the potty himself. Once the child is "clean," training him to be "dry" does not usually cause fear and resistance.

Ask your grandmother how and when she trained her children. She could give you some good tips!

CHAPTER 12

Buying Children's Shoes

Some parents feel that they must go to expensive shoe stores to buy their children shoes. Other parents go to discount shoe stores and fit their own children's shoes. Is there really such a big difference to the children?

A very well-respected pediatric orthopedist, Dr. Robert Siffert, once told me that "shoes are meant to keep the socks clean." The shoes also protect the feet from cold and injury, especially outdoors. They do not influence the way feet grow. Only the unusual child with a "c-shaped" footprint needs corrective shoes. Handicapped children may need custom-made orthotics or inserts, but arches in readymade shoes do not do anything for the child. "Support" is not important. The muscles in the foot develop strength when they are used. Walking without shoes actually strengthens the feet and ankles.

Some toddlers are loose-limbed and wobbly. High-top shoes sometimes make them feel more secure when they are first trying to walk. High top shoes are also very hard to pull off. The child will probably not be able to throw a high top out of the stroller!

Key Points

- Shoes are needed to protect the feet and keep the socks clean.
- Shoes do not influence the growth of normal feet.
- High tops help wobbly new walkers and are hard for the baby to pull off.
- The child's normal feet will not know the difference between expensive and cheap shoes.

I always tell mothers to buy inexpensive shoes, especially Shabbos shoes and sneakers, and I instruct them how to fit them:

- Estimate the size by standing the child on a Brannock, or shoe sizer.

Slip the shoe onto the foot. If it is a struggle, choose a larger size.

- Stand the child up and press the top of the shoe to find the end of the big toe. If it is closer than ½ inch from the end of the shoe, try the next size. If it is further than that, the shoe is probably too long.

  - Pinch the shoe side to side above the toes. If it "tents," the shoe is too wide; if it doesn't move at all it is too narrow. If it "gives" a little, it is okay.

  - Let the child walk in the shoes to see if they are comfortable and stay on the feet.

  - Children with feet that are not very narrow or very wide usually fit into these inexpensive shoes.

These shoes do not hold up very long, but the child usually outgrows them by the time he wears them out. For sweaty feet, sandals and soft (non-patent) leather shoes are preferable.

Many mothers are not comfortable trying to fit their own child's shoes. They should go to those shoe stores that have trained shoe-fitters and good quality shoes.

Discount or not, the children's feet will do fine in any shoes that fit comfortably.

■ ■ ■

Nutrition

CHAPTER 13

Eating and Growth

Of all of the miracles we witness every day, the growth of our children is one of the most remarkable. The growth spurt in the first year of life is truly incredible. Imagine how crazy it would be if we found ourselves triple our current weight and 50 percent taller one year from now. Yet we do not seem at all surprised when it happens to the average seven-pound newborn infant. (Smaller babies often nearly quadruple their weight, and larger babies only double their weight, but we will use the average-sized boy baby for the sake of this discussion.)

One thing we all understand is that the infant needs to eat to grow. A voracious appetite driven by the need to grow allows the baby to consume over 100 calories per kilogram every day. That is the equivalent of an adult consuming 6,000 to 7,000 calories a day! For the first few months, when the infant is still unable to move around much, the fat piles up all over the body, and the baby reaches double his birth weight. From about 4-6 months of age and on, some of the calories are burned by activity, and the baby gains weight

Key Points

- Infants need astounding amounts of food calories in the first year of life.
- The consumption tapers off in toddlerhood.
- Teenagers need a lot of extra calories during their growth-spurt years.
- Good eating habits are good for a lifetime.
- There is a much higher risk of diabetes when obesity is acquired during adolescence.

less rapidly.

This rapid growth rate tapers off at about one year of age. For the next few years, the child consumes fewer calories than he did in infancy. The increase in weight is only about 3-4 pounds, and the increase in height only about 3 inches for the whole second year of life. The appetite is considerably smaller and the activity level is relentless. The toddler only needs about 20-24 ounces of milk a day, and only eats about two tablespoons of each food at a meal.

Many parents are alarmed by this decrease in consumption. They try to feed the child even when he is not hungry. This is not wise. Many studies have shown that children will eat as much as they need if offered a variety of foods.

The real job

When it comes to food, **the most important job** that parents have during the toddler and childhood years **is to encourage good eating habits in their children**. A balanced diet of fruits and vegetables, high-quality proteins, unsaturated fats and high-fiber carbohydrates not only nourishes the child; it also gives him the enjoyment of these foods throughout life. This is the key to healthy eating as an adult.

Healthy eating habits also include eating real meals while sitting at the table, and eating about two snacks a day. Even the snacks should be at set times of day for toddlers, so that the child learns the difference between "eating times" and "play" or "sleep times." The toddler who has a continuous "nosh" all day long has a much harder time limiting his eating when he is older.

Childhood

As the child grows slowly through the ages of 3-11, he eats only about one tablespoon per year of age for typical portions of the food at his meals. He should drink about 20 ounces of milk, or eat yogurt, cottage cheese or hard cheese instead of some of these ounces. Juice should be limited to only 4 ounces a day, preferably as one drink. The rest of the drinks should be water.

The habit of always drinking sweet drinks is another cause of weight problems later on. Water is refreshing, convenient and even has fluoride to help teeth. A sports bottle filled with cold tap water is usually acceptable as a take-along drink for kids.

Adolescence

At around age 11 for girls, and age 14 for boys, another growth spurt starts, and parents are amazed at the increase in their child's appetite. This can be particularly alarming when the child starts storing fat around the abdomen before the growth actually starts to accelerate. **This is a very tricky and important time**. There is a delicate balance between the need to grow, the amount of calories used by exercise, the need to eat for social and emotional gratification, and the genetic makeup of the child. It is very important to have the child's doctor monitor the growth in height and weight during the pre-adolescent and adolescent years.

Inches and pounds

Fueling the actual growth during this last big growth spurt requires a lot of calories. The teenager gets very hungry, often later in the evening. The height increases in spurts, causing a need for extra food. Every inch a girl grows increases the weight by about 5 pounds. Every inch a boy grows increases the weight about 7 pounds. This is because the heart, liver and other organs increase in size, and the bones and muscles become longer and stronger.

To gain a pound, the body needs to take in about 3,500 calories more than the amount used. This is why I warn mothers that they must count a growing adolescent boy as two people to feed! *How much of this extra eating is enough?* How much is too much? This can depend on the build of the child. Children with broader frames gain more than children with smaller frames. The 5-7 pound-per-inch average is for average-sized kids. It is important that the growing adolescent be allowed to feel satisfied and not hungry.

The most important help you can give your growing teenager is to make sure there is real, high-quality food around when he or she needs to eat. An extra portion of chicken, a tuna sandwich, and other real substantial food will fill him up without his needing greasy snack foods. Salads and fruit alone will not be enough, since their calorie content is low.

Activity and growth

Growing bones and muscles strengthen and straighten when actively exercised. The level of activity often determines posture, as well as overall balanced weight gain during this growth period. Growing children should walk to school and back, run around and play active games during the daytime breaks, and generally not sit down during their spare time. This is a physical need of the growing body.

Delicate balance

If a growing adolescent tries to control his or her intake too strictly during this time, the final, actual growth could be stunted. Eating disorders such as anorexia or bulimia can cause a derangement of their maturation and growth that can affect the rest of their lives.

On the other hand, excessive weight gain during this growth period can lead to a lifetime of struggling to maintain a healthy body weight. **There is a particular danger to being obese as an adolescent.** The risk of diabetes is much greater than it is when the excess weight is acquired in adulthood. If there is obesity and diabetes in the family, the risk is even higher. In these families, every effort must be made to avoid obesity during adolescence.

Habits for a lifetime

We have a great responsibility to be conscious of our children's eating habits. Good habits, formed early, last a lifetime. We should consider the role junk foods play in our everyday life. If we could limit these treats for *oneg Shabbos* only, they would not be such a big factor in our children's diets. Now that we know how important eating habits are, we can make the effort to do the right thing for our families.

■ ▓ ▓

CHAPTER 14

New Ideas About Baby Food

Mothers of young babies are often not clear on when to start solid foods and which ones are appropriate. This whole subject is currently being debated by the experts as we struggle to understand the obesity epidemic and the ramifications of how we feed our infants. Baby food companies have convinced the American population that they are the only source of good nutrition for babies. These foods are expensive and certainly not more nourishing than homemade foods. There are many foods that are easily prepared for infants at home.

Key Points

- Babies love people food.
- Chicken soup and cholent make great baby foods.
- Babies need to practice finger feeding before their first birthday.
- Avoid choking hazard foods.

HERE IS MY APPROACH TO FEEDING BABIES

Breast-fed infants

If an infant is exclusively breast-fed, it is reasonable to allow him to continue until about a year of age, as long as he is thriving. From 9 months on, it is a good idea to give the child small amounts of finger foods or allow him to hold a very large food item such as a bagel, just to suck on and to practice tasting and touching food. If he is getting any bottles at all, these should be replaced by solid feedings after 9 months of age.

The reason for this: If the natural mouthing stage is passed without any chance to taste and try foods, the child might severely resist when he is introduced to foods after a year of age.

Bottle-fed infants

Although we keep nursing infants on only Mommy's milk as long as they are thriving, we usually recommend giving "solids" around 6 months of age to formula-fed babies. By gradually increasing the solid food, we slowly decrease the emphasis on formula in the diet, so that by one year of age they are down to about 18-20 ounces of formula, milk or milk products per day, and the solid foods form the basis for the daily nutrition.

Rethinking traditional baby foods

Most people assume the baby needs commercial baby foods. Infant cereals and jars of fruit have traditionally been the first foods given. This means the infant is eating refined cereals that are low fiber and made of "white" starch, and sweet fruit sauces that are primarily sugar in their nutritional composition.

Since we are seriously trying to limit the intake of "white" starches in everybody's diet, and trying to reduce the constant demand for sweet foods, it would make more sense to give the baby higher-quality foods that we hope he will enjoy eating as an older child and as an adult.

A new approach

I feel that the first foods should be chicken soup, chicken, and cooked vegetables (carrots, sweet potatoes, parsnip, squash, etc.) from the soup. Each new food should be started one at a time, with a few days in between, watching for any adverse reactions. Eventually, the soup, chicken, and all the vegetables can be blended together for a delicious, wholesome and balanced meal. If, after eating carrots and other yellow vegetables on a daily basis, the baby's skin starts looking orange, decrease the yellow vegetables to about twice a week.

One meal a day is enough in the beginning, then advancing to two meals a day after about eight months. The more the infant eats, the less formula he will take, since the calorie intake remains the same.

To advance the diet, I suggest starting legumes, such as pea soup, blended lentil soup, and, of course, cholent. Beans, barley, potatoes, and meat make great baby food! I prefer using applesauce or other fruits for dessert and snacks. Non-sweetened dry breakfast cereals that melt in the mouth make safe snack foods. Cooked cereals are also a traditional baby food. Whole grain oatmeal works fine, but it should be blended smooth when the baby is young. Other cereals such as farina (cream of wheat), corn meal grits, etc., can also be cooked for the baby. From the time we begin solids we also add allergenic foods, such as milk products, fish, eggs, peanut butter (including Bamba).

With this regimen, most babies enjoy eating, since these foods taste good and everyone else is eating the same thing. As the child gets closer to nine months of age, we give him almost any table food that is soft enough to be eaten either by fingers or spoon.

Milk

It is important to be aware of which milk products are best for a young child.

From the time milk products are introduced at around nine months, until about two years of age, whole milk products are recommended. Whole milk, 4% milkfat cottage cheese, deluxe yogurts, sour cream, and cheese are all fine. After age two, it is better to start using low-fat milk products such as low-fat yogurt, 1% milk-fat cottage cheese and 1% milk-fat milk.

Cheeses are mostly made from whole milk, and they are a good source of calcium, calories and protein. The problem is that "American cheese" is not really cheese. If you look at the label, you'll see that it is called "processed cheese food." It has a small amount of milk and a large amount of other ingredients, including commercial fats, added in the processing. It is basically a junk food. I advise parents to give Muenster, Mozzarella, Swiss, Edam, and other real cheeses. They are much more nourishing for the kids.

Most kids are eating three meals a day by the time they are about a year old. At this time they should be getting about 18 ounces of milk or milk products a day. The rest of the fluid intake should be water. Juices should be given only once a day as a treat and a source of vitamin C. (See Chapter 15, Understanding the Need for Calcium)

Choking prevention

There are some foods that are actually dangerous for young children. Nuts, raw carrots, and other foods that require hard chewing should be delayed until after 3 years of age. Grapes, frankfurters, and other smooth, round foods can block the airway, so they need to be peeled and cut lengthwise – never in wheels. Peanut butter should be given between two layers of bread or between two crackers to avoid choking.

CHAPTER 15

What Are We Feeding Our Children?

Key Points

- Eating habits formed in childhood can last a lifetime.
- Processed snack foods are not satisfying.
- Everyone needs breakfast.
- School meals should be high in quality.
- Water is the best drink.
- Save the junk for Shabbos.

We all know that eating habits formed in childhood can last a lifetime. The challenge is to know what foods are appropriate to feed our children. Recently there has been a dramatic increase in the number of obese children and adolescents. This had led to an alarming increase in the number of young people with Type 2 diabetes. Our own community has experienced this problem. Are we doing something wrong in the way we are feeding our families?

Snack foods

When you walk into any kosher grocery, you can get a hint of what is happening to our children. The shelves are full of packaged, processed snack foods. These have become a major factor in the diets of our children. Potato chips, Super Snacks, candy, and cookies have become standard fare.

There are several problems with these snacks: 1) They are full of saturated and hydrogenated oil; 2) they are mostly based on refined white starches; 3) they have corn sweeteners; 4) they have too much salt.

Snack foods make people hungry

The fact is that they are not at all satisfying, because these ingredients make the consumer desire to eat more. The **oil** is tasty and feels good in the mouth, inducing a craving for more. The **low-fiber white starches,** such as white flour and white potato, cause a rebound hunger when they are digested. The **corn sweeteners,** or **high-fructose corn syrup,** has the ability to be consumed in large quantities without satisfying hunger. The salty taste triggers the desire for more.

High-fructose corn syrup, a cheap and powerfully-sweet natural substance, is present in nearly every package of food produced, including cakes, cookies, cereals, crackers, sodas, and flavored drinks and candies. It has been implicated in the diabetes problem, since it is metabolized differently than other sugars. Check the labels! It is amazing how much of it we eat every day.

Many experts have said that if we could go back to baking our own snack foods our kids would be healthier, since the ingredients we use at home are more wholesome than those used in the factories. Using canola oil or other low-saturated fat oil instead of solid oils like shortening, and table sugar instead of corn sweetener, would be a major difference. Of course, fresh fruits and vegetables, and dried fruits and nuts also make great snack foods.

Besides snacks, we must be thoughtful about what our children eat at meals. Breakfast, lunch, and dinner are all important in establishing good eating habits.

Breakfast

Many studies have shown that eating breakfast is very important to school children and adults. A child's ability to learn and concentrate is greatly impaired by skipping breakfast. People who skip breakfast tend to eat more in the course of the day than those who eat breakfast.

Breakfast cereals can be a good source of nutrition, especially when eaten with milk. The sweetened cereals are up to 50 percent sugar, so they should be limited to Shabbos or just used to flavor other cereals that are high in fiber. Whole-grain bread and butter or cream cheese (moderate amounts) is fine for breakfast. All yogurts are good breakfast foods. Plain yogurt that has fresh fruit and table sugar added is best.

Some children are not hungry, or are too concerned about vomiting on the bus, or even too rushed to eat before leaving the house. For these kids a "take along meal" like fruit, string cheese, and whole-wheat crackers will help get the day started.

School snacks

Some schools are wisely beginning to restrict what the young kids bring for snacks. At least one of the snack times in school should be limited to "healthy," unprocessed food. Fruits, vegetables, dried fruit, and nuts are good examples. (Nuts and raw carrots and grapes that are uncut should not be given before age 4 because of danger of choking.)

Lunch and dinner

It is very important that parents be aware of what their kids are being served at school. No matter how careful we are about food at home, our kids are consuming unacceptable diets at school. This is a battle that can only be won by parental involvement in planning school lunch menus.

Lunches and dinners should be made of high-quality food. The most satisfying foods that keep a child comfortable until the next scheduled meal or snack are the ones that **have high protein content, starches that are full of fiber, and some fat,** preferably "healthy" oils. This list of course includes fish, poultry, and meats, low fat milk products, brown rice and whole-wheat bread, cereal, and crackers. In addition, there is a whole category of food that fits this description – legumes.

Legumes

These include all beans, lentils, peanuts, soybeans, and chickpeas. Legumes are high in fiber and protein, and they have high quality oils, and vitamins and minerals. Chickpeas make a great snack food that is really food. Hummus, which is made from chickpeas and sesame oil, is a good spread. Green beans, snap peas, pea soup, baked beans, bean soups, lentil soup, and parve cholent are all good legume foods. Most kids love lentil soup as much as Esav did!

Natural peanut butter, which is made of only peanuts and salt, is a very good legume food for the child who is not allergic to peanuts. (The oil must be mixed in when the jar is opened.) It is much better in quality than hydrogenated peanut butter. Peanut butter should be spread on something and covered with a "lid," since it can cause choking if eaten straight. A natural peanut butter and jelly sandwich on whole-wheat bread with a glass of low-fat milk is a very nourishing meal. (Far better than low fiber bread and Skippy with a box drink!)

Besides legumes, olives and avocados are full of a very healthy nourishing type of oil. Corn in any form is a tasty food that has oil and starch and a small amount of fiber.

All nuts and seeds in all forms are very nourishing for kids age 4 and up.

Refined white flour found in most breads and pasta and white potatoes is okay, but it tends to cause the child to be hungry much sooner than the high-fiber starches such as whole wheat, brown rice, sweet potatoes, and squash. There is a new pasta called Barilla Plus that contains legume flour and is much more nourishing and filling than regular pasta. Of course, most meals and snacks should have fruits and vegetables added.

Drinks

Drinks are very important. Most calories consumed as liquid are not noticed by the brain's satisfaction center. For this reason juices, which are full of sugar, should be limited to one glass a day, and the rest of the day the child should drink milk (about three glasses a day) and lots of water or seltzer. Sodas and box drinks along with candy and other treats are only for Shabbos party or special occasions.

Final thought

Our children grow up eating what we give them. We do not have to be completely at the mercy of what is fashionable. Just because processed and packaged foods are available and convenient does not compel us to buy them. Let's go back to plain old basics. We can reverse the obesity epidemic in our community. Shopping, eating, snacking, and drinking habits can be changed. We must think about it. It is our responsibility as parents to be aware of the long-range health consequences of consuming the foods we are offering to our families.

CHAPTER 16

Understanding the Need for Calcium

Key Points

- Our girls are not getting enough calcium.
- Adequate intake of calcium must be maintained throughout life.
- Calcium is found in dairy products and legumes.
- Osteoporosis is the consequence of poor calcium intake.

Although we are doing our best to raise healthy children, we are really neglecting an important problem. Our girls are growing up with very inadequate calcium intake. The results of this won't show until they are in their forties and fifties when they will be battling *osteoporosis.* Many mothers and grandmothers who are now at that age are just finding out that they have the problem and are at high risk for fractures as they get older.

The problem

The reason for real concern is that as we age, if we have not built up a good amount of bone mass, our bones weaken and the risk of fracture increases dramatically. This can have a devastating effect on overall health. A painful hip fracture from a simple fall can cause multiple problems including blood clots, pneumonia, depression, and other serious health problems. Spinal bone fractures cause severe back pain, nerve compression and loss of bodily functions, among other conditions.

These disabling fractures occur spontaneously, even if there was no injury from a fall. The loss of mobility and chronic pain is often the beginning of a downhill spiral in the older person's health and vitality. Weak bones can rob any person of the enjoyment of daily life and the joys of long life.

The dual function of calcium

Calcium is a mineral that is essential to our health. It is the substance that gives our bones hardness and strength. It also must be circulated in the blood to maintain heart rhythm, nerve and muscle function, and a number of delicate metabolic balances. It is so essential to life function that there must always be a steady level of it in the blood. The body removes calcium from the bones and puts it into the blood if there is inadequate intake from the diet.

Calcium requirements

To maintain bone strength and all the functions of calcium, all of our living bones go through the constant processes of bone breakdown and new bone formation. Hormones govern both of these processes. The balance of breakdown and build up is different at different ages. One thing is certain: Throughout life, a constant intake of calcium is necessary.

Variation in calcium requirements with age

During a little girl's childhood, when growth occurs, growth hormone predominates and most of the bone activity is concentrated in building up bones in length and strength. The calcium requirements are high, *1,200 – 1,500 milligrams* per day. Once maturity is reached, growth stops. The strength of her bones is at its lifetime peak.

At this point, during the young-adult phase of her life, bone density stabilizes as the amount of breakdown equals the amount of new bone formation. This is maintained by high levels of the hormone estrogen, which protects her from excessive bone loss. The calcium requirements decrease slightly to *1,000* milligrams per day at this time.

During pregnancy there is a very high level of estrogen, but the need for calcium is increased to provide material for bone growth for the unborn baby. The requirement is *1,200 – 1,500* milligrams per day.

As the woman reaches age 45 – 55, there is a natural decrease in estrogen. This allows more bone to be broken down than is built up. Calcium requirements increase to *1,200 – 1,500* milligrams per day. At that point in a woman's life, if she doesn't have a really good peak bone mass, the bone breakdown will silently lead to dangerously low bone mineral density: Osteoporosis. If this happens, fracture risk rises dramatically.

Calcium in the diet

Calcium is found in dairy products and legumes, such as soy and beans. Bones have calcium, so fish, like canned salmon and sardines with the bones left in, are a source of calcium. Most of us started out drinking three glasses of milk a day when we were children. This provided us about 1,200 milligrams of calcium each day. Over the last twenty years, the average amount of milk and milk products consumed by children and adults has decreased dramatically. The result of this change in diet is a serious decrease in bone mineral density, **especially in young women who are missing the chance to build up their bone strength during the most critical time in their lives.**

In summary, children, teenagers, pregnant women, and the elderly need *1,200 – 1,500* milligrams of calcium, while young adults need about 1000 milligrams daily. (Men and boys need calcium too, but the problem with osteoporosis starts at a later age, and is less severe than in women.)

The most important time when bones are built up to the peak adult bone mass is during puberty. *During the final growth spurt,* the young teenage girl not only grows taller, but she broadens and strengthens her bones dramatically. It is during this critical time when **a poor calcium intake can be a major mistake that will affect her bone health for the rest of her life.**

Recently, a pediatric endocrinologist tested the bone mineral density of teenage girls in our Bais Yaakov high schools and discovered that a large percentage of the teenage girls have very low bone mineral density at this critical age when they should have peak bone mass. This means that if they do not start concentrating on their calcium intake from now on, they are very likely to suffer from osteoporosis in the future.

Additional risk factors for osteoporosis

Besides calcium intake, there are several other contributing factors that put women at risk for the problem of osteoporosis.

- Family history: If a woman's mother, grandmother, sisters or aunts have osteoporosis, her own risk of developing it is higher.

- Small size: If a woman weighs less than 120 pounds, she is more likely to have a small, delicate bone structure, which increases her risk.
- Drugs such as chemotherapy and cortisone increase risk for osteoporosis.
- Sedentary women who rarely walk and exercise are at increased risk.
- Surgery, such as removal of ovaries, can increase risk.

The solution: START NOW! We can start immediately to help our daughters, and mothers, and ourselves avoid the complications of osteoporosis. Our first job is to get our children and all of us on enough calcium.

Milk products

All milks, including low-fat and skim milks, have about 400 milligrams per 8-ounce portion. Cottage cheese and yogurts have about 400 milligrams in 6 ounces. Cheeses are a good source of calcium, but sliced, processed American cheese has the least. Muenster, Mozzarella, Gouda, Edam and Swiss cheese have good amounts of calcium.

The problem with milk products is that they often have very high saturated fat and cholesterol content. Since this is not desirable in older children and adults, the best milk products are those made from fat-free milk or low-fat milk. There are other problems that some people have with milk, such as digestive intolerance and allergy.

Calcium supplements

We now have fortified juices and drinks, which contain calcium. These are good sources of calcium, but many are also very high in sugar calories. For this reason it is better to only drink Rice Dream or calcium-fortified orange juice once a day.

There are many calcium supplements, which are easy to take. Calcium carbonate chewables like Tums Ultra contain 400 milligrams in each tablet. Viactiv contains 500 milligrams of calcium plus 400 of vitamin D. Calcium carbonate comes in tablets, as does calcium citrate. There are many other supplements, although some are made from nonkosher ingredients, and some cause constipation. Most daily multivitamin supplements contain only 200 milligrams of calcium.

It is important to know that we can only absorb about 500 milligrams of calcium at a time. This means that even if we take 1000 milligrams, we will receive only 500 milligrams. The extra is wasted. **Calcium foods or supplements must be eaten at three different times in the day to be absorbed properly.**

Exercise can help prevent osteoporosis

Another factor in protecting ourselves is exercise. Weight-bearing exercise, such as walking, helps maintain bone strength throughout life. We must all try to keep active throughout our lives. In many ways exercise is the "fountain of youth."

Prescription medication

Fortunately, for those women who already have low bone density, there are new medications such as Fosamax, Actonel, Evista, and Reclast (a once-a-year infusion), which can prevent further bone breakdown. A new injectable drug was recently approved by the FDA – Forteo – which is the only drug that actually increases bone mass. A doctor must prescribe these medications if they are needed.

When it comes to osteoporosis, prevention is the best cure

Now that we understand the nature of bones and the need for calcium, we must do the right thing and take care of ourselves. When it comes to osteoporosis, "prevention is the cure." Talk to your children and your mother and your sisters about maintaining good calcium intake. By being conscientious and eating properly, we can look forward to a safer, healthier, and much more comfortable old age.

(A word about vitamin D: To maintain good bone health, children and adults need both calcium and vitamin D. During growth, a severe curvature of the legs, known as rickets, can be caused by lack of vitamin D. This problem is extremely rare now in the United States, since so many foods are fortified with vitamin D. Vitamin D is also manufactured in our own bodies when our skin is exposed to small amounts of sunlight. It is estimated that everyone needs 400 to 800 units of vitamin D a day.)

CHAPTER 17

Carbohydrates

We all know that carbohydrates are an essential component of a normal diet. We have also been thoroughly confused by the dietary medical advice given by experts. This advice is constantly changing. High-carbohydrate, low-fat diets turned out to be a major cause of the obesity epidemic. High-protein, low-carbohydrate diets caused kidney stones and other metabolic derangements. The truth is that "diets" do not even cause lasting weight loss. The only real weight control comes from good eating habits and plenty of exercise. No matter what we eat, if we eat more calories than we use, we store the excess as fat.

It is important to understand how to eat carbohydrates as a part of a healthy lifestyle.

There are three types of carbohydrates – sugars, starches, and fiber.

Key Points

- Carbohydrates are essential components of a healthy diet.
- Sugars are digested very rapidly, triggering hunger.
- High fructose corn syrup can stimulate the production of abdominal fat.
- Fiber is not absorbed. It is beneficial in aiding digestion and slowing the rate of absorption of the food.
- Unrefined starches have fiber. They do not trigger hunger.
- Refined starches have all of the fiber removed. They trigger hunger because they are digested rapidly, and they stimulate high insulin levels.

SUGARS – THE BASIC FUEL

The role of Insulin

Sugars are the simplest food molecules. They are digested very rapidly and absorbed into the bloodstream. Insulin levels rise quickly when sugars are digested. Insulin sends the sugar into the cells, lowering the blood sugar level. Insulin also goes directly to the brain to stimulate appetite. Sugar, which is the most basic form of fuel, is burned by the cells to create energy.

Sugars occur naturally in honey, fruits, roots, legumes, sugar cane, and milk.

Sucrose – table sugar

The most common sources of table sugar – sucrose – are sugar cane and sugar beets. Common sense tells use how much of this type of sugar we are consuming, since we usually add it to our foods ourselves.

Fructose

The sugar found in fruits and vegetables and grains is called fructose. Since fruits and roots also have starch and fiber, it is almost impossible to get too much sugar from eating them. Juices, which have these other components removed, are made up of water and sugar with some vitamins included. They contain a lot of sugar and they can be a real source of extra calories. It has even been shown that fructose does not reach the satisfaction centers in the brain, so people never feel full from drinking juices and soft drinks, even if they have consumed many calories.

High fructose corn syrup – a serious problem

The important thing to know about fructose is that in **very large quantities** it increases abdominal fat. There is a concentrated source of fructose known as high fructose corn syrup. It is natural, it is much cheaper than table sugar, and it tastes the same, so it is very popular with manufacturers of packaged foods. If you look at the labels of all of the packaged foods you use, you will find high fructose corn syrup in almost everything. All naturally-sweetened beverages such as sodas, teas, punch, and juice drinks (including all of the box drinks you give your kids!) are loaded with this type of sugar – cookies, crackers, cakes, candies, and even cornflakes have this natural sweetener.

Many experts now think that the obesity epidemic in the United States started when this product was developed in the 1960s. Packaged goods became much cheaper to produce, so portion sizes increased. (Sodas went from 12 ounces to a quart for the same price!)

Lactose - milk sugar

All animal milks, including mother's milk, contain a naturally occurring sugar called lactose. Lactose is only one component of the milk, which also has fats and proteins. It is not usually a source of excess sugar. Some people have difficulty digesting this sugar, a condition known as lactose intolerance.

Honey

Honey is a sugary syrup produced by bees from the nectar of flowers. It is a mixture of fructose and glucose. There are a few beneficial chemicals in honey, but it is basically the same as any sugar in the diet. Honey should not be given to babies under one year of age because of the risk of botulism.

Starches

Starches are complicated molecules, so it takes longer for the body to digest them. When they are digested, they are broken down to sugar to be used for energy. There are three types of starches – fiber, unrefined starches, and refined starches.

Fiber

Fiber, which is a carbohydrate, is not a source of calories, because fiber is not absorbed into the bloodstream after it is digested. Fiber is found naturally in sweet potatoes, legumes, fruits, vegetables, squashes, grains and quinoa. Soluble fibers dissolve in water. Insoluble fibers do not dissolve in water. All fibers are excreted with solid waste. Fiber aids digestion by maintaining the water balance in the stool. **It also slows the rate the starches are absorbed.** Fiber is considered a very beneficial component of the daily diet.

Unrefined starches

Most naturally occurring starches have some fiber surrounding them. Whole wheat, oats, barley, and beans are all full of fiber. This fiber delays the digestion of the starch, so the body absorbs it slowly. Since the sugars from the starch are not absorbed rapidly, the insulin level in the bloodstream rises slowly when unrefined starches are eaten. There is also no sudden rise and fall of blood sugar. The result is that there is less hunger after eating unrefined starches.

Although starches and sugars have 4 calories per gram, the weight of the fiber can be subtracted from the total amount of unrefined starches that are eaten when calculating calorie intake. For this reason, a cup of whole grain brown rice has fewer calories than refined white rice.

It is useful to know how much fiber is actually in the processed foods we eat. Many products that are labeled "whole wheat" are not really made of unrefined flour. Look for bread that is at least 3 grams of fiber per slice. Multi grain breads can also be made of refined grains.

Refined starches – white starches

White potatoes have very little natural fiber. The starch in them is absorbed and broken down rapidly to sugar. Similarly, when the natural fiber is removed from whole grains, the white starch that is produced is also broken down rapidly. The result is that the blood sugar rises and falls quickly, and hunger is triggered.

Pasta is usually made from refined white flour. If a higher fiber starch is desired, whole wheat and brown rice pasta can be used. A new product, Barilla Plus pasta, is made by mixing bean flour with flour, giving it a high protein and fiber content.

Even though unrefined starch has the same nutritional calorie count as refined starch once it is absorbed, there are still many good reasons to eat the whole grains and other fiber-rich foods.

Final thought

Almost all of the packaged snack foods we buy are made of high fructose corn syrup and refined starches. We should reconsider the eating habits we are teaching our children. Whole grains, quinoa, vegetables, and fruits are called "healthy foods" for a reason. Homemade snacks and baked goods can be made with whole grains, table sugar and healthy fats. (See Chapter 18, Understanding Fats)

Even those of us who are not overweight should not eat the packaged junk. No one benefits from it!

QUINOA: HOW TO USE IT

Quinoa (pronounced KEEN-wah) is a seed that looks like a grain. It grows in the high mountains of South America and Central America. It is the seed of a plant that is related to beets. It is much more nourishing and more satisfying than grains like wheat, oats, and rice. It has a complete protein and a lot of fiber in addition to carbohydrates.

Quinoa has a naturally bitter outer coating that has to be rinsed off before cooking. This is done by running cold water over the grain in a sieve until the foamy substance is no longer evident. I prefer the quinoa sold in boxes, made by the Ancient Harvest Company or sold by Trader Joe's. It is pre-rinsed, so it can be cooked immediately.

Here are my quick and easy recipes for quinoa.

All of my recipes start with making plain quinoa and then adding ingredients. I have found that the flavor is best when it is cooked in a covered Pyrex casserole in the microwave.

Basic quinoa

1 cup of dry or rinsed quinoa

2 cups of cold water

1/2 tsp salt

Combine ingredients and microwave on high for 18-19 minutes.

Or,

Quinoa can also be made by boiling the water and salt and then adding the quinoa. Cook for about 15 minutes and turn off the flame. The quinoa is fully cooked when little white rings appear as they separate from each grain. After cooking, let the quinoa stand for 10 minutes. The quinoa can then be used in the following recipes:

BREAKFAST

Hot quinoa

Heat 1/2 cup of cooked quinoa in microwave or pan.

Add butter or Smart Balance margarine, sprinkle 1 tsp of sugar, and serve as a hot cereal. Milk can be added to cool it off.

Plain, hot quinoa with cold yogurt on top makes a wonderful breakfast that has a delightful "feel" as the cold, smooth yogurt mixes with the hot cereal in the mouth.

LUNCH

Quinoa salad

(This is my favorite, but any rice salad recipe will work well.)

    1 cup of cooked quinoa
    1/2 cup of diced cucumbers, red pepper, and avocado
    Sprinkle in diced mango, craisins, or diced dried fruit, and chopped walnuts or soy nuts or pepitas
    Combine with Italian dressing or Sweet Vidalia Onion dressing (any dressing can be used).

Quinoa in pasta sauce

Heat quinoa in microwave or pan and add pasta sauce. Shredded mozzarella cheese can be sprinkled or mixed in.

SIDE DISH

    Heat quinoa and add sautéed onions or sautéed vegetables, and serve as a side dish.
    Any rice pilaf recipe can be used to flavor the quinoa.
    Plain, hot quinoa is also good as a side dish with meat or chicken or fish.

BEFORE A FAST

Mash one ripe avocado and add about 2 cups of cold cooked quinoa and salt to taste. This dish has the consistency of egg salad. It is so nourishing and filling it can be used as the main food eaten before a fast.

GOOD TO KNOW

Quinoa keeps

Once cooked in a glass casserole, the quinoa stays fresh for at least five days without losing texture or taste. It can be left in the refrigerator as an "always ready" staple to be used in single servings any time it is needed.

Quinoa is usually sold in 12- to 16-ounce packages, but it can be ordered in 25-pound bags from the health food store.

Health benefits of quinoa

■ Quinoa is a very high-fiber food that is good for constipation. It causes less gaseous discomfort than whole wheat or bran.

- Quinoa does not have gluten. It is a good addition to a gluten free diet.
- Quinoa is not a low calorie food, containing about 300 calories per cup. It is, however, very satisfying for a long time after eating, since the fiber delays starch absorption and the proteins take longer to digest.
- Quinoa is a complete food, and is a very good addition to vegetarian diets. The protein in quinoa contains all of the required amino acids for healthy function. It also has a significant amount of iron.

Final thought

Quinoa has only been available for the last few years, so many people do not know about it. Some rabbis have decided that it is even allowed to be eaten on Pesach, since it is not *kitnyos*. I feel it makes a terrific staple food. I hope you will try it in your home.

Proteins

Key Points

- Proteins are necessary in every child's diet.

- Milk has protein and necessary calcium.

- Meats, poultry, eggs, and fish have necessary iron in addition to proteins.

- Legumes are good sources of iron, calcium and protein.

- A combination of different protein sources is preferable in a balanced diet.

Proteins are particularly important in the diet of a growing child. Besides providing energy, proteins are the source of nutrients that are used to produce new tissues such as bones, skin, muscles, heart, liver, and brain tissue. As a child grows, proteins help to build the bigger body.

Proteins are also critical in all the life functions and processes such as digestion, kidney function, and brain function.

Proteins in the diet

In the newborn infant, the nutritional source of protein is mother's milk, cow's-milk-based formula, or soy-based formula. The young infant consumes large quantities of these milks and uses the proteins and other nutrients to undergo an astounding growth spurt during the first year of life. These milks are all very important sources of calcium.

Iron and calcium

Mother's milk contains adequate quantities of iron, but cow's milk and soy do not have iron, so the formulas based on these proteins have iron added to prevent anemia. After weaning and after stopping formula at one year of age, most children rely on cow's milk for calcium. Iron must be acquired from other sources.

When the child starts eating solid foods, the milk intake decreases, and other protein foods become very important. There are two basic categories of food proteins: vegetable proteins and animal proteins.

Vegetable proteins

Vegetables contain varying amounts of proteins. Most of these are incomplete for adequate nutrition, but in combination they become complete.

One example is rice and beans. Together these provide complete protein nutrition.

All of the legumes are protein-rich, and most also contain iron and calcium. This category of vegetable includes all beans: soy, peas, peanuts, lentils, and chickpeas.

Nuts and seeds are all good sources of proteins.

Quinoa, which looks like a grain but is really a seed, contains a complete protein.

Grains such as wheat, oats, barley, buckwheat, and rice contain protein, but in lesser amounts than legumes, nuts and seeds.

Animal proteins

Besides milk, the animal sources of protein are eggs, fish, poultry, and meat.

Egg whites are pure albumen protein, but only the yolks have iron in them.

Fish are all good protein foods. They are also a great source of iron.

Sardines, tilapia, flounder, whitefish, pike, and salmon are all good sources of protein. It is important to know that larger fish such as tuna have higher mercury levels than smaller fish. For this reason, we limit tuna intake to twice a week. Gefilte fish and carefully-deboned flounder and sole make good baby and toddler food.

It is a good idea to give fish regularly in the child's diet so he develops a taste for it. Eating fish is a healthy eating habit throughout life.

The **poultry** category includes chicken, turkey, and duck. These birds are excellent sources of protein. The breast meat, which is white, is almost pure protein. The skin and darker meats are also excellent protein foods, but they contain large amounts of animal fats. These fats are good, but they must be eaten in limited quantities. (See Chapter 18, "Understanding Fats")

Meats, such as beef, lamb, and buffalo are very good sources of protein and iron. The leaner cuts, such as shoulder roasts, contain less animal fat. Rib meat tends to be richer in fat. Broiling and boiling can drain off fats from these meats.

A child's protein requirements

It is very important to maintain a good milk intake in growing children. Milk foods such as yogurt, leben, string cheese and Muenster cheese are all good sources of milk protein. If there is a milk allergy or intolerance, soymilk and soy products such as tofu are good substitutes. There should be three portions of milk a day, including either 6 ounces of milk, or 4 ounces of yogurt or leben, or 1-2 pieces of cheese each time. It is okay to flavor milk to make it more interesting if the child prefers it.

Fish, eggs, poultry and meat, and legumes (including natural peanut butter) should be offered once or twice a day. The usual amount is one tablespoon of any of these foods per year of age at any meal.

When a child is given a variety of protein foods, including milk products, he will get adequate calcium and iron, in addition to the necessary protein in the daily diet. Do not worry if the child refuses occasionally. It is the overall diet over a period of weeks that really counts nutritionally.

CHAPTER 19

Understanding Fats

Key Points

- Low-fat diets that are high in white sugar and starches can cause obesity.
- Basic unprocessed foods are best.
- Saturated fats from milk and meat products are okay, but they should be limited.
- Trans fats are bad for health.
- Unsaturated oils such as fish oils, canola oil, olive oil, and nut oils, are good.
- Toddlers need high fat intake to fuel growth.

Fat is a very important basic component of a good diet. There are many different foods that contain fat, but not all of them are nutritionally ideal. Here is a discussion about fats in the diet.

The nutritional advice that has been offered by the medical profession is often **very confusing, and it changes all the time.** There are a lot more overweight children and adults than there were 20 years ago. Life-threatening diseases such as diabetes and Coronary Artery Disease are common in overweight and obese people. For the first time, the life expectancy of the American population is actually going down. There has been a lot of research into why this has happened.

High fat diets and lack of exercise have been shown to be contributing factors to the obesity epidemic in the U.S. About ten years ago, the experts started recommending that Americans try to eat a diet that is very limited in all fats. They thought that this would cause everyone to eat fewer calories in total. In response to this, the junk food industry began producing high sugar, low fat snack products in an effort to capture the snack food market. **The results were terrible!** While restricting their fat intake, people starting eating more and more sugar and starch. **The obesity epidemic got much worse!**

The experts recently changed their advice. They now differentiate different kinds of starches and fats. They now recommend that we eat a traditional balanced diet, which includes starches, sugars and fat in reasonable amounts – **but only the good ones.**

Here are the basic guidelines

The diet should be full of *unprocessed* foods. Vegetables and fruits, nuts and legumes such as peanuts and beans, and whole grains are all good. The starches should be high fiber grains and legumes and vegetables. The sugars should be mostly the ones already found in the food such as fruits and sweet potatoes. Added sugars are okay, but not in excess.

Children need fat

It is important to know that growing children need plenty of fats in their diets, because growth requires a lot of calories and fat has double the amount of calories found in proteins and carbohydrates. Because toddlers don't eat a lot at a meal, they need a higher percentage of fat in their diets to get enough caloric energy to grow on.

Unsaturated fats are desirable

The fats should be mostly unsaturated fats such as avocado, canola oil, olive oil, nut oils (not palm oil). Oils found in fish are also usually unsaturated. Most vegetable oils such as corn oil, are okay, but not as beneficial as the unsaturated oils.

Peanut oil is okay, but there is a problem with processed peanut butter. In commercial peanut butters, the peanut protein is used, but the peanut oil is extracted and replaced with trans fats, which makes the product creamier and keeps it from separating. For this reason, natural-style peanut butter, which has to be mixed and refrigerated, is a much better choice.

Saturated fats

The fats naturally found in meats, poultry and dairy products are *saturated* fats. They should be restricted by eating mostly leaner cuts and low-fat milk products. Small amounts of these animal fats are okay in a healthy diet.

Trans fats: the "bad fat"

The fats found in most packaged treats and snacks are often "bad fats."

These are trans fats. They were invented by chemists about 100 years ago. The first one was Crisco. This adulterated vegetable oil is used commercially. It makes food taste better and last longer on the shelf. Most margarines, cookies and crackers, chips, and fried foods like French fries – and even fish sticks – usually have trans fats. They are listed on the labels as "partially hydrogenated soy or vegetable oil," "vegetable shortening," and "trans-fatty acids."

Trans fats are known to cause heart disease by increasing LDL (bad cholesterol) and decreasing HDL (good cholesterol). Since the American population is addicted to eating packaged products and fast foods, the experts think trans fats may be making people both fat and sick. There is no amount of trans fat that is good. Many state and local governments are passing laws to eliminate trans fats from restaurant foods.

Final thought

The bottom line is that we should all be eating mostly plain foods that are not processed as fast or snack foods. It has always been my feeling that if we restrict candy, cake and chips, and eat them only on Shabbos, we would all consume a better diet all week, and we would enjoy the "junk" more as part of *oneg Shabbos.*

CHAPTER 20

Preventing Obesity –
Life Habits Are the Key

Key Points

- Obesity is a health hazard.
- Obesity is hard to cure.
- Obesity is preventable with key life habits.

There is an obesity epidemic in the United States. It is becoming a very serious problem in our community, too. Unfortunately, young children are becoming obese. Just look at the class pictures of children 20 years ago. There were very few, if any, obese children in each class. Now every class has at least four or five.

Childhood obesity is a terrible health hazard. The younger the obesity starts, the more medical complications are likely. Obesity actually shortens life expectancy by causing diabetes, high blood pressure ,liver disease, circulatory problems, and heart disease. Obesity even increases the risk for cancer. It also has a profound effect on the enjoyment of life by ruining the knee and hip joints and making simple walking painful. Many obese children and teens suffer from poor self esteem and social embarrassment. In our community it causes serious issues with *shidduchim*.

It is every parent's responsibility to help their children avoid this terrible problem. This is important for every family.

Unfortunately, obesity can sometimes be genetic. Families with this tendency have to try the hardest to prevent their children from becoming obese. Prevention is truly critical, because once the child has become obese it becomes much harder to get down to and maintain normal weight.

A life habit is something that is natural to the child. Children get accustomed to doing things every day without thinking about them. Life habits include behaviors like obedience, respectful conduct, manners, prayers, bathing, bedtime, and observing the laws of Kashrus and Shabbos.

There are three specific life habits that are critical to maintaining healthy body weight.

LIFE HABIT NUMBER 1

Regular exercise — at least one hour a day

A study was published recently about a group of young people of normal weight whose parents were both very obese. The purpose of the study was to find out how they avoided the genetic obesity. The researcher discovered that all of these people had one thing in common. They were athletic. They exercised regularly from the time they were small children. This key life habit had a more important effect than their eating habits.

All children need at least one hour a day of exercise. It does not have to be all at one time. This can include walking to school, recess, gym, playing in the schoolyard, dancing, jump rope, or just running around. This is a sorely lacking life habit in this community.

We cannot just shrug our shoulders and say, "That is impossible!" It is so important that the child's life could depend on it! Look at those old school pictures. Those children got much more activity than our kids today, and they went to the same schools! We must advocate for the children in this community to get more time and opportunity to exercise.

There is no point in putting a child on a diet. Diets do not help at all. Eating and drinking habits are the key.

LIFE HABIT NUMBER 2

Drink only milk or water. No juices or sweet drinks except on Shabbos

Children should drink milk, about two glasses a day if there is no allergy. This important health habit has been lost in this generation. Besides milk, all drinks should be water. Seltzer is okay, but plain water hydrates better, since the carbonation limits the amount that is consumed.

A water bottle should be the only take-along drink. This habit should be started as soon as the child starts consuming any drink besides mother's milk or formula.

Sweet drinks are for Shabbos.

LIFE HABIT NUMBER 3

Five a day! A fruit or a vegetable at every meal or snack

1 - breakfast,

2 - morning snack,

3 - lunch,

4 - afternoon snack,

5 - dinner

Many studies have shown that people who consistently eat fruits and vegetables have much less trouble controlling their weight. It is a key life habit to include either a fruit or vegetable — or both — with whatever the child is eating.

Nutrition is important

Key Life Habits 1, 2 and 3 are absolutely basic for everyone (including adults)! In this section there are numerous articles on nutrition. Understanding how to improve the quality of the foods in your child's diet is very important. If you start with the key life habits and go on to provide your family with the right foods, you are going to give them all the best chance to grow up strong and healthy — and without having to battle obesity.

■ ■ ■

CHAPTER 21

Shabbos and Yom Tov Seudos:
A New Perspective

Every Shabbos and every Yom Tov is a time for banquet-style meals, *seudos*. These meals are served in multiple courses, with elegance and style. The family dresses up in special clothing, and there is often company at the table. The majesty of Shabbos and Yom Tov are evident throughout the meal, while homemade challah, soup and foods are eaten and *divrei Torah* and *zmiros* are rendered. What a special experience it always is!

There are times when Shabbos and Yom Tov are linked, resulting in the consumption of seven *seudos* in three days! This presents us with a major challenge. How do we present the wonderful *seudos* of our holiday without causing the family to gain weight that will be very hard to lose later on?

The actual menus of the meals vary according to tradition and new cuisine. In most of the Ashkenazi community the meals are predominately *fleishig* (meat-based). The traditional Eastern European side dishes can be full of oil and potatoes and eggs and onions. Fresh and cooked vegetables are often not included, since there were few of

Key Points

- Start the meal with a salad for each person and then a non-greasy soup.
- Fill each person's plate with the main dish and side dishes in the kitchen.
- Serve dessert in unit portions and take it off the table.
- Do not leave fattening things out to tempt everyone.
- A bowl of fruit and nuts in their shells is adequate between meals.

them in the old days in Europe. It is traditional that cakes, cookies and pies are served for dessert with other treats, such as sorbets and fruit compotes.

It is really possible to prepare a series of fully satisfying and healthy *seudos* for your family and guests without causing unwanted weight gain if a few guidelines are followed.

The real key to this is to serve each person an individual portion of each course, the way food is served at elegant weddings and in elegant restaurants. Do not serve family-style with large platters of food on the table. The reason for this is that **people will continue to eat if there is more food on the table. It is the extra portions that create the excess.**

- Start each meal with a salad with olive oil or other dressing on it. These salads can be beautiful and creative and colorful. Even your non-salad eaters will probably eat the salad, since they will be hungry and the salad is all that is available at that time.
- Serve a nourishing but not greasy soup whenever possible.
- Include a vegetable dish on each main dish plate. The caterers at weddings do a lot with zucchini, broccoli, mushrooms, and other vegetables.
- The meat, chicken, kugels, and potatoes can be served as expected.
- Fill an individual plate with the main dish and side dishes for each person and bring it to the table. Make the portions appropriate in size to satisfy the person who is getting that plate.
- Have only pickles and other relishes and condiments on the table. Leave the rest in the kitchen. If seconds are requested, serve only one portion as requested from the kitchen.
- When you serve dessert, serve whatever beautiful stuff you have baked and whatever fancy dessert you have prepared in honor of the Yom Tov, but serve only one portion to each person. After the meal, take it away and put it out of sight or in the freezer until the next *seudah*.
- Between meals leave a bowl of fruit and a bowl of nuts in their shells with a nutcracker for the noshers to work on.
- Shabbos party — To enhance *oneg Shabbos* and *oneg Yom Tov*, children should be allowed to eat real junky nosh that has been saved for the occasion. This is usually later in the afternoon, several hours after the *seudah*. I have always advocated using the junk only on Shabbos and Yom Tov. That way they appreciate it more and eat a lot less of it during the rest of the week.

Final thought

Scientists have shown that **people eat whatever is available to them.** By serving in controlled portions, people will eat enough, but not too much. It is unfair to ask your overweight teens not to eat the cake you have left out on the table. Go ahead and bake and make a beautiful Yom Tov for your family. Making these small changes in the way you serve will not detract from their Yom Tov. They will be grateful when it is over if you have helped them not to overeat.

CHAPTER 22

Purim Food:
Avoiding the Pitfalls and Still Enjoying the Holiday

Key Points

- Limit all of the Purim excess to Purim itself.
- Hide or eliminate all the leftover junk food.
- Send your neighbors the foods you would want your own family to eat.
- Have a *freilichen Yom Tov!*

Purim presents a special challenge to families who are trying to eat properly. I received this letter asking for advice in the *Binah Magazine.*

Dear Dr. Schulman,

I am really working hard on improving my family's eating habits. We are all overweight. Recently we have started to become accustomed to eating healthy foods. We have eliminated low-fiber grains, trans fats, and excess sugar from our diets, in exchange for high fiber grains, healthy oils, nuts, beans, fruits, and vegetables. All of us, including my husband, three teenagers, and the three younger kids are losing weight. None of us is dieting; we are just eating better.

My question is: What should I do on Purim when my house fills up with incredible amounts of nosh, chocolates, cake, and junk foods? I do not want to deprive my family of the joy and excitement of this special Yom Tov, but I really do not want to forgo all of the gains (and losses!) we have achieved.

Perplexed by Purim

This was my reply:

Dear Perplexed,

Congratulations on your successful effort to improve your family's eating habits! The changes you have made will undoubtedly have a positive effect on your family for years to come.

Purim in the Orthodox community does present a challenge. Fortunately there has been a recent shift in the *mishloach manos* habits of the community. Many people are donating money to organizations and adding their names to prepared group packages instead of baking their own cakes and cookies. This means fewer individual gifts and baked goods. You'll probably still receive your share of packaged cookies and candies, but these are much easier to control since you can limit how many are actually opened. The sugar candies are less of a problem since they do not have very many calories and there's a limit to how many you can eat.

Here is my suggestion as to how to handle the Purim problem: *"Let them eat junk!"* (in a limited fashion). But just for this one day.

- The little kids should be allowed to eat the sugary junk without limiting them. If they really want the cookies and other treats, let them choose one or two items in each category.
- The older kids should choose whatever they want, but only a limited amount in each category. For example: either five cookies, five chocolates, one piece of a special cake if they love it, or ten candies and one small package of chips.
- The adults should do the same, but eat only the stuff they love. Make sure all of the junk and nosh is eaten on Purim, not before and not after. A good tooth-brushing is essential when the day is over.
- At the end of the day remove all the Purim nosh from the house! You may want to put small amounts of it away for Shabbos parties or the Shabbos *seudos*, but keep it out of sight and inaccessible. The reason for this is that many studies have shown that the number one factor contributing to poor eating habits is the availability of foods that are lacking in nutritional value. If junk food isn't in your kitchen, no one in your family will be tempted to eat it.

Incidentally, when Purim time approaches think about what you plan to give your own friends for *mishloach manos*. Try to give only foods that you would want to have in your own home.

Bottom line:

Make sure everyone gets their share of a *freilichen Purim!* Then return to your new, healthy lifestyle.

CHAPTER 23

Pesach:
Maintaining a Healthy Diet for Your Family

Key Points

- Pesach foods can be constipating.
- Adding high-fiber foods, such as whole-wheat matzah and high fiber fruits and vegetables can help avoid the problem.
- Quinoa, if permitted, is a great high-fiber starch and protein food.

Pesach necessitates a change of diet, which can cause digestive problems in some families. Here is a letter about this problem.

Dear Dr. Schulman,

As Pesach approaches, I am worried about a problem my family has every year. The food on Pesach always causes stomachaches and constipation. Do you have any suggestions that might help us?

Matzah Lover's Mom

This was my reply:

Dear Mom,

I have many mothers complaining about this problem. It seems that the foods like matzah and potatoes, eaten in large amounts, are not digested well by many of us. Since these foods are both made up of "white" refined starches, they constitute a very low-fiber basis for the daily diet, leading to gas and constipation. I feel that the best solution is to rethink the food we eat on Pesach.

Because there are different *minhagim*, and the opinions of individual Rabbis differ, using any of the foods I am about to suggest that you add to the family's diet for Pesach would, of course, have to be in accordance with your own *minhagim* and your own Rabbi's opinion.

Although the usual Pesach foods such as apples, bananas, meats, eggs, cheese, and other milk products are good nutritionally, they are also very likely to cause constipation. **The best way to balance out the family Pesach diet is to add high-fiber foods.**

This category includes fruits such as mangoes, grapes, melons, pineapples, pears, peaches, and plums. Canned and dried fruits have as much fiber as fresh. Vegetables are fine, but they do not all have fiber. Lettuce, tomato, cucumber, and peppers do not have much fiber. Broccoli, all varieties of squash, and sweet potatoes have a lot of fiber.

It is important to note that whole-wheat matzah has much more fiber than regular matzah. It is an easy switch to make, since most people do not notice a major difference in taste and texture.

Quinoa (pronounced *keen-wah*) is a grain-like seed that grows on the stalk of a beetroot in the mountains of South America (see Chapter 16, Carbohydrates; "Quinoa: How to Use It"). It has high-quality protein and a lot of fiber. Many Rabbanim in Israel and in the U.S. have allowed the use of quinoa on Pesach. It looks like barley or couscous, but it is not considered *kitniyos* by these Rabbanim.

Quinoa should be rinsed in cold water in a sieve before cooking, and then it can be cooked like rice. You will know when it is thoroughly cooked (after approximately 15 minutes) when little white rings appear around the seeds. Quinoa can be bought all year round in health food stores. Besides being delicious, nourishing and satisfying, it is very good for the digestive system. I often recommend adding quinoa to the daily diet of patients who suffer from constipation.

By consciously improving the fiber content of your family's Pesach diet, you will not only avoid problems, you will also help them all develop better eating habits, which can be continued all year!

THREE

Activity and Exercise

CHAPTER 24

A Plea for Exercise in Yeshivah Programs

It is well known that there are certain basic habits of health and hygiene that are essential to the growth and development of all children; parents are very concerned with proper diet, for example. They monitor carefully the amounts and types of food their children eat each day as they proudly watch them grow. Parents are also careful to ensure adequate hours of sleep to give their children a chance to recover from their days' events and labors. They keep their children clean and dress them properly to prepare them for the outside world and weather. Coats, sweaters, and of course boots and raincoats are the marks of caring, nurturing parents.

Key Points

- Exercise is as critical to good health as food and rest and warmth.
- Growing bodies need exercise to allow bones to grow straight and strong.
- Lack of exercise can cause decreased vital capacity and decreased life expectancy.
- It is our responsibility to make sure our children are allowed the opportunity to exercise regularly.

One more basic health requirement — exercise

There is one basic health need that is very much neglected in the urban Orthodox Jewish world. Although our children are fed, rested, kept clean and dressed appropriately, **they are severely deprived of a major ingredient in the formula of**

healthy body growth — exercise.

The Rambam in *Mishnah Torah* called for a person to take active exercise "[to be]…free from disease and [enjoy] increased vigor." His wisdom, of course, has been confirmed by medical science.

- In a recent study reported in the *New England Journal of Medicine*, the life expectancy of adults in different categories of physical fitness was observed. Those who did no exercise at all and would tire immediately on a simple walking test or on a treadmill were found to have a **significantly shortened life expectancy** compared to those who did even the simplest exercise, such as regular vigorous walking every day.

- Many studies on aging have shown that arthritis and the aches and pains of old age can be avoided and even reversed for many years with regular physical exercise.

A person who exercises regularly has better circulation and stronger, more effective heart activity than one who does not.

- Obesity — the American form of malnutrition — is much less common in people who exercise regularly.

- Exercise increases HDL, the "good cholesterol," and is considered almost as important as diet in preventing coronary artery disease.

- Exercise causes feelings of well-being, increased ability to cope with stress, and even an increase in ability to concentrate on complicated tasks. **Overall, exercise can improve one's physical, emotional, and mental health, and is known to be an essential good health habit.**

Especially for growing children

In growing children, exercise plays a critical role in body development. The muscles that are used regularly grow and develop normal strength and size. Muscles that are not used become thin and weak and unable to support their assigned part of the body properly. We have all seen how thin a child's leg can get when immobilized in a cast for even a few weeks. This is called the *"atrophy of disuse."* It seems logical, therefore, that as a child's body grows, all of his muscles must be exercised regularly to develop normally.

Infants and toddlers are in a constant state of motion. Just getting around their world requires a full day's exercise. Later, however, when the child reaches school age, less and less time is spent on physical activity. The legs seem to always get some use — everyone has to walk and climb stairs and some even ride bikes — but the chest muscles, shoulders, back and arms are frequently underused. As the child grows in learning and becomes a *masmid*, the day is often spent sitting down, leaning over a *sefer* for hours and hours. The muscles of the chest, shoulders and back become thin, and the spine curves forward.

Yeshivah Bachur Back Syndrome

Dr. Stanley Hoppenfeld, a renowned specialist in pediatric and adolescent back problems, states the following:

"Excessive long hours of studying in the forward bent position, as in sitting or in bending over a lectern, creates dorsum rotundum (severely rounded shoulders and back). This occurs because of the increased pressure on the vertebrae anteriorly and the stretching of the ligaments posteriorly. The lack of exercises reduces the strength of the paravertebral muscles and the muscles of the shoulder girdle, and the student is therefore unable to pull his/her shoulders back and bring himself/herself to the fully erect position. The excessive long hours of study without physical activity inflicts upon the young student who is still growing a dorsum rotundum or kyphosis, which sometimes is jokingly referred to as *Yeshivah Bachur Back Syndrome*. In reality, **it is the result of anyone studying for these long hours without appropriate exercise.**

"Many of these children also have scoliosis, or curvature to the side; however, this is completely independent of the dorsum rotundum and not related to it. On occasion, families do have slightly rounded posture on a genetic or hereditary basis. However, 99 percent of the problems that we see on a clinical basis are directly caused and related to excessive sitting in the rounded position, which causes muscle changes, vertebral body changes, and vertebrae changes.

"While at school, the students should have physical exercises so as to build up their upper body. There is a distinct wasting of the pectoralis muscles and the trapezius muscles, giving the student a smaller shoulder or body stance, compared to his contemporaries. **Unfortunately, without exercise, this thinning and rounding becomes permanent into adult life.** A regular exercise program, including back stretching, is preventive medicine, and will make difference for children throughout their life span."

Dr. Robert Siffert, former Chief of Pediatric Orthopedics at Mt. Sinai School of Medicine, and author of the book *How Your Child's Body Grows*, states the following:

"One of the major problems I see in the office is poor slouching posture. Youngsters who have loose ligaments and sit over a desk all day, and who do not develop their back muscles, are subject to progressive structural round backs so common in adult life as a result of this dangerous omission during growth. **Not only does it lead to arthritis, fatigue and poor ability to function, but can seriously endanger vital organs.** This chest and upper back deformity decreases the amount of air that can enter the lung on each inspiration (decreased vital capacity), causes crowding of the heart and major blood vessels and interferes with endurance and blood supply to the entire body."

Closer to home

In my own practice in Boro Park, I am constantly noting the terrible posture and chronic back problems in our yeshivah children. It is time to face a very painful fact. Based on these observations and those of other physicians and specialists who care for yeshivah students in our area, we can state the following:

The current tendency of not providing sufficient exercise in the elementary and high-school yeshivah day is causing harm to children and permanent damage to their backs. It also causes underdevelopment of the chest wall and general musculature and decreases vital capacity, **which can lead to a shorter life expectancy and chronic illness.**

While calling for organized exercise programs and scheduled competitive sports within the yeshivah system may have an alien ring, one must consider the alternative: Lack of any such provision is proving harmful to our children, and — beyond question — there are prohibitions in the Torah against allowing such harm to take place.

Is there a solution?

What remedy is possible? No one is "anti" exercise *per se*. Most experts agree that learning is more efficient when students are allowed to exercise. It is our assumption that our yeshivahs also recognize that exercise is important and want to give their *talmidim* every opportunity for a wholesome life. Unfortunately, they have never felt the need to emphasize this important health habit.

They do not feel that it is incumbent upon them to designate some structured time every week for this purpose. After all, it is not an issue that deals directly with Torah learning. There are however, many yeshivahs outside of New York City that do have gym and swimming facilities for their students. Such activities are considered normal and do not interfere with the intensity of Torah learning.

The New York handicap

Our New York yeshivos do have a major handicap — lack of space and lack of community facilities that could be used for such activity. For example, the Williamsburg "Y" is closed and the Boro Park "Y," built in the 1920s, is hopelessly inadequate. Many children seeking activity are "swimming" standing still in a jam-packed pool. Since these facilities are used by all groups in our area, it seems logical that newer, larger facilities should be built to accommodate the rapidly growing population of children, adolescents and adults. There are organizations, such as Hatzolah, that service all of our people, from all segments of the community. Another similar trans-community organization should be formed to come to grips with this pressing need.

It is true that summertime provides children with much more activity in bungalow colonies, day camps, and overnight camps. There is no question that these two months are good for them, but once the summer is over, the gains are slowly but surely lost, due to the "atrophy of disuse."

If we are really honest about this problem, we would see it for what it really is — **a health hazard.** We would then do our utmost to find practical solutions for this lack of exercise facilities and give our yeshivah students a proper environment for healthy growth and development, without in any way compromising on the integrity of their learning situation.

Some preventative suggestions

"Yeshivah Bachur Back" can be prevented by following the suggestions listed below:

- All desk tops should be equipped with a small *shtender* or book-holder large enough to lift a *Gemara* off the table top, up to a position where the text can be read with the student sitting straight.

- Each child — from age 5 and up — should practice a simple set of exercises. They should be done routinely every morning and evening. These exercises include sitting and standing with a book on the head, backwards stretching, and military "chin tuck" posture exercises. By stretching the body away from the forward curvature, permanent deformity could be prevented

These specific exercises should be taught to the homeroom teachers, science teachers, or gym teachers (where applicable), so they can teach them to their students.

A brief training program should be instituted for this purpose with the cooperation of physicians and therapists.

■ All children should be given ample time and opportunity each day for various types of physical activity — running, jumping, swimming, ball playing, climbing, and bike riding. These exercises will help them build stronger muscles in their upper body and shoulders, as well as increase their "vital capacity."

Proper health habits learned from childhood are our best means of helping Hashem to give us health and longevity. Exercises, started early and continued for a lifetime, can help to prevent ill health and promote well-being. Let us not be responsible for depriving our families of this simple basic part of healthful living.

(This article first appeared in the *Jewish Observer*.)

CHAPTER 25

Activities for Everyone

Key Points

- Swimming, skating and biking are skills that should be learned during childhood.
- Professional swim instruction teaches proper technique.
- Never swim alone.
- Ice skating does not require protective gear, but helmets are a good idea.
- Rollerblading requires helmets, wrist, knee, and elbow protectors.
- All bike riders need helmets.
- Walking long distances from early childhood creates an important good life habit.

There are three special skills that every child should learn during childhood. They are: riding a two-wheel bike, skating (on ice or rollerblades), and swimming.

It is ideal to learn these skills as a young child, since the learning gets much harder with age. All three activities are enjoyable throughout adult life. They also build self-confidence, coordination, and strength. Since many children can ride, skate, and swim, the child who cannot do them often feels inadequate because he or she is missing out on the fun.

Of course, **walking** is the most important activity in everyone's daily life. Although it is not a special skill to be learned, habitually walking long distances from early childhood is a very important life habit.

SPECIAL SKILLS

Swimming

Swimming, of course, is fun. But it is more than a pleasure; it is a life-preserving skill. Everyone should learn how to swim. No matter what the skill level, no one should ever swim alone.

The best way to learn proper swimming technique is to receive instruction from licensed swim instructors. An adult who never learned to swim sometimes has a real fear of the water that can interfere with normal living. Even fearful adults have a chance. They can be taught to overcome their fear of water by trained professional swimming instructors. Knowing how to swim properly is essential for everyone — both for fun and safety.

Skating

Skating on ice is basic and straightforward, since there is only flat ice in a rink. As with any new skill, a few lessons help to develop good technique and avoid bad habits. Although helmets are a good idea, no gear is required.

Rollerblading is enjoyed in a more varied terrain, including small downhills, which increase speed incredibly fast. Rollerblading requires full protective gear. Helmets, wrist guards, elbow guards, and knee guards are all essential. The skater must also learn to use the brake to control speed. Protective gear only works when it is used. Wearing gear should be required before the child starts to skate.

Biking

Biking is an activity that can be enjoyed at any age. Here is some essential information:

Helmets

Riding a bicycle requires a helmet. There is no question that helmets save lives and brain function every day. It is not a question of *if* you need a helmet. It is only a question of *when*. A young father I know recently suffered a mild concussion from a fall off of his bike while wearing a helmet. After he recovered, he noticed a dent in his helmet. When he peeled away the plastic shell, he found a crack in the helmet. The same fall, without a helmet, would probably have taken his life or left him brain damaged. His helmet will have to be replaced. The proud helmet company will send him a new one when he tells them his story.

The fit is important

Helmets must be properly fitted on the head to really work when needed. This means a fairly tight fit that situates the helmet on the top of the head. The front of the helmet must cross the forehead. The straps should be tight enough to fit only two fingers between the strap and the chin.

If your child is wearing a loose helmet that tilts up in the front to the hairline, you should adjust the helmet. The head is not well-protected. Fitting helmets is sometimes difficult to do properly. It is a good idea to ask someone in a bike shop to teach you how to do it, or ask them to fit the helmets on your kids and yourself. There is a new helmet design that has a dial on the back, which can be turned to tighten the fit around the head.

Useful facts

Here are a few useful facts about bike riding.

- Most kids are ready to learn how to ride a two-wheeler by about 5 years of age. The best place to teach a new rider is in a wide-open area, like an empty schoolyard or parking lot, not on the sidewalk. This gives him room to turn awkwardly and still keep pedaling to gain balance without going into the street. The new riders should be given a helmet, knee guards, elbow guards, and thick winter gloves. This extra gear is only to prevent the painful scrapes that discourage them. Once he or she has mastered balance, steering, stopping, starting, and using the brake to slow down, only the helmet is needed.

- The bike has to fit the rider. A bike that is too big or too small is much harder to control. The rider should be able to barely touch the ground with his feet while sitting on the seat. The seat height should be adjusted so that the rider almost, but not completely, unbends the knee when he is pedaling.

- Tires on bikes should be checked regularly to see if they have enough air. The tire should be firm when squeezed, but not hard enough to resist squeezing. A soft, semi flat tire compromises the function of the bike and makes it prone to real flat tires. To inflate the tires, use a hand bicycle pump or go to a gas station or bike shop.

- Brakes can be the source of a fall if not used properly. Bikes with handbrakes have two different brakes. The left handbrake stops only the front wheel. The right handbrake stops only the back wheel. If both brakes are squeezed, the bike stops. If only the right brake is squeezed, the bike will slow down. If the left brake is squeezed without the right, the bike often flips over and throws the rider over the handlebars. This is particularly important on bumps and downhills, and when riding fast. This means all riders must keep their hands on the handlebars near the brakes. Using the right hand to take a drink or wave to friends can easily result in a big fall if a sudden need arises to use the brakes.

- Basic riding safety is very important. Riders should go slowly and carefully when riding where there are people walking. A reckless biker can easily injure a pedestrian if he is not in control. When riding in the street the rider should use standard hand signals. Traffic lights and stop signs apply to bikers also. Riding between cars and weaving in and out of traffic is very dangerous.

Walking — the neglected activity

Most of the children in our community could walk to school if a safe walking environment were provided. Walking provides more than just exercise. It is as good for the mind as it is for the body. Everyone feels good after a walk. Starting the school day with a walk gets the day off to a fresh and invigorated start. Ending the school day with a walk allows a child to relax and unwind from a full day, and arrive home after a lot of his pent-up energy has been burned off.

There are several reasons parents do not let most of our youngsters walk to school.
1. *There is danger on the streets.*
2. *Our kids cannot walk more than a quarter of a mile.*
3. *Their books are too heavy.*
4. *We are too busy to walk them to school.*

All of these arguments are true, but maybe we could reconsider the matter. If we got the Board of Education to hire crossing guards on all of the major crossings, walking to school would be safer. The guards would also be a deterrent to unsavory adult encounters. The expense would be less than buses. We could hire teenagers to pick up little kids and walk them to school in groups, similar to the way we get kids to Shabbos programs.

It is a matter of health and safety that our children develop a positive attitude toward walking. Walking is exercise that does not require a program, a trainer, or equipment. Walking provides a good cardiovascular workout.

Why are we coddling our children? We must try to get them moving! Seven-year-olds can easily walk a mile in 20 minutes. If the books are heavy, give them rolling knapsacks. If the weather is wet, they can wear boots and raincoats like we did when we were children. Most of us walked to school. Walking was a normal part of every day. Our kids are getting the wrong message. Why do we take them everywhere by car? Even distances over one mile are not too far. Let them walk!

They can do it!

Final thought — a lifetime of fun and exercise

Walking distances every day is the foundation of fitness for people of all ages.

Swimming, skating, and biking, when learned properly in childhood, can be enjoyed throughout adulthood. Parents and grandparents can swim, skate, and ride with their kids and grandchildren. All of these activities can be a source of fitness, recreation, exercise, and wonderful relaxation for a lifetime.

CHAPTER 26

Winter Wisdom

Key Points

- Even small babies should be taken out in wintertime.
- Everybody needs sunshine.
- Cold air is better for children than heated house air.
- Frostbite prevention is a matter of common sense and proper clothing.

When the cold weather sets in and the days get shorter, we often assume that staying indoors with the heat turned up high is the best way to keep our babies and children healthy. **This is clearly a misunderstanding!**

To do our best for our children, we should get them outside every day that the weather is tolerable, try to keep the rooms as cool as possible, open windows, and humidify the air indoors if the heat must stay on.

HERE ARE A FEW FACTS ABOUT WINTER HEALTH

Sunshine — We must get our kids and ourselves outside before the day ends in early darkness.

Everybody needs a little sunshine on his or her face every day. Sunshine helps us to produce vitamin D. Whenever possible we should all get outside in the morning or midday sun, since in the winter the sun's rays hit us less directly than in the summer and they are strongest in the earlier hours of the day. Sunlight shining on the skin allows the production of vitamin D, important for healthy bones. Even though very little skin is exposed to sunlight in cold weather, 15 minutes of sunshine on the face is enough to keep up production.

Sunshine is also important to keep our spirits up. Adults, the elderly, and even small kids can become moody and restless if many days go by without sunlight. Technically this is called SADD, or seasonal affective depressive disorder. It seems that everyone needs a little sunshine. There are times when the weather is cloudy and snowing or raining for many days in a row. We must take advantage of every little bit of sun when we get it in the winter.

A recent study showed that young children who get outside regularly between the hours of 1 p.m. and 4 p.m. are better sleepers than the ones who do not. The sunlight regulates the brain hormone melatonin, which is responsible for the sleep-wake cycle.

Although we have been taught to be careful and use sunscreen lotion when we go out in the sun, it should be used less consistently in the winter (except for people with very sensitive skin), since we need to get the full benefits from our limited exposure.

Cold air

If we have a choice, it is better to breathe cold air than heated indoor air. Outdoors, the cold air may feel sharp and irritating if it is below freezing. The best solution is to breathe through a scarf wrapped directly over the nose and mouth. This humidifies and warms the air a little, and makes it easier to stay outside.

The air in winter has very little moisture. The humidity is often below 30 percent. When that air is heated indoors, the moisture level drops even more. This causes irritation and dryness of the nasal membranes, which makes it easier for cold viruses to invade. It is better to sleep in a poorly-heated room with warmer bedclothes than to sleep in a warmed room.

Setting the thermostat to turn the heat up an hour before everyone wakes up will prevent the morning chill when they are dressing.

If humidifiers — either cool mist, ultrasonic, or hot steam units — are used, they must be cleaned daily according to instructions for the unit. Usually this requires using a vinegar solution to remove mold from the machine. If this is not done, there could be real problems from breathing the moldy mist.

Preventing frostbite — using common sense

Extremely cold fingers, toes and noses are sometimes subject to a very painful spasm of the blood vessels in the skin, causing first numbness and then a severe burning sensation, known as frostbite. This can cause serious damage in severe cold exposure.

The best preventive measure against frostbite is knowing how cold it is and, on very cold days, adding layers to the clothing of the child, putting on warm, dry mittens over a small pair of knit gloves, and heavy socks with good weatherproof shoes or boots.

If it is really bitterly cold, be aware of how long the children are standing outside waiting for a bus. Just standing on a corner the children are not being physically active, so they will get colder. Strenuous activity such as running and playing warms up their bodies and makes staying outside safer. If there is a "frostbite alert" in the weather forecast, do not let them stand outside for more than a few minutes.

If anyone comes indoors with severe pain in the fingers and toes, put the painful hands or feet under warm (not hot) water immediately. This restores the circulation fast.

Do not let fear of frostbite keep you or your child indoors on most winter days. Just be aware when the weather is very severe and use common sense.

Small babies should be taken out in winter

Don't turn your infant into a "hot-house plant!"

Small babies should be taken out in all kinds of weather. Even though little noses tend to run in cold air, this does not mean they have a cold. By taking babies out in cold and changeable weather, you are getting them used to all kinds of conditions. If they are always kept in either the house or the car they are more likely to get sick when you do take them out. As always, common sense is needed when deciding how warm the outerwear must be. It makes sense to use the wind shield on the stroller if the wind is strong. If the weather is tolerable to the caretaker, there is no reason to stay indoors with the baby.

Please note that sheepskin-like liners for the stroller seat are fine, but never put the baby face down on one to sleep! The fashion of using heavy plush acrylic baby blankets for the stroller or carriage is fraught with danger. These blankets really could suffocate an infant *(chas v'shalom)*. I prefer a thermal knit blanket, which is much more breathable, on top of a warm snow suit.

Don't forget to lighten up the outer clothing on warmer days.

Sick children should be allowed to go outside if they feel up to it.

Fresh air is fine for a sick child, even in the winter. If a child is ill but has the energy to play and wants to go outside in reasonably cold weather, there is no reason to keep him indoors. The fresh air will make him feel better. He can even play with other children, because illness can't spread outdoors in daylight, since the ultraviolet rays of the sun kill viruses.

Final thought — it's all a matter of attitude

Winter does not have to be a time of imprisonment in our homes and schools. Some of us (including myself) love the cool, fresh air. With proper layering of clothing, everyone can enjoy winter. It's all a matter of having a positive attitude and common sense.

Safety

CHAPTER 27

Childproofing

In my 30 years of experience, I have dealt with a number of life-threatening incidents from preventable accidents in the home. The following is a brief list.

- A seven-year-old fell head-first out of a second story window onto the concrete driveway below when the screen he was leaning on fell out of the window.

- A 15-month-old child fell head first out of his highchair onto a ceramic tile floor and required emergency neurosurgery.

- A 9-month-old sustained third-degree burns of the hands from an oven door.

- A 4-week-old baby sustained severe burns when placed in a sink for a bath. (After the mother checked the water temperature, the hot water tap had quietly leaked into the sink while the mother was undressing the baby.)

- An 8-month-old sustained severe chemical burns when he sat in a puddle of St. Moritz oven cleaner that his toddler sister had spilled on the floor.

Key Points

- Childproofing requires careful attention and common sense.

- Even the babysitter's house and grandparents' houses need to be childproofed.

- Be aware! Quiet toddlers are unpredictable and very talented at finding trouble.

- Pesach cleaning often brings stronger chemicals into the house environment.

- A 2-year-old child required CPR when her heart stopped from an accidental overdose of her grandmother's heart medicine, which she found in a pocketbook.
- A 13-month-old baby was found with his head submerged in the toilet, which he fell into while trying to retrieve a toy.
- A 9-month-old baby was found not breathing under a plastic-covered pile of newly-delivered dry-cleaned clothing that had been left on a bed.
- A 22-month-old and the 8-month-old sibling ate 90 vitamin tablets that the older one knocked off the bathroom shelf while standing in the sink.
- A two-year-old girl turned blue while eating hot dog "wheels." (Her 10-year-old sister performed a Heimlich maneuver on her, and it popped out of her mouth.)
- A three-year-old boy sustained third-degree abrasions on his hand when he wedged it accidentally under a running treadmill.

Miraculously, with Hashem's *chessed*, all of these children survived their injuries, some of them with scars, many requiring prolonged hospitalizations.

It is well known that more children die as a result of accidental injury than from all illnesses combined. Thirty years ago The American Academy of Pediatrics and the National Safety Council proposed the concept of childproofing to teach parents how to avoid injury around the house.

Most people know that they must try to make the environment in their home safe for their children. Electrical outlet covers and KinderGard locks on cabinets have become standard in most households. There are, however, many more basic aspects of home safety that must be considered to effectively childproof a home. Here is a simple checklist.

Preventing choking

The airway of a small child can be blocked completely by any small, rounded object, like a grape or round pieces of hot dogs. This category includes jellybeans, whole baby carrots, and hard candies. All round foods must be cut in lengthwise pieces before giving them to a toddler. These foods should not be given whole or in round pieces until the child is at least three years old. All coins, buttons, balloons, wheels of toy cars and marbles can also block the airway. When any toy is labeled as a choking hazard, it is to be avoided until age three.

Nuts, corn, and raw carrots also often cause choking, and the small pieces get into the airway. These do not usually cause total blockage of breathing, but they can get stuck in the bronchial tubes and often require endoscopic or surgical removal.

Preventing poisoning

"Never underestimate the ability of a quiet toddler to climb high, and to find trouble!" All medications, including vitamins and supplements, should be kept in a locked box or cabinet, no matter high the cabinet is. Cleaning solutions, laundry products, and cleaning sprays should never be kept under a sink. They also must be put in an inaccessible place.

When there are elderly adults in the house, they must also take care to hide their medications and not leave them on their dressers or in pocketbooks.

Some houseplants are poisonous. Check yours to be sure they are safe if they are accidentally eaten.

The clear 99% pure *liquid paraffin* used in glass Shabbos candles is a **very toxic poison.** It is odorless, colorless, and tasteless and is packaged in squeeze bottles with nozzles and straws. It can easily be mistaken for a sport bottle of water. The label that is found on the bottle has a warning but it is not highlighted, so few people read it. Never leave the bottle on a countertop or table after filling the candles, and never leave it under a sink or in a lower cabinet.

Preventing falls

To have a safe home, you need proper equipment and a lot of common sense.

Windows must have window guards. Window screens do not provide any protection at all. Stairways should be blocked by safety gates. Safety straps and even five-point harnesses must be used when the child is in a highchair, especially if he or she is an escape artist. Bunk beds and toddler beds must have rails.

Never leave a baby on an elevated surface, like a countertop or a bed, without keeping one hand on him to prevent a fall. If you cannot do this, **put the baby on the floor.** (You cannot fall out of bed when you are sleeping on the floor!)

Coffee tables are low enough to cause serious injury when a child falls and strikes the edge with his head. Remove them when the babies are standing and walking and when kids are running around.

Curious toddlers can climb on top of bookcases and even refrigerators. It is essential to always know exactly where your toddler is and what he is doing.

Preventing burns

Shabbos and Yom Tov can present frequent opportunities for fires and burns to happen. Shabbos candles, hot water urns, stove top covers (blechs) are all potential hazards. Extreme care must be taken to insure that toddlers and young children are monitored during Shabbos and Yom Tov.

Radiators and oven doors must have covers. A baby will use the hot radiator or oven door to support his weight as he tries to stand up, and this can result in severe hand burns.

The hot water heater in the house must be set at 120°F — 125°F. If your tap water is hot enough to dissolve instant coffee, it is too hot.

Pot handles should be turned to the wall when you are cooking.

Never hold a child while you cook or when you have a hot drink in your hand.

Serving soup from a tureen at the table can prevent accidental burns while transporting the steaming soup bowls from the kitchen.

Electrical outlets must have snugly-fitted covers.

Matches and lighters must be out of reach.

Preventing cuts and lacerations

Knives, scissors, food processor blades, sewing needles, and other sharp items must be made inaccessible. Discard empty cans in a safe container. Glass items should not be left in easy reach.

Preventing asphyxiation

All of the following can lead to serious injury or even death: Hinged toy boxes, tight spots (such as between beds or between the bed and the wall), ropes and blind cords, plastic dry-cleaner bags, smaller plastic bags, and strings around the neck (including necklaces on babies).

Preventing drowning

A child should never be left alone in or near water, even for a second. Besides bathtubs and swimming pools, even mop buckets and toilets can be dangerous. Babies and toddlers are "top heavy," and they can fall in headfirst if they reach for something in the water. Tubs and kiddy pools should be emptied after each use.

Dealing with accidental injuries

All caregivers, parents, and grandparents should learn basic first aid for cuts (pressure) and burns (cool water), and how to do a *Heimlich maneuver* and *rescue breathing*. The few minutes' time until Hatzolah arrives can be critical to the outcome in a life-threatening situation.

It is important to remember that other homes children visit, like the babysitter's house, the grandparents' house, and summer homes must be childproofed too. Childproofing is part of our sacred job. We must all do our share to ensure the basic safety of our kids.

Pesach cleaning safety

Pesach cleaning is an overwhelming job in most households. Unfortunately, the cleaning solutions we use can cause serious harm to toddlers and children who get into them accidentally. Here is a letter to *Binah Magazine* about one mother's experience.

Dear Dr. Schulman,

Last year I spent a whole month, starting one week before Pesach, in the burn unit of the Staten Island Hospital with my nine-month-old baby. Please tell everyone to be careful with the cleaning products before Pesach. My son had third-degree burns from sitting in a puddle of St. Moritz oven cleaner.

Learned My Lesson the Hard Way

This was my reply:

Dear Learned,

Unfortunately, the pediatric burn units in the New York area have a much higher percentage of Orthodox Jewish children admitted than any other ethnic group. This is because of the Shabbos candles, *havdalah licht*, Chanukah *menoros*, cholent pots, hot water urns, and *blechs* that are found in every home. Each one of these is a burn hazard, especially when there are active, curious, unpredictable toddlers in the house. When it comes to Pesach cleaning, there is another very serious hazard that is not often recognized: oven cleaners that are not packaged according to American standards.

In the United States the government has standards of packaging that require hazardous substances — such as medication and strong, lye-based cleaning solutions, drain cleaners, and pest poisons — to be packaged in childproof containers when sold for home use. Some products, such as Easy-Off oven cleaner, are required to be less powerful than the commercial-strength products. This material, even in a low-strength solution, can cause severe burns and blindness if not washed off thoroughly and immediately after contact.

The local small groceries servicing the Orthodox Jewish community often import cleaning products from Europe or Israel. These products would not be sold in supermarkets because they are stronger than the legal limits and do not have safety packaging. One very popular example is St. Moritz oven cleaner. Cleaning the oven for Pesach is a really hard task, and many women have found that St. Moritz works better than the American products. The problem is that it is extremely strong, and it is packaged in a regular spray bottle that now contains a warning label and safety cap. Unfortunately, a persistent child may still be able to open it.

I had one three-year-old child who sprayed it into the face of her baby sister who was playing in the kitchen. The baby was screaming, and the mother could not figure out what was wrong. It took her several minutes to notice that the baby's eyelid was getting red and swollen. She finally noticed that the toddler was playing with a spray bottle in the bathroom. When she realized it was the St. Moritz, she called Hatzolah. They came and transported the baby to the hospital while irrigating the eye continuously. The baby was hospitalized for two weeks. Miraculously, the eye healed, *baruch Hashem,* with no scarring on the cornea.

Another child spilled St. Moritz on the floor and stepped in it with only socks on his feet. That incident also went undiagnosed until the mother undressed him several hours later, and there was real skin damage on the bottom of his foot. He also spent several weeks in the hospital.

Last year I had a baby brought in with St. Moritz burns on the back of his thighs and legs. The mother had cleaned his high chair with St. Moritz for Pesach and had not rinsed it off thoroughly. When she placed him barelegged in the freshly-cleaned high chair, his legs were burned. Not realizing why he was crying, she did not start irrigation until twenty minutes later. The baby was severely injured.

There are several safety points that should be remembered:
- Read instructions on all products carefully, and follow them.
- Keep all cleaning solutions and chemicals high and inaccessible to children whenever they are not in use. Do not put the container down when you are done — put it away immediately. Do not rely on KinderGard locks on the cabinet under the sink.
- Safety packaging is for your child's safety. Buying products that are not properly packaged is not wise in a household with children.
- If any skin or eye contact occurs, rinse the area under cool water immediately

and for at least ten minutes. Do not wait for Hatzolah to start irrigation. Delaying even a few minutes can make a big difference in the severity of the injury.

- When you are using strong cleaning solutions, wear latex gloves and goggles or glasses.

Using common sense and a real awareness of the burn hazards will make your home as safe as it is clean for Pesach.

CHAPTER 28

Summer Safety

Key Points

- Summer is fun but it also has its special hazards.
- Setting rules and sticking to them can prevent injury and tragedy.
- Toddlers are unpredictable. Never leave a toddler in the care of a child.
- Sunburns are preventable and are not treatable.
- Preventing dehydration requires common sense and vigilance.

Each year, as the weather gets hotter and the school year winds down, the community begins to prepare for the upcoming summer vacation season. Many families go to the country, and kids go to overnight and day camps. Summertime is wonderfully different from other seasons, since we spend more time outdoors. This means our children have much more freedom to move. There is more space to run and play, to ride bikes and roller skate, and to enjoy fresh air and sunshine. Swimming is a regular activity.

Unfortunately it is also a time of more frequent accidental injuries, sunburns, insect bites, and, on hot days, higher risk of dehydration. Many of the mishaps and injuries that happen in summer can be prevented if we use common sense and plan for a safe vacation season. We must try to do our best to have a healthy and safe summer.

Preventing sunburn

It is important to know that infants under a year of age have very thin skin. This means that they can be burned by the sun in a much shorter time than older children. For the first few months of life, the only reliable protections are clothing and shade. Floppy hats that shade the face and neck, sunshades and umbrellas on strollers are needed every day.

To protect toddlers and older children, hats and t-shirts are still a good idea. They also need sunscreen lotion, the ones made for children, with SPF#15 or more. These lotions need to be reapplied every 4 hours and after swimming.

Although some tanning is expected, it should be minimized. The more sun exposure children have, the more skin damage they have as the years go by. Light-skinned "freckle faces" are particularly vulnerable. This damage, which eventually shows as leathery, dried out skin, also makes the likelihood of skin cancer greater.

If the child does get a sunburn, there is no real treatment. Cool compresses help a little, but it has to heal on its own. Any part of the skin that has sustained a sunburn must be protected very carefully with sunscreen and shade for at least a year after the burn.

Swimming

There are a few important directives that must be enforced to prevent tragedy.
- Never, ever swim alone, and never allow anyone you know to swim alone.
- Never allow kids to swim without adult supervision.
- Supervising adults must give the swimmers all of their attention.
- Camp, school, and bungalow colony swimming pools need licensed, trained lifeguards and water safety professionals.
- Rules of conduct must be set by these professionals.
- **Everyone must listen to the lifeguards and respect these rules!**
- Passive and secure locks that close automatically must be used to lock pool gates.

Preventing dehydration

On very hot days, make sure that your day campers and campers in your overnight programs have unlimited amounts of water to drink all day long. Water sports like sprinkler running, water fights, and swimming activities are good. Allowing a child to run around in wet clothes on these days helps prevent dehydration. Since sweating causes both water and salt loss, pretzels are a good snack to prevent salt imbalance. Adults must remind counselors to keep "watering" their campers all day.

Bike helmets and protective gear

The vast majority of injuries from bike riding, scooters, skateboarding, and rollerblading can be prevented by wearing the right gear. Helmets are a must! Head injuries can be life-threatening and life-altering. There is no excuse for letting any child do any of these rolling sports without a helmet! Take away the bike if the child refuses to wear a helmet. No riding without helmets. In addition, wrist guards, knee guards, and elbow guards are all needed for rollerblading.

Bites

Here are a few important facts:

Ticks — Whenever the kids are in woods or high grass they should wear long-sleeved shirts, and tights or pants with the cuffs tucked into socks. Insect repellent containing DEET can be applied to the face, neck and clothing. At the end of the day, do a tick check, including combing the hair, to search for anything that catches on the comb or a dot that feels like it is stuck on the skin.

If ticks are found and removed in the first day or two, they are much less likely to cause Lyme disease. Simply pull them off with a fine tweezer. It does not matter if a little piece is left in the skin. If you do remove a tick you can save it in alcohol and give it to the doctor to send to the lab to see of it is infected with Lyme disease. Wash off the area with soap and water.

It is important to watch the area for the next few weeks to see if an enlarging red target-like rash develops. "Flu-like illness" in the first few weeks after tick bites should be reported to the child's doctor.

Bee stings — Bee stings hurt and sometimes cause a lot of swelling, but they are not usually dangerous. Ice helps a lot to reduce the pain and swelling.

Hives, lip or tongue swelling, wheezing or generalized itching immediately after the sting could be a life-threatening reaction known as anaphylaxis. If you suspect a more generalized reaction, give Benadryl immediately and call Hatzolah or 911. If your child has ever experienced an anaphylactic reaction to bee stings or any other substance, he should be treated by an allergist and an EpiPen should be obtained (with training as to its use).

Spider bites — Spider bites cause blistering. They are usually painless and harmless.

Mosquito bites — Mosquito infestation can be controlled with a few measures. Spraying the grounds prior to the summer is a good idea. Try to remove all stagnant water, and empty rainwater from toys and furniture whenever possible. Mosquito netting is very important for small infants. Mosquito bites are usually harmless, but scratched ones tend to get infected. The best anti-itch lotions and gels contain praxamine (ItchEx and Clear Caladryl, e.g.). Ice is a terrific anti-itch. 1% hydrocortisone creams and ointments are good for flared bites. Bacitracin or Neosporin help prevent infection in inflamed areas.

Emergency services — Every school camp, day camp, hotel and bungalow colony needs on-site personnel trained in CPR and first aid. Everyone must know who they are and where they can be found in the case of an emergency.

Toddler supervision

Toddlers are unpredictable and have no common sense. **Never leave a toddler in the care of a youngster. Do not let a tragedy happen because the responsible adult was not paying attention.**

A relaxed, active summer is a wonderful way to revitalize ourselves and our kids. With day-to-day attention to basic common sense, we can all enjoy the vacation without exposing our families to unnecessary risks.

Street Safety

As our population has grown in Boro Park, Williamsburg, and other Orthodox Jewish neighborhoods, the schools have become crowded and the schoolyards have started to overflow with active children.

When streets become playgrounds

Some of our largest boys' schools have been allowed to take over their streets for play space, blocking access to cars during the school day. The problem with this is that the children become accustomed to playing in the street. Even when cars are allowed to cautiously pass the barrier to reach houses on the block of the school, many boys have no fear of or respect for the danger of being in the street. They run around in the street, tease the driver of the car, and even push each other in its path, and throw things at the cars.

When these children go home, they play on the sidewalk in front of their homes and will often run out into the street during a game. When playing hide-and-seek, they will go to the street side of a parked car to crouch down and hide. They often do not hesitate to chase a ball or ride a bike into the street. They are not careful about cars backing out of driveways and cars backing into parking spots. They dart out between cars, never giving the drivers a chance to see them before they are in the path of their vehicle.

Adults are not careful

Even the adults do not respect the danger of the streets.

One spring evening I was driving down a side street near my home when a three-year-old on a tricycle came flying out of a driveway into the path of my minivan. Although I was going slowly, I had to slam on my brake, narrowly avoiding hitting the child and his little vehicle. I immediately pulled over and took the child out of the street and returned him to his seven-year-old sister, who was "watching" him as she and her friends played jump rope.

We all went upstairs to their mother, who was inside cooking for Shabbos. I told the mother, "Two minutes ago I almost had my life ruined, your life ruined, this little boy's life ruined and his sister's life ruined. Had I, G-d forbid, not stopped in time, who would have been to blame? The little seven-year-old girl? Me? The three-year-old? Maybe all of us, but primarily you, for not taking responsibility for his safety!"

Lack of experience adds to the problem

All drivers know how difficult it is to avoid an accident when the car must stop unexpectedly. A child, or a parent who does not drive, might not realize how dangerous a moving car can be. Many of our school-age children are taken everywhere in a car or bus. They do not have the walking experience to learn the dangers of the streets and how to cross intersections safely

It is time we go back to basics and teach ourselves and our children about street safety.

Strollers

Infants are often placed in grave danger as they are pushed in a stroller into the street in front of their mothers. The stroller should not leave the sidewalk until all the oncoming traffic has stopped and it is safe to cross. Waiting in the "gutter" for a break in the traffic and then dashing out into the street with the stroller leading the way is fraught with danger.

Young mothers and babysitters should remember that street signs and streetlights must be obeyed. It may take longer to get where they are going, but it is essential to cross only when it is safe. This also means looking both ways, even on a one-way street, and noticing any cars that are signaling that they intend to turn. There is never an excuse to push a stroller out into the street from between two parked cars. It is not their own lives they are risking, it is the life of the child in the stroller.

Crossing the street with little ones

Toddlers and young children should hold an adult's hand whenever crossing the street. The adult should always demonstrate looking both ways and watching for the walk sign. There should always be enough time allowed for the toddlers' little legs to get across safely. They cannot walk as quickly as an adult. If the toddler must hold on to the handle of the stroller, instead of holding an adult's hand, he should walk very close to the adult to allow control of impulsive behavior until everyone has reached safety.

Toddlers are impulsive and unpredictable

They *always* need adult supervision, especially when they are outside. (We would never leave diamonds outside in the care of a seven-year-old child. Toddlers are worth much more!)

School-age children

Everyone should be shown how to have a healthy respect for the dangers of the street. All children must learn that a car can come down any street at any time. They must learn how to be careful. Certain rules always apply:

- Always cross at corners.
- Always obey traffic signs.
- Always look both ways every time you enter the street, and wait until there are no cars coming from either direction.
- At an intersection, look for cars that are signaling that they intend to turn.
- Be extra careful when it is raining, since it is harder for the pedestrian to see cars coming, and harder for the drivers to see people in the street. It is also much harder to stop a car.
- Never enter the street from between two parked cars.
- Never play in the street unless it is closed to traffic and an adult is supervising.
- "Let the ball roll" until there are no cars in sight.

- If there is traffic and the intersection is hard to cross, ask an adult to help you cross to the other side.
- If you are playing in a street that is closed off and you see a car coming, get onto the sidewalk that is nearest to you.
- Never throw anything at a car.

These rules, which should be second nature to all children, must be reinforced in school. They should be taught in preschool and enforced by the teachers and administrators. If children are found doing dangerous things like throwing things at cars or running in front of cars when they come down the street near the school, they should be strictly disciplined.

It might be a good idea for Hatzolah to go into the schools every year and do a street safety program to help emphasize the importance of these rules.

All adults must remember that we teach by example. We all must obey these basic rules ourselves! It is our responsibility to educate the children about safety. We must not rely on miracles to avoid accidents and injury every day. Hashem in His mercy protects foolish people and children, but we still must do our best to keep everyone safe.

CHAPTER 30

Maintaining a Safe School Environment

Key Points

- We are responsible to provide a safe school environment.
- Maintenance, cleanliness, and lighting and ventilation are important.
- Safety includes a safe nutritional environment.

Every September as the new school year approaches, parents should take time to think about the school environment in which their children will soon find themselves. They will spend many hours a day in school in the coming months. Parents are always careful to make sure that our homes are safe and clean. It is logical that they ensure that the same standard is maintained in the schools the children attend. There are many different factors that should be considered.

Cleanliness

The most important areas to be maintained are the bathrooms and the school kitchens. The maintenance of school bathrooms requires frequent cleaning and provision of supplies. Toilet paper, soap, and paper towels are essential. Cloth towels are not acceptable since they spread bacteria. If you can smell your way to the bathroom in your child's school, it is not being cleaned with proper frequency and thoroughness. Despite the fact that budgets are tight, this kind of maintenance is literally essential to the health of the children. In our community especially, there have been numerous epidemics of Shigella Dysentery that have been traced to bathroom hygiene.

Hand sanitizer has been found to be very effective in controlling the spread of these germs. It would be a good idea to have a dispenser at the exit of each bathroom. One quick squirt that is rubbed on the hands and air-dried is all that is needed.

School kitchens must also be kept meticulously clean. This is usually well-done in our community.

Maintenance of the physical plant of the school

Broken windows and window guards, broken steps, peeling paint on walls and ceilings, broken desks, faulty wiring and other such hazards must be repaired — not only at the end of the school year, but as they are discovered. Boilers and heating systems need constant maintenance.

Lighting and ventilation

In order to ensure optimal learning conditions, there must be good lighting and ventilation. Windows should be easily opened safely. Window guards should be installed when needed.

Fire safety

All schools are required to have fire evacuation plans, fire extinguishers, and fire drills. These requirements are not to be taken casually.

Schoolyard safety

There must be good supervision in every schoolyard while the children play. Some schools have trailers and buses parked in places that are accessible to the kids. These areas must be monitored to make sure the children are safe. There can be unsafe hidden activities going on under and in these vehicles during recess. If the "schoolyard" is a blocked-off street, supervision is required to make sure that the cars that do get through do not endanger the children.

Bus safety

There should be an adult monitor on buses that carry small children. The sight of children standing in their seats, fighting and hanging out of bus windows is terrifying to all of us. Short stops happen without warning. We must do our best to ensure that our kids are safe on their buses.

Nutritional environment

Besides the physical safety of our children, we should also be concerned that they are in a good nutritional environment during the school day. The obesity epidemic in America is definitely affecting our community. There are more obese and overweight children in this generation than ever before. The health risk of obesity is much greater when the obesity occurs in childhood. Obese youngsters develop diabetes much more quickly than adults who develop obesity later on.

It has been clearly shown that nutritional environment is a critical factor in this epidemic. This includes the foods that are given to the kids, the foods that are made available to them, and how their eating habits and tastes and preferences are developed during childhood. Even drinks are very important — water and milk should be the choices. Soda and juices are liquid sugar. The machines found in most schools should not sell soda or candy.

Since even our toddlers spend significant time in school, the food in school is a very important factor. Healthy snack policies are a very good start. Rewards and parties that emphasize sweets and greasy junk food set terrible precedents as the kids develop their taste preferences. School lunch and suppers should be planned with good nutrition in mind. We cannot simply wring our hands in despair about the candy and junk in school. We owe it to our kids to work on their nutritional environment in school.

CHAPTER 31

Purim Safety

Purim presents parents of teenage boys with a special challenge. This is a letter from the parents of a young boy who wrote to the *Binah Magazine* for advice.

Dear Dr. Schulman,

Please help me to settle a family controversy. Our oldest son is in yeshivah high school. He is looking forward to spending Purim going around the neighborhoods with his friends collecting money for *tzedakah.*

I do not want to ruin his Purim, but I am uncomfortable about this, since I know that many of the kids get drunk. Since they have a driver with a van who will take them around, I'm not concerned about drunk driving. But we are worried about the exposure to alcohol and the behavior that it causes. How should we handle this?

Worried Parents

This is an important question.

Key Points

- Talk to your boys often, especially before Purim, about how you feel about drinking on Purim.

- Your children want your respect and approval. Let them know how proud you will be of their common sense and good judgment when they make the right decisions on Purim.

- Make sure they can call upon you to help them leave if the situation feels wrong.

This was my reply:

Dear Worried Parents,

Talk to your son! And have that conversation before Purim!

I think it is reasonable to tell him that he is only allowed to drink alcohol at home, and even then no hard liquor, only wine. Many Rabbanim, including Harav Avraham Pam, *zt"l*, have emphasized this in the last few years.

We all know that letting kids get drunk is not good for them.

These kids vomit to the point of dehydration, develop severe headaches, experience changes in level of consciousness and often fall down and injure themselves, all due to alcohol. The emergency rooms in Brooklyn and in Israel fill up with many cases of acute alcohol intoxication in teenagers on Purim. A mother who has spent her Purim evening sitting by a stretcher in the emergency room can tell you how awful it is.

If the child does his drinking at your own *seudah,* consuming only wine, you can watch him and limit his intake. **If he is drinking with friends, he will probably keep going even if he feels terrible, due to peer pressure.**

There is another danger to allowing your son to binge on Purim. It is now known that the adolescent brain is more prone to developing addictions than the adult brain. Many teens who are addicted to alcohol got their first "high" on Purim. They get over the illness of their first binge and act upon an urge to try it again.

On a side note, the same is true of smoking. Many addicted teen smokers report that their first cigarette was given to them on Purim. (There are still places where even 7-year-old boys are "treated" to cigarettes on Purim.)

Collecting *tzedakah* with a team of boys can be an uplifting experience. They will probably collect the most money if they make a great impression on people by singing songs, dancing, and acting like real respectable yeshivah *bachurim*.

You can probably trust your son to do what you ask. **It is important to talk openly about the drinking before Purim.** Tell him what you expect of him. He will not want to let you down. Let him know that if the situation does not feel right to him, he should call you and you will gladly pick him up.

CHAPTER 32

Smoking Addiction

Our community has a real problem. Large numbers of adolescent yeshivah *bachurim*, age 13 to 18, are starting to smoke. This is nothing new. There have always been a lot of smokers in the yeshivahs. We have always accepted it as an unfortunate fact of life. We say, *"What can we do?" "How can we prevent it when so many adults in the yeshivah world smoke?" "It is not forbidden according to Jewish Law." "There is no way to stop boys from doing what their peers do."*

The tragic reality is that most of these boys will not be able to stop smoking

Is there really nothing we can do to stop our precious young boys from becoming chronic smokers for the rest of their lives? It is time to take a different look at the nature of this problem.

Scientific research reveals that smoking creates health problems

Until 50 years ago, the association of tobacco and illness was only vague. When

Key Points

- Smoking is bad for anyone's health.
- It is a major risk factor for cancer, heart disease, lung disease, and many other illnesses.
- Smoking is an ADDICTION!
- Boys start smoking for social reasons and find themselves addicted for life.
- Girls do not smoke for social reasons.
- Our community should take steps to change the social acceptance of smoking in boys.
- We must not stand helplessly by while our sons make a horrible mistake that will impact the rest of their lives.

researchers in the 1960s first began to show evidence that smoking was causing *lung cancer,* the medical world started looking more closely at the population of smokers.

Since that time, new medical information has piled up year by year. It is now known that smoking dramatically increases the risk for *heart attacks, stroke, cancer of the lungs, mouth, throat, and bladder, pneumonia, bronchitis, emphysema, and asthma.* The risks of breathing secondhand smoke have also been demonstrated.

Now we know — it's an addiction!

The most startling medical revelation is just becoming common knowledge. That is, that smoking is an **addiction**. Although the tobacco companies have been aware of this, they concealed the information for decades. It became public knowledge only recently, during the legal confrontations between the tobacco victims and the companies.

We now understand why it is so hard for a smoker to stop, even when told that his life depends on it. We now understand why so many fathers and husbands spend the last few minutes before Shabbos standing outside or sitting in their cars smoking and inhaling deeply. We now know why a perfectly normal man will go out of his office building on a miserable, wet, windy day to stand huddled together with all types of people with whom he has nothing else in common. **It's the addiction.**

Not just a bad habit

Smoking is not just a "bad habit" like nail biting. It is different in a very basic way. Habits can be broken with some behavior modification. **Addictions are changes in the "hardwiring" of the brain.**

In smoking addiction, the drug, nicotine, is the major component. The smoker's brain develops a dependency on the drug as it affects his feelings and sense of comfort. The urge to smoke is generated by a discomfort associated with withdrawal of the drug.

The smoker needs to smoke to take away the discomfort. Without it he feels edgy, restless, irritable and sometimes anxious and depressed. **Satisfying this need is so important that the smoking addict will sacrifice his own money, health and well-being to continue smoking.**

Breaking the addiction is very hard

Overcoming this addiction is extremely difficult. All Orthodox smokers stop for Shabbos, but they usually hurry to light up immediately after *Maariv.* **Even when the**

smoker manages to stop smoking, the urges have to be dealt with for many years to come. Smoking addiction is now considered a medical illness by insurance companies and medical experts.

Most smokers wish they could stop — but they can't

The fact of the matter is that most smokers wish they could stop. Many have tried repeatedly and failed. When a study was done of attitudes of people purchasing cases of cigarettes at a discount depot, 85 percent of them answered *No* to the question, *"Are you happy to be a smoker?"* and the same percentage answered *Yes* to the question, *"Would you stop smoking if you could?"*

Why, when, and how do our *bachurim* start?

With so much now known about the bad consequences of smoking, why do our *bachurim* start smoking? Most boys will report that they were first introduced to cigarettes in yeshivah. Some started on Purim or with *chassan* cigarettes. Most started when an older *bachur* gave them a cigarette and showed them how to inhale.

Even nowadays, when some yeshivahs have become stricter about smoking, the boys in each school can easily show you the stairwell or rooftop where the smokers go to smoke. The adolescent boys feel that it is socially desirable to smoke because **it makes them feel grown up and important.** They look up to Rabbanim who smoke and older cool boys who are their role models.

Starting to smoke is very unpleasant, but they persist

Starting to smoke requires effort and determination. When a boy first tries a cigarette, it makes him cough and gag. He feels a little lightheaded and nauseated. He decides to keep trying until the choking stops and he can enjoy the good feeling. He says, *"If everyone else can learn to do it, I can too."* By the time he gets used to the smoking, he is starting to feel the pull of the next cigarette.

Social reasons for smoking in boys and against smoking in girls

The most important point is that this whole process starts for social reasons. None of these boys start by needing to smoke. They start by needing the social acceptance of their peers. **They end up with an addiction and a peck of trouble.**

One thing is sure. Peer pressure is so important to adolescent boys that **if a *bachur* knows that smoking would make him a social outcast, he will think twice before starting to smoke.** How do we know this is true? Look at the girls in our society. Not one girl in the social mainstream would even think of starting to smoke.

Why the girls do not smoke

The girls do not smoke because it is socially unacceptable. A girl who smokes is not considered "fine and good." It is strange that a boy who smokes can still be the "best *bachur* in the yeshivah." **If boys would be held to the same standard as the girls, a lot of lives could be saved!**

The obvious solution

We must change the social acceptance standard in our society that allows a boy to be considered socially desirable even if he smokes.

It is up to the parents and the schools to set the acceptable norms

Young people have a tendency to think of themselves as being immune to consequences. They tend to see themselves as invincible. Adults know better. That is why we as parents and teachers have to set guidelines and restrictions when it comes to adolescent behavior.

We give them dress codes and behavior codes that have to be followed to maintain their social status as good and acceptable. We must include *not smoking* as one of the standards of adolescent behavior.

We simply must not stand by and allow these kids to make a mistake that will have a negative impact on the rest of their lives!

Social solutions

Since the problem starts as a social issue, it needs a social solution. I see several things we can do to cause the necessary change in attitude.

Including the smoking adult in the solution — It would make a lot of sense if the adults who smoke can be a major force in preventing *bachurim* from starting to smoke. We must ask these fine people to look upon themselves and the example they are setting. They must always be aware that merely by smoking in front of children, they could be responsible for attracting them to starting to smoke.

They could tell the children how sorry they are to be stuck with this terrible burden. What an impact it would have on the students if a *rebbi* looked at them directly and said, "*Beloved bachurim, I was young when I first started smoking. I never dreamed I would not be able to stop. I didn't know it would cause addiction. No one knew it in those days. It was the biggest mistake I ever made. I want to stop. I am still trying, but it is so very hard! Please forgive me for setting such a bad example. Don't make the same mistake I did!"*

Everyone will look upon these men with sympathy and concern, not disrespect.

Prevention is the cure — Parents must talk to their boys before age 10, long before they are offered a cigarette. Tell them about all of the negative facts regarding smoking, including how addictive it is. Tell them you will be very disappointed if they ever start to smoke. Repeat this often throughout adolescence. Your words will remain with them and give them strength to resist.

Explain that **many wonderful people smoke, but that they wish they had never started. We must look up to them, but we must also feel sorry for their affliction.** When you see a young, frum person smoking say, *"That person doesn't look cool. He looks like a person who has made a big mistake. He thinks he is holding that cigarette, but he is wrong. The cigarette is holding him!"*

Shidduchim — Parents should consider smoking as a very serious issue when looking for a *shidduch* for their daughter. *Not smoking* should be included on her list of desired characteristics. By age 45, the smoker could very likely have real medical problems. These girls have a right to have a healthy husband and father for their children after 20 years of marriage.

The girls should be made aware of all of the important facts regarding smoking, even though they don't smoke. It is only fair that they know about the medical illness of addiction and all of the consequences of smoking.

They should know that if a boy says, *"I will stop smoking as soon as we get engaged,"* it is probably **not true. He is an addict.** She should say, *"If you can stop smoking, you should do it immediately, and if you are successful you may let me know after 6 months of being 'clean.'"* If a boy hears this often enough and decides to really stop, the pain of this rejection could save his life. If the girls collectively refuse to be matched to smokers, the boys will be much less inclined to smoke.

Change the rules in yeshivah — All of the major yeshivahs should get together and agree to a new set of rules that will discourage boys from starting to smoke.

1. The first cigarette should be *treif* for a yeshivah *bachur*. No one who is not married should be allowed to start smoking. Once he is married he must ask permission of his wife to make such a huge decision.

2.. **The elementary and high schools should expel a student** who is **seen** anywhere, anytime, **smoking.** *Not smoking* should be included in the formal rules of dress and behavior that allows a boy to be included as a student of the yeshivah. For example, they must wear white shirts, dark dress pants, a jacket, and a black hat. They must not talk to girls in the pizza shop; they are not to drive in the country. They must not smoke.

3. **The adult faculty** and employees of the yeshivah, including *rebbeim*, teachers, administrators, and even maintenance crew, **should never smoke in front of the students,** even outside the school setting.

The smoking *bachur*

The young *bachurim* who are among the unfortunate who have already started smoking must be helped to stop — the sooner the better! Even though it is difficult, it must be done. They must stop, because they will soon realize that their whole future really depends on it, socially and medically. Most smoking addicts are helped with a combination of medication and therapy.

This will not only save these *bachurim,* it will have a major impact on the problem. If there are no older *bachurim* smoking, and no role models who smoke, the younger generation of boys will not even be tempted to try smoking.

Final thought

We now understand that this is a different type of problem than we ever dreamed. Until this community wakes up and takes the social actions needed to **discourage children from starting to smoke,** every child who picks up smoking from now on is our responsibility. We cannot throw up our hands and give up on our sons. We owe it to them to get this problem under control before more lives are ruined. We, as a community, as parents, as teachers, and as Rabbanim, have it in our power to do it. The fact is, **we must do it!**

CHAPTER 33

Ensuring Your Child's Personal Safety

When we live in a wholesome, family oriented, religious community such as ours, it is often assumed that our children will be safe from predators. We certainly shelter them from outside influences in our modern-day society. Unfortunately, even in our own community, there are people who have urges to do unseemly things to children. We call this *"child personal abuse."* The definition of personal abuse is when an adult uses a child to gratify himself.

Personal abuse can be like a contagious disease. A small percentage of the abused children grow up to become abusers as adults. Each abuser can affect the lives of many children. If we could prevent our children from being victims of abuse, the incidence of abuse would disappear in the coming generations.

Our children can also be subjected to bullying and physical abuse in the school environment. The best way to protect our children from being abused this way or in any way is to prevent the child from getting into an ongoing abusive relationship. Here is a basic program that parents must learn and implement with their children.

Key Points

- Child personal abuse can happen in our community.

- The abuser is usually familiar to the child.

- Communication between parents and children is the key to preventing abuse and its consequences.

- Ignoring this problem when it happens can only make it worse.

Who would do such a thing? **The abuser is usually familiar to the child.**

Everyone is aware of the "stranger danger" concept, and children should certainly know not to go along with a stranger. But despite what is commonly thought, most child abusers and child personal abusers are not strangers — they are familiar adults or older children in the child's life. Personal abuse can happen with close family members, bus drivers, teachers, neighbors, shopkeepers, or anyone the child knows. The predator takes advantage of the child's natural trust, and gradually builds up a relationship that entraps the child.

The most important thing to do to protect your child is to make sure that he will always come to tell his parent immediately if something unusual happens. Every child must know that his parents want him to talk to them. Opening the critical lines of communication must start very early.

Toddlers

When a child leaves home to go to nursery school or playgroup, his mother and father should sit down and talk to him. This conversation should contain the following elements:

1. Your mommy loves you.

I will always love you. Nothing you will do will ever take that love away from you.

I want to hear about things that happen in school — all the good things, and even the bad things that happen.

If you have done a bad thing, I may not like what you did, but I will always love you.

2. There are three kinds of touches.

The **Yes** touch (like when Mommy hugs you and you feel good)

The **No** touch (like when your friend hits you — it hurts!)

The **I Don't Know** touch (this is when someone touches you and it doesn't hurt, but it makes you feel funny). If someone touches you and you feel funny, go away from them and tell Mommy about it.

3. No one is allowed to hurt you or make you sad or scared.

If someone is hurting you or making you feel bad at school, tell me about it. I will find out what is happening and I will stop it.

4. The area that is covered by your bathing suit is your private area.

Sometimes when you are little your teacher may help you in the bathroom. That is okay. Other than that, you are not allowed to touch someone else and no one is allowed to touch you in the area covered by your bathing suit. You are not allowed to show anyone and no one is allowed to show you. If anyone does this, you can say, **"No! My mommy doesn't let me!" Go away** from that person and **tell your mommy** what happened.

5. If anyone tells you, "Do not tell your mommy," tell Mommy right away!

I will give you the biggest hug if you tell me about it.

6. If anyone hurts you or scares you, you should come and tell Mommy.

Someone might say, "If you tell your mommy, I will hurt you or hurt your mommy"; do not worry. They might say that something terrible will happen if you tell your mommy. You still must tell me. I am a grownup and I will protect you. (The most creative threat I have ever encountered was, "If you tell your mommy, you will melt the next time it rains!")

Eye contact and a couple minutes of your time

The most important thing you can do as a parent is to stop what you are doing, look the child in the eye, and ask him, "How was your day?" He might not tell you much, but if you consistently show him that you are interested, he will remember this when he needs you.

If you are always busy in the kitchen or on the phone, he might feel that he does not want to bother you. The larger the family, the more important it is that you give a few minutes a day of eye contact and keep the channel of communication open. That way when something does happen he will feel comfortable telling you about it.

This line of talk should be gently reinforced periodically with the child.

Behavioral signs

When a child is being subjected to personal abuse, there might be certain behavior changes that would alert you.

- The child may seem unusually interested in the private areas of other people's bodies.
- The child may draw pictures of hidden body parts.
- The child may show signs of stress, such as sleep problems, appetite changes, behavior changes, tantrums, restart bed-wetting, fears, and irritability.
- The child may become unusually afraid of, or unusually attached to, an adult in his life.
- The child might give verbal hints or even describe the abuse to the parent. **It is critical that the parent actually listen to the child, and if a hint or a statement is heard it must be taken seriously.**

The older child

The same points as were made with the toddler should be restated as the child starts school or goes away to camp. He must know that he should tell you if anything unusual happens.

Girls must be made aware of the laws of *yichud* by age 10. Emphasize the need for walking in groups, and how it is not permitted to get into an elevator alone with a man. Even when babysitting, if the father comes into the house, she should leave if there are no other people around. She should also be made aware of how the laws of *yichud* apply to relatives in certain situations, even brothers or uncles.

Unfortunately, the older child might try to handle difficult situations independently. As a result, they can become entrapped in an abusive situation and feel there is no way out.

Because the abuser is frequently nice to the victim, gaining his loyalty and confidence before starting to take advantage of him, the child may have affection for the abuser and feel that he is enjoying the relationship, even though he knows it is not right. The confusion only adds to the stress. These relationships go on for a very long time, until someone intervenes or circumstances change.

Parents should realize that an older child should not have very strong feelings toward or against any casual adult in his life, like an uncle or a neighbor. If he has such inappropriate feelings about someone, the reason for this should be investigated.

The older child and teenager need the same reassurance as the little ones. Reassure your child that you are there for him and that you always want to hear about his experiences — good and bad. Tell the child that you will always love him.

Consequences

If a child has been a victim of personal abuse, the statistics show that about 1/3 of them just laugh it off or forget about it; 1/3 will show symptoms of stress initially and then get over it; and 1/3 go on to have problems for a lifetime.

These problems can be both psychological and physical. Depression, anxiety, insomnia, problems with marriage and relationships, and, unfortunately, actually becoming an abuser are all common in the lives of these victims. Migraine headaches, abdominal pain, eating disorders, and stress-related intestinal disorders such as inflammatory bowel disorders have been found to be common in victims of personal abuse.

Revealing abuse can be nearly impossible in the Orthodox world. Victims are blamed for accusing their elders. The occasional incidence of suicide in young teens is usually a result of personal abuse. Many victims never reveal their abuse experience. In general, the earlier the abuse is identified and stopped, the fewer long-term effects the victims have.

It is amazing how long the abuse experience continues to live on in a person before it is told to anyone. Many experts have noted that a period of 15 to 20 years of keeping the secret is not unusual. The abused child is afraid of the consequences of revealing the abuse, so the child carries the burden himself. He knows that the abuser's family will suffer and he will be blamed for not remaining silent.

Many times it is an adult who tells about abuse he experienced as a child. When a victim reaches adulthood, he feels he will be taken seriously if he tells his story. He also feels responsible to stop the abuser, who may still be in contact with children. By this time, the abuser's family has grown up, so the victim feels freer to talk.

It is very important to know what to do if you find out that your child has been abused. The first reaction must be to reassure the child that you are not angry with him, and that everything will be okay. The second reaction must be to make sure that this person will not abuse the child anymore. This may require dealing with the school, the neighbor, or even with close family members.

A knowledgeable Orthodox rabbi should be consulted for guidance.

There are special therapy groups for Orthodox child personal abusers in our community.

If there is a disturbance in the child's mood or behavior, the child may need to be treated by a social worker or counselor who has had special training in treating personal abuse in children.

When the child is protected, reassured, and counseled, he will put it all behind him and go on to lead a healthy and normal life. This is our goal as parents, and as a community. We must do all we can to make sure that personal abuse is dealt with properly.

Years of bitter experience have shown that personal abuse is a problem that does not just go away. An abuser who is not stopped can abuse hundreds of children over a lifetime. Some of these victims go on to perpetuate the abuse against the next generation of children. We have the power to stop this unending cycle by acknowledging the problem and dealing with it as a community.

Pediatric Problems and Solutions

CHAPTER 34

Understanding Short Stature in a Growing Child

Your child is shorter than the other children in his class.

Is this *short stature* normal or is it a medical problem?

Growth is the special job of childhood. All of the child's physiology is geared to growing from conception to the end of puberty. Optimal growth depends on nutrition and good health. It is obvious that some children grow faster and taller than others, and their ultimate heights are determined by genetic factors. No one seems to worry that a child is growing on the tall end of the spectrum. When a child is growing slowly and is shorter than his or her peers, there is often more concern. Although short parents tend to have short children, sometimes the slower growth is due to actual medical problems that could be corrected.

Key Points

- Optimal growth is influenced by many factors.
- Genetics play a big role.
- Nutrition and metabolism are critical factors.
- Natural delay in puberty can cause apparent growth problems.
- Growth hormone treatments are safe and effective when indicated.
- Short, healthy people lead normal lives.

Growth charts

As a child grows and develops we carefully watch the *pattern of growth* to make sure that it is normal. Growth charts are plotted to follow the increase in measurements as the child gets older. These charts show the growth of normal children. They were created by measuring thousands of normal children over their whole childhoods. Separate charts were made for boys and girls.

The growth chart is recorded in percentiles — for example, if you measure 100 random healthy children, the very tall ones are taller than 95 percent of the group so they are in the 95th percentile; the average children are in the 50th percentile, and the shortest ones are in the 5th percentile. The curved lines on the charts show the expected pattern of growth for each percentile.

Expected height

Tall children usually come from tall families, and average or short children also follow their family patterns. The actual adult height percentile is usually somewhere between the height percentile of the father, and the height percentile of the mother.

Each child is measured regularly as they grow and the height is plotted on the chart to see how their growth compares to the lines in the growth chart. Normal growth follows these lines. *When the child is about 2-4 years old, the percentile line he is growing on is a fairly good predictor of the percentile line he will end up on when he stops growing.*

When a small child is growing along his percentile curve in a percentile similar to his parents, we usually do not worry. However, if his growth drops off the curve and goes to a lower percentile, or if he actually stops growing, there is cause for concern.

Factors that contribute to growth

Many things play a role in growth. Parental height, genetic diseases, prenatal problems, prematurity, nutritional intake, kidney function, intestinal function, endocrine function including sex hormones, growth hormone, adrenal hormones, thyroid and pituitary hormones, bone structure, and timing of puberty. All interact in the growth of a child.

The role of genetics

Many different genes interact to allow growth. Because so many genes are involved, there is no way to determine the height by looking at the genes. Obviously the pattern of height can run in families. In families where both the father and mother are short, there is little likelihood of producing tall children. A mixture of heights in the parents can produce variable heights in the children. There are some genetic diseases that have predictable short stature. Children with Turner's syndrome, Blooms syndrome, Down syndrome and other genetic diseases are usually very short. Some of these children with genetic diseases can be treated with growth hormone if it is indicated.

Diet and digestion

If the child is having a poor weight gain, a careful nutritional history must be taken. Poor growth can be secondary to lack of calories in the diet, or a gastrointestinal problem such as celiac disease, malabsorption, vomiting, eating disorder, or poor appetite. Often when the intake is improved and the intestinal problem is cured, the growth improves. These problems can be addressed by a Pediatric Gastroenterologist.

Endocrine and metabolic factors

When the growth failure has no obvious nutritional cause, the child will be referred to a Pediatric Endocrinologist, who will do a series of tests and x-rays to see what the source of the growth problem is. One of tests is called a *bone age*. This is an x-ray of the wrist to determine the maturity of the child's skeleton. If the bone age is delayed, it sometimes means that the child will grow more slowly than expected.

The endocrinologist will do blood tests that check the function of all of the hormones which have effect on growth. Kidneys, hypothalamus, pituitary gland, adrenal glands, and gonads are all assessed.

Constitutional delay of growth and puberty

If the workup does not show any dysfunction of the child's endocrine system, and if the bone age is delayed, the diagnosis of *constitutional delay of growth and puberty* is often made. These children are often known as "late bloomers." They are smaller than their peers because their growth and physical development (not mental development) are on a slower time table. They can look much younger than their classmates in the sixth, seventh and eighth grade, because their puberty has not yet begun. The big growth spurt during puberty makes their friends grow much faster than they are growing. These children will show the earliest signs of puberty later, but when they start to grow as their puberty sets in, the growth spurt will last until an older age, so they often out grow their peers.

The problem is, it is sometimes hard to differentiate whether the child will grow well later or not. This is true especially when a child is a late bloomer and has small parents. This child can appear to be very short — even shorter than his small family would predict.

The endocrinologist will try to predict what the ultimate height will be. If it is possible that the child will be abnormally short, the medication called growth hormone could be used.

Vitamins – not an effective therapy

Good nutrition is important for growth, but there are no specific vitamins, minerals or supplements that actually boost growth.

Growth hormone

Growth hormone is a daily injection which is easily tolerated by the children. It is known to be safe and has been in use for over 20 years. It stimulates the growth of the bones. Since this treatment could cost as much as $30,000 a year, insurance companies are reluctant to pay for it. They require certain tests to be done to see if there is really a growth hormone deficiency before they will allow it.

In some short families there is no deficiency at all, but the hormone can sometimes be effective in gaining extra inches,. The amount of extra height gained by these children is probably not more than two inches.

The hormone is safe and effective. It is given daily until the child stops growing at the end of puberty. It will not be effective at all if it is given after puberty is complete, so there is a need for careful timing and decision making if the child does not start to grow as expected in puberty when the final growth spurt is supposed to occur.

Quality of life

There have been many studies to try to determine if being normally short (4 feet 9 inches in a girl, 5 feet in a boy) causes a poorer quality of life. Interviews of many people seem to show that there is really no difference in the quality of life for people who are short. Most of the parents of our short children feel that as long as the child is healthy they do not want to try to make him taller.

Because it is important for a healthy child to grow to his full potential, it is imperative that children be seen regularly for well-child checkups, which include growth measurements. Since growth stops when puberty advances, it is very important to have all children monitored, including babies, children, preteens, and teens. If a growth problem arises, it must be corrected before it is too late to help it.

■ ■ ■

CHAPTER 35

Understanding Blood: Normal Functions and Blood Problems in Childhood

Key Points

- Blood is one of our most important organ systems.

- Blood is produced in the bone marrow.

- Red blood cells carry oxygen — anemia is a deficiency in the red blood cells.

- White blood cells help defend us from infection — leukemia is cancer involving white blood cells.

- Platelets help the blood to clot — thrombocytopenia is a deficiency in platelets.

- Donating blood can save lives — there is always a need for donors.

One of the most unappreciated and important systems in the body is the blood. The blood that courses through our arteries and veins has several different components. Each one performs different critical functions that keep us alive and healthy. The following is an explanation of the blood components and a discussion of what happens when a problem arises in this system.

The bone marrow—our blood cell factory

Although before birth the liver and spleen produce blood cells, for most of our lives, the blood is produced in the bone marrow of our long bones. The bone marrow lies in the hollow core of each of our long bones. Cells arise and mature in the bone marrow and they are released into the circulatory system. Each blood cell has a limited life span: A red blood cell lasts only 120 days, so new blood cells are always being produced to maintain healthy quantities all the time.

The red blood cells

The red color of blood comes from the iron-containing protein known as **hemoglobin,** which is found in the **red blood cells.** The hemoglobin carries oxygen from the lungs to all the tissues of the body, and after it has delivered the oxygen, it carries carbon dioxide (a waste product) back to the lungs to be exchanged for more oxygen. Life completely depends on this critical function.

Anemia — deficiency in the red blood cells

Red blood cells usually comprise about 36-40 percent of the total volume of blood (the *hematocrit*). The normal amount of hemoglobin in a milliliter of blood (the *hemoglobin)* is 11-14 grams. Anemia occurs when these two values go down to less than 33 percent, and less than 10.5 grams. This deficiency is usually caused by a lack of iron in the diet, an elevated serum-lead level, prematurity, or an illness that causes fever. Illnesses of any type can suppress the bone marrow and lower the red blood count. These anemias are easily identified and corrected. When iron deficiency is the cause, the child is usually placed on iron and vitamins.

Anemia in the newborn can be caused by hemolysis due to blood type incompatibility. This is a breakup of the red blood cells due to antibodies that are produced by the mother which cross the placenta and attack the infant's red blood cells. This condition often causes significant jaundice in the newborn.

The most severe and life-threatening incompatibility is due to Rh, which is now prevented by giving the Rh-negative mother Rho Gam if the baby is incompatible. Because of this wonderful medication, this condition is unheard-of in our current generation.

The most common incompatibility is the one seen when the mother is type O and the baby is A, B or AB. This can cause jaundice and anemia in the newborn. It usually corrects itself within about one week of birth.

Diet and anemia

Mother's milk is a good source of iron in a totally-breast-fed infant. Formulas now have iron in them. After six months of age the infant can be fed solid foods if it is deemed necessary. Despite the fact that baby cereals have iron added, the best first baby food is meat or chicken that has been cooked and ground or blended. The iron in these foods is absorbed very readily, and the proteins in the meats are high quality.

Eggs, fish, and legumes have lots of iron and protein.

The problem arises when a child over one year of age switches to cow's milk from formula or breast milk. Cow's milk has no iron at all. Milk and all milk products are very important as a source of calcium and protein, fats and carbohydrates. However, the child's diet must be balanced by including meats, poultry, fish, eggs, and legumes to provide adequate iron. A diet of too much milk can cause anemia.

The recommended amount of milk is 3 six-ounce portions of milk a day, and one portion of leben, yogurt or cheese or cottage cheese.

The white blood cells— leukocytes

The bone marrow also produces white blood cells. These are cells that circulate in the bloodstream and protect us from infection. There are two basic categories of white blood cells, the granulocytes (also known as *neutrophils* or *polys*), and the lymphocytes.

Granulocytes

The *granulocytes* are the majority of white blood cells. They provide the defense against bacterial and fungal infections. These cells identify and attack these organisms and actually "eat" them and kill them by digesting them. During acute bacterial infections, the number of granulocytes increases, resulting in a high total white blood count. These cells die after they ingest a few organisms, so they must be replaced by the bone marrow very rapidly during an acute infection. When a large amount of dead granulocytes accumulate in an area of infection, the debris is known as pus.

A small portion of the granulocytes are *eosinophils*. These cells attack parasites and also become numerous in allergic reactions.

Another small number of these cells are *basophils*, which explode and release histamine during allergic reactions.

Lymphocytes

Lymphocytes are usually smaller in number in the bloodstream than the granulocytes. During viral illnesses the total number of lymphocytes will often outnumber the granulocytes. They are also found all over the body in the lymphatic systems. Lymphocytes are subdivided into *B cells* and *T cells*.

B cells produce antibodies. Antibodies are proteins that bind to dangerous organisms (called pathogens) and cause their destruction. These antibodies are the mechanism of our immune response.

B cells can also be memory cells that provide protection by producing antibodies when a previous pathogen tries to re-enter the body.

T cells coordinate the immune response and defend against viruses and some bacteria.

Another type of lymphocyte — the *monocyte* — also consumes organisms, and performs the function of presenting pieces of the organisms to the T cells so they can initiate the immune response.

Problems with the white blood cells

When the bone marrow produces excessive numbers of immature white blood cells, the cause is often a malignant condition called *leukemia*.

In children the most common leukemia is the leukemia in which the excess and abnormal cells are lymphocytes. This cancer is known as *Acute Lymphocytic Leukemia*, or *ALL*. ALL is often curable with chemotherapy or, in more-resistant cases, bone-marrow transplant. Currently the cure rate is over 90 percent in most subtypes of ALL.

When the excess and abnormal cells are granulocytes, the cause is usually *Acute Myelogenous Leukemia -AML*. This leukemia is more resistant to treatment, but in recent years the survival rate has improved dramatically, with newer approaches to chemotherapy and bone-marrow transplantation.

During chemotherapy treatment regimens, the actual number of white blood cells can drop dramatically, even to near zero, leaving the patient vulnerable to infection. This condition is known as *aplastic crisis*. This common complication can be treated with a medication that stimulates production of white blood cells. Infections acquired during these crises require hospitalization.

Rarely, drugs that are not chemotherapeutic agents can cause aplastic crisis. These drugs are usually in the category of immunosuppressive medications that are used to treat autoimmune conditions.

Some infections, such as Infectious Mononucleosis, and Pneumococcal Pneumonia, can cause extremely high white-blood counts that may appear similar to leukemia. These white blood cells are normal ones with no evidence of malignancy. This condition is called leukemoid reaction. When the underlying infection resolves, the white blood counts return to normal.

Platelets — Thrombocytes

Platelets, also known as *thrombocytes*, are small, round structures that circulate with the red and white blood cells. They are essential for clotting and wound repair. The usual number of platelets in a cc of blood is 150,000 to 400,000. They only live about one week in the circulation, so the bone marrow must produce them continuously.

PROBLEMS WITH PLATELETS

High platelet counts

Abnormally high platelet counts (over 1,000,000) can result in an abnormal tendency to form clots in the veins. The platelets can also contribute to blockages of arteries in the heart and in the brain. To decrease the ability of platelets to adhere to each other, the drug *aspirin* is helpful. Very small doses of aspirin daily are needed to perform this function.

Low platelet counts

Low platelet counts can cause a tendency to bleed excessively with injury and even without injury.

Thrombocytopenia (low total number of platelets)

The most common childhood condition that affects platelets is *Ideopathic Thrombocytopenic Purpura, ITP.*

This condition presents as purple bruises on the skin (purpura) which result from a decreased platelet count (thrombocytopenia.) The actual cause is unknown ("ideopathic").

ITP is usually not a serious illness, but if the platelet counts go very low, medications are given to raise it to safe levels. Occasionally, the condition becomes more long-term and requires longer courses of medication.

Viral illnesses, such as infectious mononucleosis, can lower platelet counts temporarily. This rarely requires treatment.

Serum

Serum is the pale yellow liquid component of blood. It carries nutrients and blood cells in the blood stream. It contains many substances which are critical to life function.

Serum Clotting Factors

There are proteins in the serum which are needed for normal clotting function. These are called factors. Factor VIII and IX and von Willibrands Factor deficiencies are caused by genetic conditions. The most common mild deficiency is known as von

Willibrands Disease. Frequent severe nosebleeds and bruising and bleeding after major or minor surgical procedures such as dental procedures are the usual presentation. This condition can be treated by use of medications prior to procedures or during bleeding episodes.

Factor VIII deficiency is known as classical Hemophilia. This genetic disease can cause severe bleeding into the joints and other parts of the body. This is treated by factor VIII infusions, which control the bleeding. Factor IX deficiency is a milder form of hemophilia. It is also easily treatable.

Blood loss - hemorrhage

Blood loss from surgery or trauma.can be life-threatening. To maintain blood pressure and volume, transfusions are often required. People have four different major blood types: A, B, O and AB. In addition, the Rh factor is either positive or negative in each of these types.

O-negative blood is the rarest type and it cannot be replaced by any other type. However all other types can be compatible with it, making it a universal donor type. O positive blood can be given to anyone who is not Rh negative.

A, B, and AB blood can be replaced by same type blood — as well as by O blood that is also Rh compatible. AB can be replaced by A, B, O or AB blood, as long as it is Rh compatible.

There is a chronic shortage of blood for transfusion in surgery or emergencies. It is very important for people who are healthy and able to donate units of blood occasionally in order to build up the blood banks in the local community. This procedure is not painful and can save a life. The blood that is donated is replaced quickly by the healthy bone marrow of the donor, so there are no serious risks to the donor.

Good nutrition, adequate fluids, and a healthy lifestyle are essential for the whole body, including the complicated blood system. We must try our best to take care of ourselves and appreciate the gift of normal health.

CHAPTER 36

Understanding the Child
With Abdominal Pain

Key Points

- The nature of the abdominal pain helps us to know when to worry.

- Abdominal pain can be crampy, continuous, burning or sharp.

- Abdominal tenderness means that the pain worsens when pressure is applied.

- The location of the pain in the four quadrants of the abdomen can help determine the cause of the pain.

- Continuous pain and tenderness in the right lower quadrant can be caused by appendicitis.

Every parent has heard the words, "my belly hurts me." This common complaint is usually not a sign of serious problems. Most bellyaches are transient, but some can be recurrent and can even interfere with daily functioning. We all know, however, that sometimes the pain represents a serious problem, like *appendicitis.* How do we know when to worry?

Here is an overview of abdominal pain in children. This discussion is limited to children who can express themselves, usually over the age of 2 years. The best way to understand abdominal pain is to know the identifying features of the pain. The discussion will characterize the following aspects of the pain: *the nature of the abdominal pain, the timing of the pain, the presence of tenderness,* and *the location of the pain.*

The nature of the abdominal pain

Crampy abdominal pain: intermittent, tight or squeezing discomfort that is intense and then eases in repeated cycles

Continuous abdominal pain: a dull ache or a stronger pain that remains constant and does not decrease, even with change of position,

Burning pain: a burning discomfort in the stomach or esophagus

Gas pain: very intense and sharp discomfort that is crampy in nature.

The timing of the pain and associated circumstances

It is useful to note the timing when the pain occurs. For example, if the pain always comes after eating milk products, it might be caused by lactose intolerance. A bellyache that only occurs before a test in school is probably caused by anxiety. It is important to take note of these factors, especially when the problem is recurrent.

The presence of tenderness

The term "tenderness" means increasing pain when manual pressure is applied over the region of the pain.

Location of the pain

Noting the area of the pain can be useful in determining the cause and treatment. The "map" of the abdomen has 5 areas: the *middle* or *periumbilical area,* and four sections called *quadrants*: *the right* and *left upper quadrants*, and the *right* and *left lower quadrants*.

Crampy pains that shift around the abdomen or stay around the navel

It is often said that the closer the pain is to the bellybutton, the less likely it is that it will have a serious cause. If you ask the child where it hurts, he will often rub his hand over the middle of the belly. These pains are most often caused by excess gas and/or by constipation.

It has been shown that in over 80 percent of cases in which children are brought to the emergency room for abdominal pain, constipation is the primary cause of the pain. Besides the gas pains associated with constipation, excess gas can also be caused by swallowing air, or by food intolerance such as lactose intolerance, fructose intolerance, cruciferous vegetable intolerance, and other digestive intolerances.

Right-upper-quadrant pain

If the pain is intermittent or constant and is located in the upper abdomen on the child's right side, it is usually gas pain, but it could rarely be caused by gall bladder disease. If the pain is very intense and does not pass quickly, the child should be seen by a physician.

Left-upper-quadrant pain and pain in the upper middle of the abdomen

The stomach is located in the left upper abdomen, extending across to the upper midline. When the pain originates in the stomach, the child will often complain of an intermittent squeezing feeling in this area. If the feeling is accompanied by nausea and vomiting, the cause is usually a viral illness.

Stomach pain can be caused by excess acid. This frequently causes a burning pain, but often it is also a tight feeling. Sour burps and "heartburn" which travel up into the chest are also signs of excess acid or reflux. The pain is increased by pressing on the stomach in the left upper quadrant or in the upper midline. When this problem persists or is recurrent, the child should be seen by a doctor.

Gas pains can also appear in this area, since the transverse colon is below the stomach. When there is excess gas, tapping on the belly will often produce a hollow sound, and the abdomen can feel tight, like a volleyball full of air. When this is noted, inducing a burp and/or a bowel movement sometimes gives relief.

Left-lower-quadrant pain

When the pain is in the left-lower quadrant, it is usually caused by gas or constipation. These gas pains can be acute and very intense, but they are intermittent. If the crampy pain is followed by a bout of diarrhea, it is usually caused by a viral or bacterial infection. If these pains become chronic, they might be a sign of colitis. A doctor should be consulted.

Right-lower-quadrant pain

Although gas pains can occur in any area of the abdomen, we worry more about pain in the right-lower quadrant. This is because the appendix is located in this area. When the appendix becomes inflamed due to an infection, the illness usually starts with a dull ache in the area of the navel and gradually shifts to the right and towards the lower abdomen. This is usually accompanied by a lack of appetite and some nausea. *The pain in appendicitis is described as continuous.* It does not intensify in a crampy pattern. It is very uncomfortable but not acute or stabbing. The child will lie quietly curled up in one position or shift slowly to try to find comfort. When the child has appendicitis, the *abdomen is tender.* The pain is intensified by pressing the belly. It also might hurt when the manual pressure is quickly removed — "rebound tenderness." The child with appendicitis will often walk tilted to the right and bent over.

When a child has continuous pain with tenderness that lasts for more than an hour, a physician should be consulted.

Chronic conditions

There are many intestinal problems that can present as chronic abdominal pain: *acid reflux, H. Pylori gastritis* (an infection in the stomach lining), *chronic constipation, parasitic infestations, irritable bowel disease* (caused by hypersensitive nerves in the intestine), *inflammatory bowel disease,* such as *ulcerative colitis,* and *Crohn's disease, gluten sensitivity/celiac disease* and *gastrointestinal allergies*. When a child has frequent abdominal discomfort that interferes with quality of life, mood, schooling, sleep, and appetite, a doctor should be consulted. Once a source is identified there is usually a solution that can be employed to control the problem.

Non-abdominal causes of pain in the abdomen

Abdominal pain can also be caused by conditions that are not actually in the abdomen. A *strep throat* can cause abdominal pain and nausea. Pain on either side of the lower midline can be ovarian in origin. *Urinary tract infections* and *kidney stones* often cause abdominal pain. *Bacterial pneumonia* can cause severe abdominal pain, vomiting and high fever without any cough. *Henoch-Shoenlein purpura,* a purple rash on the legs, can cause severe abdominal pain. Rare genetic conditions like *Gaucher's disease,* and *Familial Mediterranean Fever,* can present with abdominal pain. Whenever the pain is very intense or is associated with high fever, a doctor should be consulted.

Final thought

As we all know, proper eating habits, and a high-fiber diet can often be the best way to avoid digestive problems. However, even in the properly-fed family, children get bellyaches all the time. Pinworms, a benign chronic parasitic infestation, can cause abdominal discomfort even if there is no rectal itching.

Parents have to know the nature of their children. Some kids might even complain that they have a bellyache just to avoid eating a food they do not want, or to get attention. Any life stress can cause abdominal pain. If this is suspected, the cause of the stress should be sought.

It is the parent's task to try to estimate how serious the abdominal pain is. In acute pain, the location and nature of the pain should guide the parent in this assessment.

Any bellyache that is persistent or chronically recurrent should be investigated by a physician. Many of the underlying causes are treatable.

CHAPTER 37

Celiac Disease in Children

Celiac disease, also known as gluten-sensitive enteropathy, is an autoimmune disorder that can cause multiple health problems throughout life. Once thought of as only a type of diarrheal illness, celiac disease is now known to cause chronic nutritional deficiencies, growth failure, bone weakness, fatigue, diarrhea and constipation and even lymphomas and intestinal cancer.

The problem arises when the child starts producing antibodies against the protein **gluten,** which is found in wheat rye and barley and some oats. This antibody can become a problem as early as the second year of life, but the diagnosis is often missed.

Key Points

- Celiac disease is an inability to tolerate gluten in the diet.
- Celiac disease is genetic.
- Gluten is found in wheat, barley, and rye, and in some oats.
- The diagnosis is made by blood tests and endoscopy.
- Celiac disease can cause many symptoms, including failure to grow normally.
- A lifetime gluten-free diet is the only treatment.

Celiac disease is a genetic disorder

Celiac disease runs in families. The gene that causes celiac disease is an autosomal recessive. This means that it will only show itself if the person inherits two copies of the gene, one from each parent. Close family members of people with known celiac disease should be tested, since symptoms can be subtle and easily missed. Many people do not feel that they have symptoms, but once they realize that they have this condition, they are amazed at how much more energy and strength they have on the gluten-free diet.

The antibody attacks the lining of the intestine

The celiac antibody attacks the intestinal lining, causing a chronic inflammation in the lining of the small intestine. The absorption of nutrients is less-efficient in the inflamed bowel and nutritional deficiencies develop. The deficiencies are subtle. They can cause failure to thrive, abdominal pain, anemia, and weakness.

Symptoms that can be caused by celiac disease in children

- Persistent diarrhea
- Chronic constipation, recurrent abdominal pain, or vomiting
- Dental enamel abnormalities- poor development of permanent teeth
- Failure to grow normally
- Significant pubertal delay — no evidence of the early signs of puberty by age 14
- Iron deficiency anemia not responsive to supplementation
- Recurrent mouth ulcers
- Chronic fatigue

Making an accurate diagnosis is very important

When a child has these symptoms for more than 3 months, the blood test for celiac disease should be done. If the blood test is positive the child must be evaluated by a pediatric gastroenterologist who will do endoscopy and intestinal biopsies to see if the actual celiac lesions are present.

The child *should **not** be taken off gluten grains until after the diagnosis is confirmed by biopsy.* This is because the lesions might disappear on the gluten-free diet. It is important to make a proper diagnosis. Once celiac disease is confirmed, the gluten-free diet is maintained for a lifetime. This is not the same as a wheat allergy, which might go away with time.

Principles of a gluten-free diet

The person with celiac disease is cured completely by the gluten-free diet. As long as the diet is maintained there is no disease. If the diet is not maintained, celiac disease will cause intestinal damage. Even if the person feels fine, the damage will be continuous.

Occasional mistakes in the diet *will not cause immediate problems*. It is important that the diet be adhered to once the mistake is realized.

The cornerstone of treatment of celiac disease is the elimination of gluten in the diet. The principle sources of dietary gluten are wheat, rye, and barley. Some oats are a problem, but some are *certified gluten-free*.

Malt, which is a barley product, contains gluten. Many breakfast cereals have this ingredient. In our community, Kosher for Passover foods that do not contain matzah meal are all gluten-free. Many people use this as a good guide for gluten-free packaged foods. Even kitnios are gluten-free, so foods that are Passover-certified for those who eat kitnyos are all gluten-free.

Celiac disease is not a tragedy

Years ago, the people with this disease were ill and had a very poor quality of life. Once the source of the problem was discovered in the 1950s, the prognosis changed totally. People with this condition now lead long and healthy lives. The diet is restricted, but it is only a mild inconvenience, not a life-changing disaster. It is important to make sure that the parents and the child with celiac disease do not create a sickness out of this intolerance. These kids are not sick at all. Once the diet is established, no medication is needed.

The gluten-free diet is just a regular diet that does not contain wheat, spelt, barley and rye and some oats. That leaves us with fruits and vegetables, potatoes (including chips), rice, corn, quinoa, milk and all of the milk products, meats and fish. Even candies and chocolates are usually gluten-free. There is no reason why a child with celiac disease cannot lead normal life, grow as tall as he is destined to grow, and feel energetic and strong.

CHAPTER 38

Constipation in Children

Key Points

- Constipation is a real problem at any age.

- Young babies often need anal stimulation, such as glycerine suppositories, which are not habit-forming at that age.

- Adding molasses or brown sugar to formula can soften stools.

- Toddlers often withhold stools while being trained.

- High-fiber foods prevent and treat constipation.

- Bananas, white rice, and apples can be very constipating.

- Milk and milk products are sometimes constipating.

- Severe constipation should be brought to a doctor's attention.

The miserable symptoms of constipation can occur at any age. The problem is defined as difficulty passing bowel movements. Constipation can also cause poor appetite, irritability, abdominal pain, rectal pain, and bleeding. Here is a basic overview of this common problem.

NORMAL DIGESTION — HOW THE WHOLE SYSTEM WORKS

The upper GI tract

When food or drink is swallowed it enters the esophagus, which immediately conducts it down to the stomach. The food does not fall down merely by gravity's pull. The muscular, rhythmic, serial contractions, known as *peristalsis,* make it possible to swallow food even if the person is standing on his head. These contractions propel food all the way through the digestive tract from entry to exit.

Once in the stomach, the liquid that is swallowed is quickly absorbed, digestive juices are mixed with the remaining solid content, and the food is passed on to the small intestine. During the long trip through the three areas of the small intestine, liquid enzymes are secreted by the pancreas and liver, which break down the food into absorbable nutrients.

Proteins, fats, and carbohydrates are further broken down into their smallest components, which are then absorbed. During this process, all of the food's nutrition is extracted and transported into the bloodstream through the complex structures in the walls of the small intestine. Whatever is not broken down and absorbed is considered by the body to be waste. This is passed along to the large intestine, the colon. At this stage, the consistency of the waste is semisolid sludge.

The lower GI tract— the colon

In the colon, the waste is slowly pushed along by peristaltic contractions, while the remaining water in it is slowly reabsorbed. During the passage through the colon, water is absorbed, and the waste becomes solid. When the solid waste reaches the very end of the colon (the *rectum*), the nervous system sends signals to the brain that elimination is needed. In a normal situation the person feel the urge to defecate and begins pushing and relaxing the *anal sphincter* to move his bowels.

Constipation is when something goes wrong and the stool is retained. When the stool remains longer in the colon, it becomes drier and more difficult to pass.

Constipation occurs in children at different ages

Newborn infants — It is normal for newborns to move their bowels several times a day during or after feedings. As the infant gets a little older, this reflex decreases to one to two times a day. Formula, which produces thicker waste than mother's milk, can sometimes cause constipation by turning hard in the colon if the bowels do not move daily. For these infants it is sometimes necessary to add molasses or brown sugar to the formula to soften the stools.

Babies who are exclusively nursed never have hard stools, but they sometimes go several days without passing a bowel movement. This is acceptable after the first month of life if the infant is not uncomfortable. If the child is trying to push and no stool comes, some help is appropriate.

It is reasonable to use *glycerin suppositories* or *Pedialax liquid glycerine applicators* to facilitate defecation. Babies do not become dependent on these simple interventions.

It eventually teaches the baby to relax the right muscles and move his bowels easily.

Occasionally an infant is born with a defective anus, which is closed or has only a tiny opening. This is corrected surgically when it is detected. There is a rare congenital defect known as Hirschprung's Disease, which presents with difficulty moving bowels in infancy. Thyroid deficiency causes constipation. If the constipation is severe or chronically persistent, a physician should be consulted.

Babies and toddlers

The problem of constipation in babies and toddlers in diapers is usually caused by certain foods in their diet, which form very hard waste in the colon. **The most effective prevention of constipation is a high fiber diet.**

The school-age child

It is not unusual for a school-age child to resist the urge to move his bowels and hold back stool in his rectum. The reason is often that they do not like to use school bathrooms, which can be unpleasant. The symptoms of constipation in this age group are difficulty passing stools, anal bleeding, bellyaches, lack of appetite, restlessness, gassiness, and poor bladder control. Children who have difficulty controlling their bladders during the day should be evaluated for possible constipation, since it is often the underlying cause.

There can even be leakage of stool into the underpants from constipation. This problem, known as *encopresis,* can be very confusing. It appears that the child has diarrhea, since he has liquid stool coming out without the child being able to control it. What is really happening is that the rectum is distended with a wad of retained stool and the nerves that signal an urge to move the bowels have become stretched and stop signaling.

The only stool that escapes is the liquid that leaks around the wad. When this happens, a physician should be consulted. This must be treated as a severe case of constipation. The leakage stops when bowel habits become normal for at least a month to allow the nerves to return to function.

GOOD EATING HABITS

The fiber story

Insoluble fiber, which is found mostly in natural grains and vegetables and fruits, is not broken down by the small intestine and it has no nutritional value. The fiber maintains a soft,solid consistency of the waste since it absorbs and holds onto excess water (even in diarrhea),and it does not allow much water to be absorbed by the wall of the colon. It is the prevention and the cure.

Whole grains such as whole wheat, brown rice, oatmeal, and kasha are good sources of fiber. All breads, crackers and cereals that are made from whole grains and their brans are full of fiber. Quinoa, a grain-like seed, is very high in fiber. If the food has at least 3 grams of fiber per serving, it is a genuine high-fiber food.

The vegetables with the highest fiber content are legumes like beans and chickpeas, squashes, sweet potatoes, and cabbage, broccoli and cauliflower. (Lettuce, tomatoes and cucumbers have minimal fiber content.) Most fruits and nuts are good sources of fiber. Dried fruits such as prunes and raisins are just as good.

Problem foods — apples, bananas, white rice, and milk

For some children, apples, bananas, and white rice are constipating. Apples and bananas have plenty of fiber, but they also have *pectin,* which acts as a binder. White rice tends to harden badly in the colon. Milk products sometimes form very hard calcium complexes, resulting in rock-hard stools. Eating a fiber food at the same time as the milk food can help.

Toilet training — A common source of toddler constipation is the fear of using the toilet during training. There have been some interesting studies that suggest that delaying the age of training increases the risk of this problem. Most of the world's children are trained at about 12-16 months of age, and this age group is much less fearful of using the toilet. (See Chapter 10, The Timing of Toilet Training)

If a child has a painful bowel movement he can become very afraid, and he will hold back when he has the urge to push. This can make the problem much more difficult to overcome. Any stool that is not eliminated is likely to get drier and harder with time, and a painful bowel movement reinforces the fear.

Laxatives — These constipated children should be helped with laxatives. Glycerine suppositories are sometimes helpful. Enemas are not ideal for children, since there is a potential problem with salt imbalance. Although mineral oil, prune juice, Senekot, Metamucil, and milk of magnesia have been used for years, they can be difficult to administer, and they all have side effects.

I find that the new osmotic non-prescription laxative, MiraLax, GlycoLax, or Polyethylene Glycol 3350, is the best. It is a powder that disappears totally into any drink, even clear water. It is tasteless and has no texture. Given once a day, it is not absorbed at all; it simply travels through the digestive tract and is eliminated totally with the waste. It mixes with the waste material and does not allow it to harden.

It has been shown to be effective (using more frequent doses) in even the most constipated children, with minimal side effects. It is also safe to use it as often as needed, since it doesn't affect the bowel function; it only softens the stool.

The importance of good habits

Good eating habits are very important. When a child eats fruits, vegetables, whole grains, and legumes from an early age, he will very likely enjoy eating these foods as an adult. We owe it to the kids to get them started on the right track.

Exercise is a very good stimulator of normal bowel function. We must do our best to make sure our children have a chance to get lots of activity.

Timing is important

The body works at its own rhythm. The colon usually contracts and moves waste along after meals. For this reason, it is beneficial for the children to become accustomed to **allowing time for the bathroom after a meal.**

Final thought

It is important to contact the child's doctor if constipation is persistent. This problem can become chronic and lifelong. It may affect the child's whole personality and sense of well-being. Even though the topic is embarrassing, children should be reassured that if they are having problems in the bathroom, they should tell you about it so you can help solve the problem.

CHAPTER 39

Bedwetting

Many children wake up with dry underwear from before the age of two years. For some, the process of becoming dry at night takes much longer. This "problem" is known as *bedwetting,* or *enuresis.*

For many years we have felt that bedwetting is caused by laziness or immature behavior. Countless children have suffered shame and ridicule because they could not control their bladders in their sleep.

For many of these children, bedwetting is a shameful secret that has to be kept from others. Their younger siblings who are dry at night make fun of them. Their parents are angry with them.

Until the era of effective larger disposable underwear, mothers were burdened with excess laundry and the child's room smelled of urine all the time.

Why are these kids so hard to "train?" One thing must be understood. **It is not a matter of will or desire to be trained.** Many kids would give up all their birthday

Key Points

- *Enuresis,* or *bedwetting,* is common in normal and healthy children.
- Most bed-wetters are deep sleepers with small bladders who produce too much urine in their sleep.
- It often runs in families.
- As the child's body matures, bedwetting is outgrown.
- Medications can be used when needed.
- Disposable overnight underwear, like Pull-Ups, is very helpful.
- Enuresis is nobody's fault. Both the child and the parents need reassurance.

presents just to be dry. They simply cannot stop it from happening during sleep. *"It just comes out."*

Many parents have tried to avoid night wetting by restricting fluids at night and waking the child up to go to the bathroom late in the evening. For some children these methods are effective in keeping them dry, but many are still having wet nights.

■ It is important to understand why enuresis (the medical term for bedwetting) happens, why it is normal, and why we have to be patient and reassuring until it stops by itself. Now that we have access to them, there is nothing wrong with using disposable underwear, such as Pull-Ups or Goodnites, to avoid the smell, discomfort, and excess laundry.

AN OVERVIEW OF ENURESIS

Predisposing factors

There are four factors that predispose to bedwetting.
1. The child is a **deep sleeper** who does not wake up even if there is noise or disturbance.
2. The child has a **small bladder, which holds very little urine.**
3. The child produces **large amounts of dilute urine** during the night. This is caused by the lack of a hormone produced by the brainstem that tells the kidneys to concentrate urine during the overnight fast.
4. **There is a family history of bedwetting.**
5. Many bedwetters have all four factors. **Physical growth and maturity is the cure for each one.**

Incidence

One out of five healthy children are still "wet" every night at the age of five. Every year after that, about one out of five of those "wetters" outgrows his enuresis. This leaves a significant number of bedwetters even at age nine and ten. **Remember, these are normal, healthy children.** They need reassurance that it will stop eventually.

It has been my experience that if the child is still wet every night at age seven, it often takes until age eleven to see the difference. The onset of early puberty, with growth of other related organs, often brings the maturation needed for night control. I usually do not recommend taking away the Pull-Ups until there have been a few dry nights.

Treatments

There are medications and other methods that control bedwetting in older children. I prefer not to use them unless the child, despite our reassurance, is upset by the persistent wetting. If the bedwetting is causing him to feel badly about himself, I consider treatment. This could happen when he sees the younger children becoming dry, or going to a friend's house to sleep becomes a problem, or if going away to camp worries him. There are several options to try. Each one addresses a different aspect of the problem.

1. Alarm systems — These are devices that will vibrate or ring when wetness is first detected on the undergarment. The child will be awakened and will stop urinating and get up and go to the bathroom. This method works by causing the child, who has been awakened on the first few nights, to sleep at a lighter level in order to avoid being woken. Often the alarms fail to waken the deeply sleeping child, so there is no improvement. The earliest age when it is worth trying these alarms is five to six years of age. They sometimes work.

2. DDAVP — This is a synthetic replacement for the brain hormone needed to signal the kidneys to make smaller amounts of concentrated urine. It comes in pills or nasal sprays, which are given at bedtime. DDAVP is a very safe medication, but it cannot be used if the child has had a lot to drink right before bed. Doses should be increased if the initial dose is not helping. The maximum dose is 4 tablets or 4 sprays per night. It only works on the night that it is taken. We often use it just for sleepovers or for camp in the older kids.

3. Imiprimine — This is an antidepressant, given in small doses, which has two beneficial side effects. It causes the bladder to hold urine longer and stretch to a larger capacity. It also causes the child to sleep a little lighter so he will notice the full bladder. Imiprimine is an old drug. It works well in some children. We can add it to DDAVP if either one doesn't work alone.

DDAVP and/or Imiprimine can be used every night or intermittently as needed. They should be stopped every three months just to see if they are still needed.

Recurrence of bedwetting

It should be noted that if a child was fully night-trained and becomes a bedwetter at a later time, the management is completely different. The doctor should be consulted and the urine checked for infection. It is not unusual for an emotional problem to cause this secondary bedwetting. Family discord, illness or death in the family, or school problems sometimes are the source.

Daytime wetting

Daytime wetting is **not at all** the same problem. **Children over age four who are day wetters should be evaluated by a physician.** They sometimes have bladder spasms or are constipated, or have dysfunctional voiding, which interferes with bladder control.

Final thought

The most important thing to remember is that bedwetting is not anyone's fault. A child who is a deep sleeper with a small bladder should not be shamed or punished. His or her parents should not feel frustrated or inadequate. **This problem often runs in families.** If grandparents are asked, they will often tell of having the same problem with their kids. If everyone stays cool about it the child will not perceive it as a major problem and will emerge with his self-esteem intact. The parents will also have saved themselves a lot of unnecessary aggravation.

■ ■ ■

CHAPTER 40

Allergy in Children

Allergic reactions in children can be manifested in many different ways. In their mildest form, they can cause a runny nose or a dry itchy patch on the skin. In their most severe form, they can cause catastrophic swelling of the airways and/or shock, which can be fatal. Here is an overview of childhood allergies.

What are allergies?

Allergies arise from an abnormal immune response to an allergen, which could be a food, an environmental material, or a drug. Normal immune responses are beneficial because they are directed against disease-causing targets, such as bacteria and viruses. The immune response in allergy is not beneficial to the child. Instead of providing protection, it actually causes illness and problems. The normal immune globulins that are produced in

Key Points

- Allergic reactions are produced by *IgE antibodies,* an abnormal immune response.
- The nose, eyes, throat, and bronchial tubes can react to environmental allergens.
- The skin can react acutely, with hives, or chronically, with eczema.
- The gastrointestinal tract can react with vomiting, abdominal pain, and bloody diarrhea.
- *Anaphylaxis* is a severe allergic reaction that causes generalized itching, hives, and swelling of the lips, tongue, and throat. It can also cause extreme difficulty breathing and shock.
- Anaphylaxis can be fatal. It must be treated as an acute emergency.
- Avoidance of the allergen is usually the best way to prevent allergic reactions.
- Identifying the allergenic substance often requires evaluation by a physician.

response to infection are IgG (also known as gamma globulin), IgM, and IgA. Each globulin is directed against specific targets. For example, anti-Measles IgG protects against Measles.

For some reason, some people are abnormally sensitive, and they produce an unwanted Immune globulin, called IgE, when exposed to certain allergenic substances. These unwanted globulins cause reactions. For example, anti-egg white IgE causes a reaction when egg whites are eaten or touched. If only small amounts of IgE are produced, the reactions are likely to be mild. If very large amounts of IgE are produced, the reactions can be very severe, even life-threatening.

What problems can allergies cause?

Here is a list of conditions that can be caused by allergies.

Hives, also known as *urticaria* — This is an itchy, blotchy skin reaction. The bumps are irregular in shape and are pink and white. About 25 percent of hives are caused by allergy. The rest are caused by viruses and other conditions.

Eczema — This itchy, irritated skin rash is often caused by food allergy.

Allergic rhinitis — Sneezing , itchy, watery, runny nose and nasal congestion are common symptoms of allergic rhinitis. This problem is usually caused by allergens in the air, such as pollens, mold, and dust. What time of year is the worst? Outdoor allergies are seasonal. The spring allergies (mistakenly called *rose fever*) are caused by molds, tree, and grass pollens. The late summer and fall allergies (mistakenly called *hay fever*) are caused by ragweed, pollen, and mold. The indoor allergies to dust and dust mites, cockroach, and mold occur year-round. (These are correctly called *perennial rhinitis.*)

Allergic conjunctivitis — The allergen causes red, itchy, watery eyes with swollen eyelids.

Allergic cough — This cough originates from an irritated throat during allergy exposure.

Asthma, *or hyperreactive airway disease* — In this condition, the allergen causes congestion, excess mucous production, and swelling of the lining of the bronchial tubes, while also causes spasm of the muscles around the bronchi. This combination of reactions results in cough and difficulty breathing. Asthma, which can be mild or severe, requires long-term medical management to prevent complications.

Allergic gastroenteritis — This is a local reaction in the gut, due to an ingested food. This reaction appears as vomiting, abdominal pain, and sometimes, bloody diarrhea soon after the food is eaten.

Serious otitis media, or ear fluid — Some children with chronic ear problems are allergic to foods in their diet, which cause dysfunction of the Eustachian tubes, leading to ear fluid and infections. (See Chapter 38, Ear Problems in Children)

Seasonal irritability — Some young children will be abnormally irritable during allergy seasons, even before the other symptoms develop. This is usually noted in highly-allergic families. Treatment with antihistamines can restore the child to his usual happy temperament.

Anaphylaxis — This is a systemic reaction to an allergen, which can be life-threatening. See below for a detailed discussion of this condition.

What is an allergic reaction?

When an allergen (an allergy-inducing substance) is encountered by a sensitized person, two types of inflammatory cells are activated: *mast cells* and *basophils.* These cells release a cascade of substances, including *histamine.* Histamine causes trouble in many different areas of the body. In skin, it causes hives, itching, and dryness, as well as weeping, open blisters such as poison ivy rashes. In the nose, it causes watery discharge, sneezing, and congestion. In the mouth, it can cause swelling of the lips, tongue, and throat. In the airway, it can cause swelling and spasm of the bronchial tree, known as asthma. In the gastrointestinal tract, it can cause vomiting, diarrhea, bleeding, or obstruction. In the cardiovascular system, it can cause severe loss of blood pressure known as shock.

Why are some people allergic, while others are not allergic at all?

There is probably a genetic predisposition to developing allergies, since some families are more allergic than others. There are also environmental factors that make people become allergic more easily. If an allergen is in the environment, the specific allergy can be more common. For example, farm children are more likely to be allergic to chicken feathers.

Which foods and drugs are most allergenic?

In children, the most **commonly eaten protein-containing foods** are the most common allergens. These are **milk, soy, egg, fish, peanuts, tree nuts, and wheat.** Obviously, these nourishing foods cannot all be avoided.

When a food allergy is *acute,* like hives, the foods that were eaten right before the reaction are the ones to suspect. When the reaction is *chronic,* like runny nose, cough, chronic ear problems, or eczema, the everyday foods, like milk and soy in formula-fed babies are the ones to investigate. A doctor should be consulted to help find out what food is causing the problem.

Drug allergy

The drugs that most commonly cause reactions are penicillin products (including Amoxil), sulfa medications and cephalosporins (particularly Ceclor), aspirin, and ibuprophen. When drug allergy is suspected, the drug should be discontinued immediately.

Are allergies lifelong?

No. Most food allergies are outgrown within a few months of stopping the exposure. Even severe allergies can disappear over time. If the reactions are not severe or life threatening, the food can usually be reintroduced into the diet again in about six months if it is tolerated. Severe allergies should be managed by an allergist, and food "challenges" should be done under controlled circumstances in a hospital or doctor's office that is specially equipped. Some allergies, such as peanut, can be persistent, but not in every case.

How are allergic reactions prevented?

The issue of when to allow a baby to start eating allergenic foods is controversial. In Israel, where Bamba, a peanut-flavored treat, is often given to babies, peanut allergies are very rare. In America, where most children do not eat peanut butter before 9 months of age, peanut allergy is common. New studies have shown that it is advisable to start peanut, egg, fish and milk products at an earlier age (six months) than was traditionally thought . Probiotics, such as Culturelle, and acidophilus have been shown to prevent the development of food allergies when given regularly. (See Chapter 34, Probiotics, and Chapter 5, GERD and Colic in Infants)

Avoidance

Food allergens — The most-effective prevention for a food allergy reaction is **avoidance** of the offending food **once it has been identified.** This allows the IgE level for this food to decrease. Since even small exposures can stimulate IgE response, it is best to completely avoid the allergy food for a few months.

Environmental allergens — For environmental allergens, such as pollens, the preventive approach is geared to minimizing exposure by having the child sleep in a dust-free room with an air purifier. During allergy seasons, it is a good idea to have the child take a shower, wash his hair, and change clothes when he comes inside on a bad allergy day. This eliminates the pollen he has brought home with him.

Preventive use of medications

Sometimes, a medication must be administered continuously during allergy seasons to prevent symptoms or keep them under control.

Desensitization

For persistent and severe environmental allergies, including severe bee sting allergy, desensitizing allergy shots, which can be given over a period of months and years, can ameliorate the problem. Lately, a new process of oral desensitization has been found to be clinically useful.

What is allergy testing?

Blood tests — RAST testing, which measures specific IgE levels for each suspected allergen, is done by simply drawing blood and sending it to a reliable lab. This is not very accurate if it does not show positive results in young children, since it takes until at least one year of age to get the IgE level high enough to measure. It is very helpful if the levels are high.

Skin testing — Skin testing can be done by scratch testing or intradermal testing. It is done in a physician's office.

Elimination diets — This method is a useful test in young children. The foods that are suspected are eliminated until the symptoms subside, and then reintroduced gradually to determine which one was the cause of the symptoms.

Kinesiology and other alternative medicine testing — These procedures are not known to be based on any scientific principle. The testing is probably a sham. Their providers usually advise elimination of foods that are commonly known to be allergens.

Contact sensitivity testing — This type of test is usually done with a patch. It is used to determine which substance, such as latex, causes local symptoms when it comes in contact with skin. This is done in a physician's office.

How are allergic reactions treated?

Here is a list of types of medications that are useful in treating allergy symptoms.

Antihistamines — These are drugs that block the effects of histamine.

The older antihistamines, such as Benadryl, Atarax, and Clortrimaton, are stronger, but they have several drawbacks. They only last about 6 hours. They can cause drowsiness, poor school performance, and dizziness. The newer antihistamines, like Claritin, Zyrtec, Allegra, and their generic counterparts, are long-acting and less likely to have drowsy side effects. These medications are not as powerful as the older ones. There is one antihistamine that is used in eye drops and nasal spray, and has little absorption. This drug, Asteline, leaves a funny taste in the mouth after use, but it is very effective in controlling nasal symptoms. There are several antihistamine eyedrops, which control the symptoms of eye allergy.

Steroids — The strongest anti-allergy drug is actually *cortisone.* Since oral cortisone, if used for a long time, has serious systemic side-effects, its use must be limited. Very high doses can be given over short periods of time to treat serious allergic problems, such as acute asthma, without serious side effects. Lately, newer forms of cortisone, such as Budesimide and Fluticasone, have been invented. These are sprayed into the nose or inhaled into the airway and they have a beneficial, long-lasting local effect on these areas, with very little chance of systemic effects.

Cortisone creams in varying strengths are used for all types of allergic skin rashes except hives. The more potent ones must be prescribed and monitored by a physician. Inappropriate use can result in permanent skin damage and even absorption of the cortisone, causing systemic side effects.

Leukotriene inhibitors — Singulair, the only leukotriene inhibitor approved for babies and children, is a new type of drug that is effective in allergy. It works through a different mechanism than antihistamines. Instead of blocking histamine, it prevents the release of histamine. This medication has almost no side effects. It tastes delicious and is only given once a day. It does not work during an allergy episode. Singulair works by preventing. It should be taken for two weeks prior to and then over the entire allergy season to be most effective. It is recommended for long-term use in children with recurrent wheezing, and also for seasonal nasal allergies

Epinephrine — This medication is administered by injection in an acute anaphylactic reaction.

What is anaphylaxis?

Anaphylaxis is a severe allergic reaction that can develop very suddenly and affect every system in the body. **Anaphylaxis is life-threatening.** It can be caused by foods, drugs, and some insect stings. Itching all over the body, hives, swelling of the tongue and throat, wheezing, feeling faint, and feeling a sense of impending doom are all symptoms. Whenever the reaction seems to be inside the body and not just on the skin, anaphylaxis is suspected.

Anaphylaxis can cause death if it is not treated immediately. If a person of any age is having an anaphylactic reaction, **he should be given three medications immediately while you are calling Hatzolah.**

1. **An EpiPen injection,** followed by oral dose of
2. **Benadryl,** and then
3. **Cortisone,** as quickly as possible. He should then be **rushed to the emergency room. There is no time to wait and see how bad it will get.** His life may depend on doing everything immediately, while you get him to an emergency room. This is really a case of *"It is better to be safe than sorry."*

EpiPens

EpiPens are auto injectors of epinephrine that are preloaded and easily used. Epinephrine works almost instantly when it is injected into the skin anywhere on the body. Since no needle is visible, it is not scary to administer. If a child has experienced an anaphylactic reaction, the home, the car, and the school should all be supplied with EpiPen Jr. Someone in each place should be trained in giving the EpiPen. It is not very painful at all — just a little prick. Older children and adults can easily learn to administer the EpiPen to themselves. There is no reason to worry about giving it by mistake. The effect is not dangerous and it can be lifesaving. EpiPens should be replaced every year, since they expire.

Extreme sensitivities

One of the hardest things to comprehend about anaphylaxis is just how sensitive a child can be to the allergen. A highly-sensitive child can anaphylax from just smelling the food. As a camp doctor, I treated a fish-allergic child who anaphylaxed while passing the plate of fish at the table. I have treated an egg-allergic child who collapsed seconds after a drop of cake batter from the mixer splattered on his neck. I have treated a peanut-allergic child who collapsed from picking up an empty wrapper from a peanut chew.

Peanut allergies can be among the most severe in children. Since the highly-allergic child is really in danger from even traces of peanut in the environment, it is advised that his school be peanut free. If there is no tree nut allergy accompanying the peanut allergy, almond butter or cashew butter or pea butter are safe substitutes for peanut butter. Nosh and foods brought in from home should be carefully screened.

Overdiagnosis of food sensitivity

Although food allergies are quite common, there are many children who are thought to be allergic who really are not. This mistaken perception by some parents has led to the elimination of valuable nutrients from the child's diet. If your child has a suspected food allergy, talk to his physician about it. It may be permissible to continue giving the suspected food. Milk, eggs, nuts, and fish are all nutritious components of the child's diet.

Final thought

The extreme anxiety experienced by parents of severely-allergic children cannot be underestimated. They need a lot of support from family and friends to cope with the tensions created by the fear of anaphylactic reactions. Support groups, such as IMA in Brooklyn, have been created to network families with severely allergic children. There are also new allergy-diet kosher cookbooks available, such as *Simply Tempting*, created by Blimie Frank, the mother of a severely allergic child.

Allergies are mostly just inconveniences, and even in their most severe form, the reactions can be managed so that the child can lead a normal life. A health "para" is often needed in school to ensure that the severely allergic, anaphylactic toddler does not come into contact with the allergenic foods. The para is also trained to administer the EpiPen, Benadryl, and cortisone, should a reaction occur. Fortunately, most infantile and childhood allergies lessen with time. If everyone does their share in protecting the severely allergic children in the community, both the children and the community will benefit from the consideration.

Behavioral Health Issues

CHAPTER 41

ADD / ADHD

A mother came in to my office recently to show me the certificate her eleven-year-old son had earned as *Talmid Hashanah* in *Gemara*. We were both thrilled. His story is a real example of what can happen to an ADD child.

When he was nine years old, the child was brought in by his mother after he had been thrown out of yeshivah for the third time. As a little boy, he was very active, bright, and cute. He had been a polite child, but in the past year his classroom behavior had become impossible. He was annoying his *rebbi* and his classmates with constant playing around and getting out of his seat.

When he was reprimanded, he talked back in a disrespectful way. He was not keeping up with his schoolwork. At home he was angry and irritable and refused to do homework. He hated school. He was miserable. An evaluation showed that he had ADHD.

The following discussion is about childhood ADD/ADHD. I am limiting the

Key Points

- ADD is Attention Deficit Disorder.
- ADHD is Attention Deficit and Hyperactivity Disorder.
- ADD is an inability to slow down and filter stimuli, which causes distractibility and prevents focusing.
- Hyperactivity is restlessness and impulsivity.
- These conditions are caused by a problem in the function of the brain.
- Changing the school environment to smaller classes sometimes helps.
- Medications can be very effective in helping ADD and ADHD.

scope to include only children who have normal intelligence and who are not learning disabled. I use "he" to refer to the child, but girls are also affected.

What is ADD/ADHD?

Attention deficit disorder (ADD) and ADD with hyperactivity (ADHD) are both caused by dysfunction in the front part of the brain that controls focusing, concentration, and impulse control.

In the first few years, these children seem to be progressing normally. The problem becomes noticeable in the second or third grade, when the schoolwork gets harder and they are required to spend increasing amounts of time sitting and listening to the teacher. The ADD child has difficulty functioning and learning in a classroom setting.

What is wrong in the brain?

The frontal area of the brain works like "brakes" that slow down the movement of stimuli such as sound, sight, and sense of touch into the brain. When these "brakes" are not working, everything bombards the brain all the time. **The child in the classroom feels the way we all would feel at a** *simchah* **when the band is playing too loudly.** Thinking and processing become impossible. The ADD child is distracted by everything, even his own thoughts.

Although ADD children are often normal, even superior, in intelligence, they may perform far below their potential capabilities. They can be quiet and not disruptive, but **they literally cannot concentrate.** They have difficulty focusing on a page for more than a few lines of reading. They are often found "daydreaming," because they are unable to follow what is going on in the class.

Adding hyperactivity to ADD

If the child with ADD also has hyperactivity (ADHD), the problem is much more noticeable. Hyperactive children are impulsive and restless, with irritating, aimless fidgeting and disruptive behaviors. This obvious lack of control and "bad" behavior makes life miserable for the teacher, the classmates, the parents, and the child himself.

Everyone berates these children for not behaving more maturely. *"Just sit still!" "Pay attention!" "You're so smart! Why don't you know the work?" "Why are you acting so stupid?" "Grow up!"*

The children cannot answer. **They don't know why they are doing these things.** They really cannot help it. **They only know they are not worth very much, since people** are always disappointed in them.

Negative feedback

They go through their formative school years with a huge amount of negative feedback and very low self-esteem. They feel persecuted, angry, and frustrated. Some become bullies. Many feel depressed. Some grow into "at-risk" adolescents. They feel that they are "losers" who do not belong in our society. Some even go off the *derech*, begin to abuse illegal substances and alcohol, and become involved in criminal behavior.

Is this a new problem?

The genetic tendency has probably been there all along. In past generations, Jewish children grew up on farms, in small towns, and in less-crowded cities, with schoolyards and parks to play in. They were not in the classroom for more than a few hours a day. The schools were less structured and had smaller classes.

It is only recently that our kids are required to attend school from a young age for so many hours a day. We put them in classrooms with 30 children and give them very little physical activity such as gym and outdoor recess. Although many normal children can function well in this setting, the child with ADD and ADHD is taxed beyond limits and cannot perform properly.

Small classes and individual attention

The ADD/ADHD children do better in small classes where the teacher can give them individual attention. They need frequent breaks that allow them to run around and burn off physical energy. In many circumstances, they can be helped in a school with "resource room" support, but the time in the mainstream class is often frustrating and unproductive.

All children want approval

All children are born wanting to learn and, most importantly, they naturally love to earn approval from their parents and the other important adults in their lives. They do not want to be "bad." **The ADD child is often a normally intelligent person who is smart enough to know he should be doing better.** Most of these children are not truly "learning disabled." They could learn and process schoolwork if they could only focus without all the distractions in their unfiltered brains.

Now that we understand the nature of the problem, we need to understand the possible solutions we can offer a child and his family.

HELPING THE CHILD WITH ADD/ADHD

Treatment options

When parents come to me with a child who has been evaluated and is found to have ADD, I try to help them understand the possible solutions for the problem. Since this child's brain is neurologically "wired" differently from those of most unaffected children, just letting him continue in his current situation is not really a viable alternative. He has to get through 15 years of classroom learning and come out a normal, happy, self-confident person. The years of negative feedback and frustration can, as we know, lead to real problems as the child grows up.

There are two approaches to resolving the situation:

1. Change the learning environment to meet the needs of this child's brain.

This is very difficult to do successfully in our community environment. Learning Torah is not merely a choice, it is the essence of the school program.

Taking a child completely out of school is not usually an option. These ADD children do not belong in "special education" programs for learning-disabled and intellectually-challenged children.

The ones with milder cases can sometimes manage in small classes in regular schools. Tutors who work with the child one-on-one can be very helpful in maintaining learning at the class level. The child will need frequent breaks with physical activity.

There are some schools with very small classes and more individual attention, with specially-trained teachers. There are very few programs like this for normally intelligent children, and they are very costly.

2. Change the child's brain to make him more suited for his normal school environment.

This can only be done by using medication to help the front part of the brain function normally.

The medication option

Sometimes the best way to find out if this approach will help is by trying it. The benefits are immediate when the proper dose is reached. If the child's teachers and parents, as well as the child himself, notice improvement, the drug can be continued.

If the child feels no difference or if he does not feel well, the medication can be stopped immediately.

Since there are several preparations, if one is not working, another can be tried. This only takes a week or two.

Most of the currently used medications are "stimulants," based on the drug *methylphenidate,* known as Ritalin, which enhances the child's ability to focus and concentrate, and makes his behavior less impulsive. Despite its name, a stimulant does not make the ADD child wild. It can stimulate the brain to be more alert and activate the "brakes" that slow down stimuli as they enter the brain. Another class of stimulant drugs, amphetamines, is sometimes used in addition to Ritalin. Some medications combine both types in the same pill. (Strattera is different, and I am not discussing it here.)

Over the last few years, long-acting forms of Ritalin and other ADD medications have become available. Concerta, Ritalin LA, and Adderal are examples. These preparations are given in the morning and usually last about 8 to 10 hours. They do not need to be used every day, and they only work on the day they are given. Some people prefer to give medication only on school days and not on Shabbos or vacation days.

Before one of these medications is tried, a child should be examined by his physician and his **height, weight, blood pressure, and pulse noted.** These should all be monitored periodically while the child is on medication. If appetite suppression is a problem, growth must be carefully monitored.

Side effects

Some children complain of headache or stomachache in the first few days of medication. This is very temporary when it happens. Another side effect is appetite suppression. It is important to advise the parents to give the child a big breakfast before he takes the pill and a big late dinner after it wears off. It is also important to give the pill early in the morning so it wears off by bedtime to allow normal sleep.

If the stomach upset does not subside quickly another form of methylphenidate, a patch preparation — Daytrana patches — can be used.

If a child develops tics while on Ritalin that do not resolve, it may be necessary to stop the drug.

There have recently been reported very rare cases of cardiac problems resulting in death. These events happened mostly with the drugs that had amphetamines added to the Ritalin, such as Adderal. The incidence was less than 1 in one million prescriptions written.

Most parents are concerned with possible long-range side effects.

"Will medicine affect the child's future ability to raise a family?" No, it will not.

"Will the child become a substance abuser?" These medications are not addictive and can be stopped any time. The interesting fact is that ADD/ADHD children who are treated with medication have a lower incidence of alcohol, tobacco, and drug abuse than those who are not. They also grow up with fewer psychosocial problems than those who are not treated.

"How long will he have to take medication?" ADD/ADHD usually does not go away with maturity. However, most adults with this condition do not need medication unless they are in a job or learning environment that requires focus and concentration. The drugs can safely be used periodically, occasionally, or long-term, so the adult with ADD can use them as needed.

Should we "drug" our children?

Many people in our community are against using drugs at all. There is a fear of toxic chemicals and unnatural products. The fact is, Ritalin has been on the market for over thirty years. When used properly, it is safe.

Very few educators and psychosocial professionals who care for children are against the use of ADD medications. They have experienced the dramatic improvements in many of these kids. The child who responds to medication functions normally and becomes much happier with himself. Everyone in his life is also happier.

As you have probably guessed, the boy who became *Talmid Hashanah* was given Concerta. His yeshivah refused to take him back, so he was started in a new yeshivah. The change in his school life was immediate. His *rebbi*, friends, and family are all very pleased with him. His life was truly salvaged by treatment of his ADHD.

It is true that some children are wrongly diagnosed with ADD/ADHD. Not every child who is doing poorly in school or shows difficult behavior has this disorder. A professional evaluation and follow-up are necessary to determine if the child is being treated appropriately.

Final thought

One thing is certain. Understanding the problem gives everyone more patience and empathy. It also gives hope. With proper help and support, many of these kids can grow up to meet their full potential as students and as people. They can then go on to lead normal lives.

■   ■   ■

CHAPTER 42

Childhood Phobias

Key Points

- Phobias are "life benders."
- Unreasonable fears that affect the normal flow of life are called phobias.
- Phobias start with a fearful experience or thought that intensifies to the point of causing very uncomfortable physical symptoms.
- In order to avoid feeling that way again, the phobic person will go to great lengths to avoid exposure to the fearful experience again.
- Gradual exposure with supportive help often resolves the phobia.
- Cognitive Behavioral Therapy trains the person to control the fear.
- Medications are sometimes needed.

I am often asked to advise a parent about a child who seems inappropriately frightened of something that does not cause fear in most people. Here is a typical example:

"I do not understand my 8-year-old daughter. She once had a little dog playfully jump up on her, and she was very frightened. That was when she was three years old, and she has never liked dogs since then. As time has gone by, she has gotten more and more afraid of dogs.

"Lately, she won't take a walk with the family on Shabbos because she is afraid there might be a dog. She recently ran out into a busy street when a girl walked toward her with a dog on a leash. She wants someone to drive her to a friend's house that is only a two-minute walk down our own block.

"Everyone tells her she is being silly, but she is really terrified. What's going on? What should be done to help her get over this growing problem?"

This child has developed a *phobia*. Here is an explanation of phobias.

Normal fears

Every child has fears. Fear of the dark, clowns, vacuum cleaners, and other common things are normal. As parents, we try to use reason to reassure and teach the child not to be afraid. The frightening thing will become less frightening as time goes by.

Exaggerated, unreasonable fears

Although it seems that she is being unreasonable, **the little girl's fear is beyond the realm of reasoning and thought.** She seems to have developed a real phobia. Her early experience with the little dog created a fear that has escalated recently to an overwhelming terror that is interfering with her normal life activities. **Whenever a fear causes a person to change the normal flow of life activities, it is a phobia.**

How a phobia develops

A fearful moment. It is important to understand the way a phobia differs from an ordinary fear. In the following explanation I am using the word "you," since this experience can happen to anyone. Every time you feel afraid, you experience a little quickening of the heartbeat and a slight tightening of the stomach. (*"What was that loud noise?"*) These physical reactions are caused by certain chemicals released in the brain in response to a fearful thought. Most of the time you can reassure yourself and rapidly calm down. (*"It is nothing dangerous. A balloon just popped."*) When the calming thought happens, another set of chemicals is released that cancel the first ones. The heartbeat slows, and the other symptoms quickly disappear. Fear is not pleasant, but it is a tolerable feeling.

When the fear lingers too long in the mind

If, due to a person's naturally anxious nature, the fear is not rapidly dissipated, the original set of chemicals goes on to cause more physical symptoms and even more exaggerated fearful thoughts. (*"It must be a gunshot!"*) **The physical symptoms escalate to pounding heartbeat, rapid breathing, tightening of the stomach and throat, shaking, sweating, etc.** If the fear persists, even worse thoughts come (*"I am going to die!"*), and the symptoms get even more intense.

A bad memory of the intense fearful feeling is produced

Eventually the situation resolves and calm returns. (*"Everyone is laughing about the noise, so I guess I'm not in danger."*) The memory of the fearful event will be very intense and long-lasting, because it was accompanied by intense emotion and very uncomfortable feelings.

That feeling must be avoided at all costs!

Since the fear was a very unpleasant experience, it is not surprising that you do not want to feel that way again. Phobias develop when you will go to any length to avoid experiencing that awful feeling again. The mere sight of a balloon makes you feel tense. You start refusing all invitations to parties. Your life is changed by your desire to avoid that noise.

There is no logic

Even if you can rationally understand that there is nothing to be afraid of, you still will not go into a room where there are balloons. This is not a matter of logic. You can believe that there is no danger, but no one can promise you that you will not feel that terrible fear again.

Lifebender

A phobia is what I call a **"lifebender."** It can be a lifelong burden. For example, the fear of water can cause a person to avoid going away to camp. This phobia can even make taking a bath or dunking in shallow water a terrifying experience. Often a person with phobic fear of water will construct her life around avoiding going into water.

A serious matter that needs attention

It is my feeling that whenever a phobia is identified, it should be taken seriously. The little girl could really get hurt running away from a dog by running into traffic. She also will never enjoy her time outdoors if she is always wary of the possibility of encountering a dog. Gentle and persistent exposure to the feared experience will eventually help the person to gain control of the overwhelming fear. Petting a little dog, or going to a pet store to see the cute puppies would be a good start. Once she sees that her terror is not happening during these exposures, she will be less afraid. Remember, a major part of the fear is a fear of feeling terrified.

Cognitive behavioral therapy

If simply exposing the phobic individual does not relieve the intensity of the phobia there is a very effective modality known as Cognitive Behavioral Therapy (CBT) that can be utilized. The CBT therapist is a personal trainer for the mind. The therapist teaches the person (it can be used at any age) to use his own mind and certain behavioral techniques to break down the phobic thinking and turn away from it. (*"That dog is not so scary. He is wagging his tail. It is only the 'Worry Monster' in my brain that is making me feel scared. Get away from me, you silly Worry Monster!"*)

The training is done gradually, first teaching the person to recognize that he is beginning to react to a fear that is not a rational thought. Then, relaxation techniques are taught to help calm the reactions as they occur. Eventually, the person is taught to think about fearful scenarios and to practice the counter thoughts that will be needed to handle them.

There is no magic in this training. It takes some work and effort to strengthen the mind's "control muscles." The results are very gratifying.

CBT has been found to work on many other conditions related to anxiety, including obsessive-compulsive disease and generalized anxiety disorder. It is also effective in treating depression. Since many of these conditions are the result of a tendency to rigid thinking, a lot is accomplished by simply allowing for more flexibility in the anxious person's thinking. Because it teaches the person to master his own thoughts and feelings, it has long-lasting effectiveness.

Medications are sometimes needed

Some people are so overcome with fear that they need medication to help them before they can begin to work with the therapist. Anti-anxiety medications can be prescribed to help the patient gain control as he goes through therapy.

Final thought

Phobias are a terrible burden. If the family of the person recognizes that it is really a phobia, they should make every effort to help the person get treatment. In the meantime, the fearful person will resist any discussion of the fear, since even talking about it is painful. With love, support, and reassurance, real relief is possible.

People who have conquered phobias often say that they feel like they have taken off a knapsack full of rocks!

■ ■ ■

CHAPTER 43

Headaches in Children

Key Points

- Headaches are common in children and are usually not serious.

- The least-common causes are tumors, aneurism, meningitis and major head trauma. These conditions have additional warning signs.

- The most common causes of headaches in children are infections (like strep or viruses), minor head trauma, sinus disease, tension, and TMJ.

- Migraines are common in children and can be triggered by lack of sleep, inadequate hydration and certain environmental factors.

Many parents are very alarmed when their child complains of a headache. The occasional stories of children who have suffered terrible conditions which started as a headache create the impression that all headaches are dangerous. The fact is, headaches, even migraine headaches, are very common in children. They are rarely serious. There are many causes of headaches. Often the type of headache points to the source of the problem. Here is an overview of the causes, types, and treatment of childhood headaches.

LEAST-COMMON CAUSES OF HEADACHES

Tumors

Brain tumors are very rare. They are the least-likely cause of an occasional headache. When a tumor is the cause, the headache can be in the back of the head, early in the morning, and associated with vomiting. This type of presentation is repeated every day with some resolution during the day.

Aneurisms and vascular malformations

Rupture of an aneurism or arterio-venous malformation in children is extremely rare. The headache associated with bleeding from rupture of an aneurism is usually extremely intense. The child is screaming in pain. There might be weakness of one side or speech or cognitive impairment. This is an extreme emergency.

Meningitis

Meningitis, which is an infection of the lining of the brain and spinal cord, causes fever, headache, vomiting, rigidity of the neck, and sometimes seizures. *Viral meningitis* is usually mild and does not require treatment. *Bacterial meningitis* can be life threatening and can cause severe brain damage and complications. Fortunately, the most common causes of bacterial meningitis over one month of age — HIB and Pneumococcus, have been nearly eliminated by the HIB and Prevnar vaccines that are given in the first six months of life. The rare and devastating meningitis, *Meningococcal Meningitis* has also become rare because of the Menactra vaccine given at age 11. Since the introduction of the three vaccines the incidence of bacterial meningitis has dropped by 95%.

Serious head trauma

A hard bump on the head can cause a headache. If the injury is associated with loss of consciousness, confusion, or loss of memory for the event, the condition is called a *concussion*. If there is bleeding in the brain from the head trauma, the child will complain of headache and vomit repeatedly. Children with a concussion or repeated vomiting after a bump on the head should be seen in an emergency room.

Cluster headaches

Cluster headaches are very intense headaches that are accompanied by teary eyes and runny nose. They occur in clusters with headache-free periods between headache periods. They are very rare in children. Although these headaches are very troublesome, they are not dangerous. A neurologist should be consulted for treatment of cluster headaches.

COMMON CAUSES OF HEADACHES

Common infections

One of the most common causes of headaches in children is viral or bacterial infections, such as flu, strep throat, or any illness than can cause fever. The child will often complain of head pain before the rest of the symptoms arise. The illness that is causing the headache will usually declare itself within a day. These headaches can be treated with Ibuprophen or Acetomenophen in the recommended dosages.

Minor head trauma

A bump on the head can cause a mild headache. As long as there are no other symptoms as described above, the child just needs pain medication and observation.

Tension-type headaches

A tension-type headache is described as a tight feeling in the scalp. It often starts in the "hatband" area of the head and spreads to the whole head including the back of the neck. These headaches can be caused by emotional stress, fatigue, lack of sleep, hunger, or any type of stress on the child.

In some children, problems with the *Tempero Mandibular Joint (TMJ)*, eye strain, and grinding of the teeth can cause tension-type headaches. Tension-type headaches in general are usually mild and are treated with food, fluids, relaxation, massage, and pain medications. Removing the source of stress can be the best cure.

Sinus headaches

Sinus headaches are usually described as a feeling of pressure in the mid-forehead and in the face above and below the eyes. This headache can cause nausea, and often feels worse when the head is bent forward. This type of headache can be caused by the viral congestion of the sinuses which accompanies a cold. If the headaches and pressure do not go away with the cold, there may be sinusitis caused by an infection. The treatment for sinus congestion and infection should begin with saline (salt water solution) sprays to irrigate the sinuses. Decongestant nasal sprays help a lot but can only be used for two days to avoid dependency. Pseudoephedrine (Sudafed), an oral decongestant, can be used in children over two. Most children do not need antibiotics for sinusitis if the saline irrigations are used, but if the symptoms are persistent for more than two weeks, antibiotics are sometimes required. Many children and adults suffer sinus headaches during barometric changes when the weather is about to change, or after they have been crying. These headaches can be relieved by decongestant nasal sprays alone or with pain medications.

Sinus headaches can be dull and very persistent. They often interfere with the child's ability to function in school.

Migraine headaches

Migraine headaches can appear as early as two to three years of age. The tendency to have migraines often runs in families. This type of headache is described as a severe pounding pain starting in the temples. In children, the headaches are often on both sides of the head, while in adults the pain is usually on one side.

Migraine headaches are often accompanied by excessive sensitivities to light and noise, nausea and vomiting. Some people have a warning sign before the headache begins. Visual disturbances such as spots or zigzag lines are common. These visual disturbances persist when the eyes are closed.

The treatment for migraine headaches includes lying down in a cool dark and quiet place. Fluids and food should be given as well as pain medications. The headache is relieved by falling asleep. Once the person wakes up the headache is gone.

In children, the most common causes of migraines are lack of sleep and inadequate water intake. Young children need about 12 hours of sleep and older children need about 8 hours of sleep. Children who are prone to migraines should also take along sports water bottle (8,16, or 32 ounces depending on the size of the child) when they go to school or camp, and they should be encouraged to finish it throughout the day. Special care should be given to maintain good hydration on hot summer days. Foods like certain cheeses and wines can sometimes cause migraines.

If migraines are frequent, a neurologist should be consulted and preventive medications and treatment can be prescribed.

Final Thought

Most headaches in children are not serious. If your child has a headache, try to assess the type of headache and treat it appropriately. If the headache is very severe or if it comes with the signs of serious head injury, meningitis, seizures or neurologic impairment, a physician should be consulted immediately and the child should be taken to an emergency room.

For the child with migraines and tension-type headaches, a good sleeping and eating schedule and a reduction of stress in school and at home often stops the headaches.

CHAPTER 44

Childhood Seizures and Epilepsy

Key Points

- Seizures are a result of abnormal electrical activity in the brain. They usually do not affect intellect or personality.

- Febrile seizures are common in childhood and they do not cause damage to the brain.

- Epilepsy or seizure disorders are conditions that cause recurrent non-febrile seizures

- Most seizure disorders are treatable

When a child has a grand mal seizure, also known as a convulsion, the people who witness the event often feel that the child is in grave danger. The violent jerking of the body and the arms and legs, and the loss of consciousness, is an awful thing to see. Fortunately, despite the scary appearance, the seizure does not harm the child. Actually, one out of every ten people experiences a seizure at some time in their lives. Here is an overview of the subject of seizures in childhood.

What is actually happening during a seizure?

A seizure starts when abnormal and excessive natural electrical impulses discharge in the brain. This surge of electrical stimuli causes the child to experience a sudden event involving any or all of these brain functions:

1. **Behavior** like staring or doing strange things
2. Abnormal **body movements** like falling, stiffening, or jerking
3. **Loss of consciousness**.

What causes a seizure?

A seizure is always triggered by an abnormal electrical impulse in the brain. When there is no known cause, the seizure is called *idiopathic*. When fever is the trigger, the seizures are called *febrile* seizures. Brain damage, tumors, brain injury, poisonings, and diseases such as meningitis can also cause seizures.

Definitions

There are several terms which are important to understand when we discuss seizures.

■ **Epilepsy** – The term epilepsy is frightening to hear, but it really only means that the person has had more than one seizure. Most children with epilepsy outgrow the tendency to have seizures during childhood. Most epilepsies are treatable with anti-seizure medications.

■ **Aura** – warning sensation before the seizure

This is an abnormal sensation, like a bad smell or a bad feeling, which goes on to develop into a seizure.

■ **Post-Ictal state** – recovery stage after a seizure

After a generalized seizure, there can be a period of confusion, headache, and sleepiness which can last minutes to hours.

■ **Tonic** – This means there is a stiffening of the body and limbs.

■ **Clonic** – This means there is jerking of the body and limbs. The motion is usually one jerk at a time, not shivering or shaking.

Types of seizures

■ **Petit mal or absence seizures** – These little 2- to 20-second seizures are *staring spells* with occasional mouth movements. They occur in normal, healthy children. More than 75% of children with petit mal outgrow the seizures.

■ **Generalized or grand mal seizures** – This type of seizure affects the whole brain, and there is loss of consciousness. They are the typical *convulsions* with stiffening *(tonic)* followed by jerking motions *(clonic)*. There is always a *post-ictal* state following a generalized seizure.

■ **Partial seizure** – This is a short seizure that only affects one part of the brain, so the patient is conscious. When a partial seizure progresses and causes a convulsion, or when it lasts several minutes, it is called *complex* partial seizure.

■ **Myoclonic jerk** – This is the quick "startle" type of jerk movement that occurs normally while falling asleep. When the jerks occur in clusters, when the patient is awake, they are abnormal.

■ **Infantile spasms** – These seizures occur at 3 to 7 months of age. An attack has clusters of spasms. The infant bends forward with arms that are outstretched and then brought together. The infant often cries with each spasm. These *rare* seizures can lead to deterioration in development. Early treatment with adrenocorticotropic hormone (ACTH) injections can sometimes stop the spasms and improve developmental prognosis.

■ **Benign rolandic epilepsy (BRE)** – These seizures occur in children aged 3 to 13 years. They begin at night. They start with mouth twitching and progress to the face and on to the arms and legs. The child is usually conscious, looks frightened, and might have difficulty talking. Rarely, they progress to a generalized seizure. Although these episodes are unpleasant, they do not cause any damage, and they are usually outgrown.

■ **Juvenile myoclonic epilepsy (JME)** – This seizure disorder usually starts in the teenage years. There is no effect on the intellect. The seizures are of variable types. In the beginning, the attacks start in the morning after awakening and consist of multiple myclonic jerks. With time, grand mal or petit mal seizures develop. Although these seizures are rarely outgrown, they usually respond well to medications. JME tends to run in families.

■ **Febrile seizures** (seizures caused by fever) – Febrile seizures are very common, occurring in 3% to 4% of children. These convulsions occur between the age of 6 months and 6 years. They usually happen within the first day of the fever. The fever causing the convulsion is usually 102 degrees F or higher. Often the child has the seizure when the temperature rises suddenly at the very beginning of the illness. Roseola, a very common viral illness, has been found to cause most first febrile seizures. Febrile seizures are *tonic clonic convulsions*. The child stiffens and loses consciousness, although the eyelids remain open. The child will usually jerk both arms and legs repeatedly. After the seizure, the child will be sleepy and dull for a while – the *post-ictal state*.

When seizures last less than 15 minutes, and when they only occur once in 24 hours, they are called *simple* febrile seizures. When they last more than 15 minutes, or if they recur within a day, they are call *complex* febrile seizures.

Febrile seizures do not cause brain damage. They often happen repeatedly until the child outgrows them. Parents and caregivers should know the basic first aid for seizures.

Basic first aid for seizures

1. Lie the patient on his side in a safe place.
2. Move any sharp or hard objects away from the patient.
3. Look at the clock to note the time the seizure starts and stops.
4. If the child has difficulty breathing, emergency aid should be called.
5. If the seizure is a first seizure, or if the seizure lasts more than 5 minutes, emergency aid should be called, and the child should be transported to an emergency room.
6. Do not put anything in the child's mouth during the seizure.

If a fever is noted in a child who is prone to febrile seizures, fever-reducing medications, such as ibuprofen or acetaminophen, should be given if possible.

Seizures commonly happen at the onset of fever, without warning. If this happens, do not attempt to give oral medications until the seizure stops.

Parents of children with recurrent seizures are usually provided with Diastat (diazepam rectal gel), which can be given at home to stop a prolonged seizure.

Important facts about febrile seizures

Febrile seizures generally **do not** lead to epilepsy. They often run in families. They **do not** cause brain damage. In general, if the child wakes up after sleeping off the seizure in the post-ictal state, and is acting normally, there is probably no serious infection of the nervous system, such as meningitis. The cause of the fever should be evaluated by a physician or nurse to determine if antibiotics are needed. Most children outgrow febrile seizures by age 6.

Medical tests

The neurologist who is evaluating a patient with seizures that are not associated with fever may want to do tests to determine the type and nature of the seizures.

• **EEG** (Electroencephalogram) – This test actually reads the electrical activity in the brain. Small leads are taped to the patient's scalp in various areas of the head, and the patient lies quietly while the machine reads the signals. The tracings are often done while the child sleeps.

• **Video EEG monitoring** – If a regular EEG is not informative, a new technique, *video EEG*, is employed. By video-recording the actual events while recording the brainwaves, the neurologist can determine if the events are seizures, and if they are, what type they are.

This EEG is done while the patient is in a special setting in the hospital. The leads are placed on the scalp and the child is observed by video camera -awake and asleep, eating and playing, quiet and crying – while a continuous tracing is recorded. This usually requires a day or two in the hospital, so that an event will happen and be observed simultaneously on an EEG tracing and a video recording.

▪ **CT scans** – CT scans are sometimes requested by the neurologist to determine if there is bleeding in the brain, a blood clot, stroke, tumor, or other structural abnormalities after trauma or during an acute episode of seizures not associated with fever. CT scan are quick (usually less than a minute is required), but they are x-rays, so they do expose the child's brain to radiation.

▪ **MRI** (Magnetic Resonance Imaging) – An MRI is often requested in order to look at the brain in detail, to determine if there is a tumor or structural abnormality. This is a very useful test which does not expose the child to radiation. The problem with MRI is that the child must remain still for at least 15 minutes in the machine to get an accurate picture. This often requires an anesthesiologist to administer general anesthesia and monitor the child during the test.

▪ **Lumbar puncture** (spinal tap) – This test is used to obtain a sample of the fluid that bathes the brain and spinal cord. It is usually only done if there is a suspicion that there could be an infection in the lining of the brain or spinal cord known as *meningitis.*

The test is done by inserting a needle in the back between the lower spinal bones and draining out fluid to be tested. This test is not dangerous at all in infants. It is not any more painful than a blood test.

Treatment of seizures

Most seizures that are not caused by fever require treatment with anti-seizure medications. There are many different drugs approved for the treatment of seizures in children. The actual drug that is chosen depends on the type of seizure. Many seizure medications have side effects such as sleepiness or irritability, but these effects usually wear off with time. Since not all children respond alike, it is sometimes necessary to try several different medications, even employing more than one, until the seizures are well controlled.

Once control is accomplished, the medication is usually continued until the child is seizure-free for two years.

Final thought

Most normal children with seizures outgrow them. Even those *normal* children who do not outgrow them *go on to lead normal lives* with medication to help control the seizures. It is a blessing that these medications are now available.

In past years, when seizures were mysterious and frightening, a terrible social stigma was placed on the epileptic person. Now, in our times, seizures are recognized as an ordinary, treatable physiological malfunction in the brain, not a curse or a character disorder. In our time, we have learned to respect a person for his or her *middos* and abilities. We understand that epilepsy is an inconvenient problem, *but that is all it is.* We value these people as we value all of the other normal members of our community.

■ ■ ■

CHAPTER 45

Scary But Benign: Understanding Breath-Holding Spells and Fainting

Key Points

- Breath-holding spells are not dangerous.
- Some breath holders faint, but quickly regain consciousness.
- They always start breathing again.
- Fainting can have many causes.
- Fainters should lie down ASAP if they feel it happening.
- Repeated episodes should be checked out by a pediatric cardiologist.
- Fainting is usually not a sign of serious illness.

Anytime a child turns blue or loses consciousness it causes extreme panic in the parents or whoever is witnessing the event. Of course, if the child is choking, he needs immediate first aid, such as sweeping the mouth and the Heimlich maneuver. Often, however, the child is crying and simply stops breathing for a few seconds. This is called a *benign breath-holding spell.* Other times, a child can faint in response to certain stimuli. This common and benign problem is called *vaso vagal syncope.* The following is an explanation of these two distressing entities.

Benign Breath-Holding Spells

Sometimes, when a baby cries intensely, he will sometimes end the cry with a tightening of the vocal cords that blocks the inbreath. The baby can actually turn blue in the face until he relaxes the vocal cords and breathes *in* to start the next cry. This *benign breath- holding spell* is terrifying to observe but it does not cause death or brain damage. Usually after a few long seconds, the child lets the vocal cords relax and starts crying again. In extremely intense breath-holders, the spell can end in a loss of consciousness — the child faints. This results in immediate relaxation of all his muscles and relaxes the vocal cord spasm so the child starts breathing again. He will usually regain consciousness in a few seconds.

Causes

Why do some children do this? They are known as benign breath-holding spells, but they are not so benign for the person caring for the child. Grandparents have had heart attacks watching the crying child turn blue if they are not accustomed to this habit.

Breath-holders tend to run in families. It is often passed directly from parent to child. One lady in my practice called it the *"blessing* of the grandmother." When her own child used to scare her with breath-holding spells, she used to say *"I wish that you will be blessed with a little one just like you!"* Obviously, when he grew up, he had a little breath-holder just as his mother wished upon him.

The spells can show up in the first few days of life, or they may start a little later. Usually there is a strong stimulus causing the cry, like frustration, pain or anger or fright.

Sometimes the child cries because of the pain of a bump on the head. If he then faints from a breath-holding spell, it is sometimes difficult to distinguish the episode from a concussion causing loss of consciousness. If the event was witnessed, there is usually a clear history that the child cried out and then held his breath, then fainted. If a concussion had occurred there would not be a cry of pain.

Treatment

The treatment for the child having a breath-holding spell can be benign neglect — doing *nothing.*The child will start breathing on his own with no assistance. One quick trick that sometimes works to break the spell is to blow hard in the child's face, or to throw cold water in his face, stimulating a reflex that causes the baby to take a sharp breath in when he feels cold on his face.

Behavioral caution

Beware of the child who knows how upset his caretaker will be if he cries and holds his breath. If the child knows that his breath holding terrifies the parent or grandparent or babysitter, he can get anything he wants from them. "If you do not give me what I want," or "if you put me to bed," "I will cry and hold my breath." Such a child can develop into a little monster. Everyone involved in his care should learn to tolerate an occasional breath-holding spell without any emotional input. These spells are not dangerous. "You cannot have the treat right now," "If you hold your breath, it will not scare me. I know that you will be okay."

Most children outgrow the spells around age 2-3.

DO NOT WORRY! THEY ALL START BREATHING AGAIN!

Fainting – *Vaso Vagal Syncope*

Fainting spells — also known as *vaso vagal syncope* — occur at any age, but they are more common in toddlers and in adolescents. Like breath-holding spells, the tendency to faint runs in some families.

Causes

The vaso vagal response is triggered by dehydration in most cases. Just getting the child to drink water more often and eat some salty foods (a few pretzels) during the day will often make the fainting spells stop occurring. Other common stimuli are fear, panic episodes, pain, crowded hot rooms, the sight of blood, hot showers or even standing in one position with feet together for a long time.

Warning symptoms

There is usually a warning a few seconds before fainting. Typical ones are: a feeling of dizziness, nausea, weakness, hot and cold feelings, muffling of hearing, ringing in the ears, seeing spots or having blurred vision, or pallor of the face and ears right before the child faints.

Get down ASAP

Teach the fainter to lie down immediately and put his feet up on a chair or wall if he feels like he is going to faint. This precaution can decrease the likelihood of losing consciousness. and it also prevents injuries from falling if he does go on to faint.

After the fainter recovers

The fainter regains consciousness within a minute or two, but he can feel tired for a little while after that. A cold drink of water will help him feel better quickly. Occasionally the child will actually have a *grand mal* siezure, or convulsion, immediately after fainting. This is normal and does not need evaluation by neurologist, unless the seizure is limited to one area of the body.

Follow up and evaluation

The first time the child faints, the pediatrician should be called. After that, if it keeps happening, he should be seen by a pediatric cardiologist to rule out any heart problem that could be responsible.

These problems are very rare. The vast majority of these children will be found to have only *vaso vagal syncope* and no treatment or further investigation is needed.

Final thought

It is very important for everyone in the community to have updated courses in first aid. I also recommend classes in CPR for everyone. The knowledge gained in these courses is very important to make help immediately available to everyone in the family and community. I also feel that it builds self confidence. Knowing what to do and when to call for help is very empowering. Breath-holding and *syncope* are very distressing to witness. A well-trained first aider will keep a level head and will know what to do, and will also know that there is really no serious danger.

CHAPTER 46

Understanding Autism

Key Points

- Autism occurs in children with a wide range of intellectual ability
- The key features of autism are: problems with social interaction, problems with communication, and unusual behavior patterns which are restricted, repetitive, and stereotypical.
- Three types of autism make up the autistic spectrum:
  - Early Infantile or Classic Autism – the severe form of the disorder
  - Pervasive Developmental Disorder Not Otherwise Specified (PDD-NOS) – the less severe form of autism
  - Asperger's Syndrome – impairment in non-verbal and social skills without impairment in language and communication
- Early diagnosis is very important, since early intervention can make a big difference in social and behavioral development

It seems that the diagnosis of Autistic Spectrum Disorders has become very prevalent over the last 10 to15 years. As a long-time primary care pediatrician I have watched this trend very carefully. From my perspective, there is no increased incidence of this disorder. There were always children who exhibited the symptoms and signs of Autistic Spectrum Disorders, but, except for the severely affected, we did not know what we were seeing. We labeled many of them as socially inept when they were high functioning, and mentally retarded when they were low functioning. It is only recently that the variations in the severity and manifestations have been recognized and defined.

This new recognition has been very important, because the early intervention strategies that can now be applied have improved the prognosis in many children with milder forms of the disorder. The earlier these children are identified and referred, the more effective the treatments. Children or adolescents who do not have the benefit of early intervention may not get optimal improvement with therapies aimed at their Autism.

Some children seem to develop normally and then suffer regression of their abilities after one year of age. Some show signs from early infancy. It is important for the primary care pediatrician to watch out and inquire about signs of autism at each checkup.

An Overview of Autistic Spectrum Disorders (ASD)

There are three conditions that make up the majority of Autistic Spectrum Disorders:

1. Early infantile or *Classic Autism* – the severe form of the disorder
2. *Pervasive Developmental Disorder Not Otherwise Specified* (PDD-NOS) – the less severe form of autism
3. *Asperger's Syndrome* – impairment in non-verbal and social skills without impairment in language and communication

Three defining impairments

There are three defining categories of problems in children who are identified as *on the autistic spectrum:* Problems with *social interaction,* problems with *communication,* and unusual *behavior patterns* which are restricted, repetitive, and stereotypical. The severity of the impairments can vary.

Note: Many of the features of autistic spectrum disorders can occur in normal children as they develop. The diagnosis of ASD is based on the presence of all three of these key impairments.

SOCIAL INTERACTION

1. Poor eye contact and other *non-verbal behaviors*

These children often have very poor eye contact. This is because they cannot understand eye contact, facial expressions, gestures and body posture. They often are unable to recognize emotions in themselves or in other people. They might see a child crying after falling down, but they do not recognize that the child is unhappy and in pain. This problem might not be noted until age 2 or 3.

2. Peer relationships

Children who are on the autistic spectrum have trouble making friends. The toddlers tend to want to play by themselves. The older children may want to have friends but they lack basic understanding of how to interact with others. They do not have a clear understanding of simple unspoken rules like taking turns. They might lack an understanding of "personal space."

Many of these children do develop close relationships in their own families, but they are often thought to be aloof or "independent" even within the family.

3. Joint attention

Toddlers who are on the autistic spectrum lack a desire to get the parent, babysitter, or sibling to pay attention to whatever they are interested in. They do not seem to want to share their experience. They do not look for approval or disapproval. A normal toddler will look at his parent as he touches an electrical outlet, obviously knowing he will get a "No!" If he sees a doggie when he is in the stroller, he will point and try to get his mommy to look at it too. The autistic child will not have any need to share his excitement in this way.

4. Social reciprocity

One of the hallmarks of autism is the inability to sense another person's feelings. Instead of *"Hi! My name is Josh. What is your name?"* an autistic child will say *"Hi, my name is Josh. I live down the road. I like to eat eggs."* He will not make any effort to hear what the other person has to say. The child might also not understand taking turns.

Communication

Children who are on the autistic spectrum have difficulty communicating from an early age. Parents will often first seek help when their child does not start talking or even babbling by one year, or does not even start using gestures to indicate his needs and desires. The child will not try to communicate his needs because he does not realize that the caretaker is really there to help him. He just cries hopelessly because he does not recognize that people are people.

In many autistic children, the development of both receptive and expressive language is delayed. They do not understand words. They often do not even respond to their own name by age one year. They do not understand simple questions or directions. They will not imitate "bye-bye" or "clap your hands."

The degree of language impairment is variable. The more severely they are affected by the autism, the more language impairment they have. Some will speak but only to repeat words they have heard (*echolalia*). Higher-functioning children do speak, but even they will have trouble sustaining a conversation. They also might talk excessively about things that interest them. They do not understand humor or sarcasm. If you say "hold your horses!" instead of "slow down," they will not understand what horses you are referring to.

Even some of the children who have good language skills will have unusual voice qualities and odd speech patterns, like sing-song or monotone speech.

Behavior patterns

Children on the autistic spectrum often have *rigid and repetitive* behaviors. Although present in many typical children, these behaviors are often very intense and, along with the social and communication problems, are important to the diagnosis of autistic spectrum disorder.

1. Preoccupations

The baby might become intensely interested in looking at edges, lights, fans, or strings, or in looking at things out of the corner of the eye. The older child might become intensely interested in a particular topic like train schedules or maps or phone numbers.

2. Rituals

The child will insist on always doing things in a set order, like putting on the shirt before the pants, or eating foods in a particular order. Changing that pattern will cause him acute distress, triggering violent tantrums. He will often exhibit obsessive behaviors like not stepping on cracks in the sidewalk.

3. Motor mannerisms (stereotypies)

These are movements like hand flapping, rocking, swaying, and toe walking.

4. Play

These children do not have spontaneous imaginative play or pretend play. They sometimes imitate a video, but they do not do anything imaginative on their own. When they play, they often line things up or stack things, or play with only one part of the toy – like constantly spinning the wheel instead of zooming the toy car.

OTHER FEATURES

Sensory perception

About half of children on the autistic spectrum have abnormal sensory perceptions. These vary from child to child. Some are hypersensitive to textures – avoiding some and obsessively seeking others. Some sniff or lick everything but food. Some kids will react very strongly to a distant fire engine but not pay any attention to a loud noise in the same room. Some kids cannot tolerate light touch, but they feel good when touched with deep pressure. They often will not allow anyone to touch them, even in affectionate touch, since they perceive the touch as distressing.

Cognitive skills

Cognitive intelligence can range from severely mentally deficient to very intelligent in children on the autistic spectrum. The skills in a child on the autistic spectrum can be very uneven ("splinter skills"). They may do well on mechanical skills but do poorly on reasoning or abstract thinking. Some children have extremely high levels of ability in certain skills such as mathematical calculation, memorizing lists or schedules, or musical talent. Some learn how to read very early.

Pervasive Developmental Disorder –
Not Otherwise Specified (PDD-NOS)

This term is used to describe children who meet some but not all of the criteria for autism. They may be identified late, or they may be unusual or milder in presentation. This label is given to many children who need special services in the areas of social interaction and language. If the children continue to develop these skills, they might lose the label of PDD-NOS and go on to mainstream education, but they often still have difficulty socializing. Some PDD-NOS children manifest further evidence of autism as they grow older.

Asperger's Syndrome

Children with Asperger's do not have delays in language development, and they are not cognitively delayed. They do have features of autism which are recognized at around 4 to 6 years of age. They have unusual social development, including lack of social awareness, difficulty socializing, and Asperger's children do not understand the subtleties of language. They are literal and concrete – they do not understand jokes or sarcasm.

The Asperger child is often seen as the "strange" one in the class. He will start talking about a subject that interests him when no one is interested. He will sometimes talk down to his peers like a "little professor." He will tattle-tale without regret since he sees the world as black and white.

Treatment

Children with autistic spectrum disorders need early and intensive intervention in the toddler and preschool years. Therapies such as Applied Behavioral Analysis (ABA) and other behavioral approaches can help the children learn to socialize and communicate step by step. The goal is to teach the child's brain social and behavioral skills that are present from birth in typical children, such as eye contact and reciprocal conversation.

Although some ASD children will need medication to treat anxiety, aggressive behavior, or Attention Deficit Disorder (ADD) that accompany the autism, *there are no drugs that treat or cure the autism itself.*

Many therapies, some of them dangerous, have been tried to "cure" this problem, but they have fallen out of favor.

Early intervention and behavioral training has been shown to be the most useful intervention. Scientists are trying to find the basic defect that results in autism. Most evidence points to a defect in the way the brain is "wired."

Sensory abnormalities are treated with some success by occupational therapy strategies like sensory integration and desensitization.

Controversies

There have been many controversies over the cause of autism. Lately, an unscrupulous doctor in England claimed to have proven that it is caused by the measles vaccine. His claims have been scientifically disproven, and he has been recently charged and convicted of *falsifying his data!* He was paid over $100,000 by people who wanted a report that would help them to sue a vaccine company.

The unfounded fear that he spread caused a drop in immunization levels which led to epidemics. Although his license to practice medicine has been removed, and he has been thrown out of the medical society in England, the impact of this false report has not disappeared. *Measles vaccine was never a cause for autism*, but the disease itself is known to be dangerous. Unimmunized children are suffering encephalitis, deafness, and brain damage from measles – a vaccine-preventable disease.

Thimerisol, a vaccine preservative, was also suspected, but this has also been disproven. There was no difference in the rates of autism in the children who had thimerisol in their vaccines than the children who did not. Thimerisol is rarely used any more, but *it was never a cause of autism.*

A very good review of the history of autism controversies can be found in the book *Autism's False Prophets* by Dr. Paul Offit.

Final Thought

The most elemental disability at the core of autistic spectrum disorders is that the autistic child has great difficulty realizing that other people are real people with reactions and feelings and perceptions like his own. This creates profound effects on all of his interactions with others in his life.

As time goes by we are understanding more and more about the identification and treatment of the child on the autistic spectrum. It is our responsibility to recognize the child with social, communicative and behavioral impairments at an early age. It is also our responsibility as a community to be accepting and supportive of these children as they struggle to achieve a place in our "normal" society.

PANDAS

CHAPTER 47

PANDAS

PANDAS

We have known for many years that the bacteria known as *Beta hemolytic group A Streptococcus* causes sore throats with fever and swollen lymph nodes in the neck.

We also know that there are rare and serious complications that can occur when this infection is left untreated. These are *acute rheumatic fever* (inflammation of the heart, joints, skin, and nervous system), and *acute glomeruonephritis* (a kidney problem). Milder forms of arthritis are also often traced to Strep.

These conditions arise when the child's immune system produces excess amounts of antibody in an effort to fight the Strep. This excess antibody can mistakenly attack the heart, brain, joint lining, or kidneys, causing disease. The fear of these complications has led to the development of throat cultures and fast Strep tests that can be performed in the office or lab. When group A Beta Strep is identified, antibiotics are prescribed.

Key Points

- Strep can cause complications in some children who are overproducers of antibodies.

- One of these conditions is PANDAS: **P**ediatric **A**utoimmune **N**euro-psychiatric **D**isorders **A**ssociated with **S**trep.

- Acute onset of tics, Tourette's, OCD, or other psychiatric symptoms in a child should trigger an evaluation for Strep.

- Antibiotics can eliminate the tics and the psychiatric symptoms in some children.

It has long been noted that about 50 percent of cases of rheumatic fever had no history of sore throat or fever prior to the attack. It is assumed that not all Strep infections cause an identifiable illness, and not all are in the throat. Sinusitis, ear infections, and some other infections can be caused by group A Strep. These often go undiagnosed and untreated, because they do not usually cause fever and systemic illness.

In 1998 Dr. S. Swedo from the National Institute of Mental Health described another pediatric problem caused by Strep — *Obsessive Compulsive Disorder*. She described a group of patients who developed the psychiatric symptoms during or after a Strep infection. These children were all pre-pubertal and did not respond to the usual psychiatric medications. They all had extremely elevated levels of the anti-Strep antibodies DNAse B and ASLO.

Some of them improved dramatically after treatment with antibiotics.

Since that time, other neuro-psychiatric disorders in young children — including tics, Tourette's Syndrome, anxiety disorders, depression, and major behavior changes — have been attributed to Strep infections. The syndrome was labeled **PANDAS** (**P**ediatric **A**utoimmune **N**euro-psychiatric **D**isorders **A**ssociated with **S**trep).

There are large studies going on now in major medical centers to study PANDAS. They are trying to determine if the patients really do improve on antibiotics, and whether they need long-term prophylactic doses to prevent relapse. Meanwhile, many pediatricians are considering Strep when one of their young patients suddenly develops a neuro-psycychiatric disorder.

The symptoms can vary in different children. The most obvious one is tics, which are involuntary facial and body movements such as eye-rolling, grimacing, or tapping hands or feet. Other symptoms include involuntary noises such as snorting, squeaking, coughing, or even yelling.

Some of the children develop strange habits such as running to the bathroom every few minutes in fear of wetting themselves. Some have more classic obsessive thoughts such as fear of germs or guilt over trivial transgressions, and compulsive behaviors such as hand-washing, or even excessive *davening*.

Sometimes the child will have a sudden change of personality or behavior, for example, a naturally even-tempered child becoming irritable, impulsive, oppositional, or obnoxious.

Some of the children develop severe anxieties that interfere with normal functioning, for example, fear of leaving home. Many of these children experience joint pains and headaches along with the change in behavior.

When a parent complains of a dramatic change in a child, it is now known that this child needs a throat culture and a blood test for the ASLO and DNAse B antibodies. If either test result is abnormal, the diagnosis of PANDAS should be considered.

PEDIATRIC ACUTE ONSET NEUROPSYCHIATRIC SYNDROME (PANS) (PANDAS WITHOUT STREP)

PANS children are diagnosed based on the acute onset of their condition regardless of source. Tests for other infections such as Lyme disease and mycoplasma are warranted, since they too can cause PANDAS symptoms.

It is not always possible to diagnose PANS/PANDAS by blood tests.

If the clinical symptoms are typical, it is worthwhile to treat as PANDAS anyway.

The treatment for these children should be a course of antibiotics (See Chapter 33, Understanding Antibiotics). Which specific antibiotic to use is not well-delineated. Many doctors are using Amoxicillin or Keflex; however, there is some evidence that azythromycin can result in a quicker and more dramatic return to normal behavior.

The pediatric psychiatric community is not yet in tune with this diagnosis. Any pre-pubertal child who experiences a deterioration in his or her psychiatric functioning should be tested for the ASLO and DNAse B antibodies and should have a throat culture. If either of these test results is abnormal, a course of antibiotics (in my experience, azythromycin) should be attempted before a psychiatric referral is made, since it often results in cure.

PANDAS is still a new and somewhat unproven concept. The fact is, however, that in our community we have seen many examples that seem to fit the diagnosis and respond well to this "unusual" treatment.

The problem can recur with subsequent Strep infections. When the PANDAS behavior starts to become evident again, another treatment with antibiotics usually resolves the problem. Some doctors feel that after a recurrence, a 6- to 12-month course of low-dose Amoxil two times a day, or Zythromax once a week, should be given to prevent Strep infections.

Even though we, as pediatricians, are trying hard not to use antibiotics unnecessarily, this is one instance when we must consider treatment as critically important. Although most kids with tics and even childhood OCD improve with time, the PANDAS symptoms can, if left untreated, become permanent.

It is important to realize that everybody suffers when a PANDAS child is suffering

— the parents, the siblings, the classmates, the teachers, and the friends.

This is, admittedly, a strange new idea, but for the parents of a child with PANDAS, the relief experienced when their child returns to normal is indescribable.

CHAPTER 48

Dr. Susan Schulman's Protocol for Treating Suspected Mild to Moderate PANDAS/PANS

Diagnosis

Suspicion of mild to moderate PANDAS (Pediatric Autoimmune Neuropsychiatric Disorder Associated with Strep) comes from the history and clinical picture — not laboratory confirmation. Although these patients do not all meet strict research criteria for PANDAS, they still warrant consideration and clinical trial of treatment.

Symptoms

Symptoms include *unexplained and abrupt* **onset of any** *persistent deterioration in the child's behavioral health*. Common symptoms include: high irritability — both emotional and sensory — regression to babyish behavior, anger, explosive behavior, tantrums, emotional lability, sleep disturbance, anxiety symptoms, fears, phobias, panic disorder, Obsessive Compulsive Disorder, frequent urination, urinary accidents, depression, deterioration in cognitive function, poor focusing skills, and deterioration in handwriting and drawing ability. Motor tics and vocal tics, and new-onset stuttering, can be noted alone or with behavioral symptoms. Not all children with suspected PANDAS have tics.

Beta Hemolytic Strep Group A

Most children with PANDAS have a history of strep infection or a current positive culture, or exposure to other children with strep. Often the anti DNASE B antibody titers are markedly elevated. The ASLO titers are elevated if the strep exposure is recent, but they are less reliable. Some children, even those with history of repeated strep infections, have unusually low titers. If there was a history of strep associated with the onset of the condition, they still warrant a trial of treatment.

Following titers after initial evaluation is not necessary, since clinical signs and symptoms are the only criteria for judging effectiveness of therapy.

Other infections — PANS

Infections with other organisms can trigger the same symptoms as the ones caused by strep. **Mycoplasma Pneumonii** and **Lyme Disease** are both known to cause this problem, as are other infections. The new term PANS (Pediatric Acute-onset Neuropsychiatric Syndrome) has been adopted.

Anecdotal experience

The following protocol is based on my clinical experience with many PANDAS children (more than 200) over the last 10 years. I have found that it results in dramatic improvement in most patients, often obviating the need for psychiatric medication.

Starting dose — clinical trial

After checking for other stressors like bullying, family strife, and abuse, if PANDAS is *suspected,* I prescribe **azythromycin** to assess the effectiveness. I use 30 days as a *clinical trial.* This is just to see if there will be any response to therapy.

It is important to observe the child to assess lessening of tics, and/or anxiety symptoms. The first sign of improvement is usually a decrease in irritability.

If there is absolutely no improvement, discontinue the azythromycin.

Note — There are no liquid preparations that are effective except Pfizer's Zythromax brand.

Maintenance

If any improvement is noted (e.g.: decreased frequency or intensity of tics or lessening of irritability or phobic or anxious behavior), continue the azythromycin for three more weeks.

Reassess at three-week intervals and continue as long as there is improvement.

Note: A flare-up of behavioral and neurologic symptoms can occur during the treatment when a viral illness occurs. This usually responds to ibuprofen 2 times a day, or naproxen sodium 2 times a day until the intercurrent illness subsides)

Taper

Once the child has reached baseline or has plateaued in improvement for four weeks, consider tapering the dose by reducing the dose by one-quarter, per dose, weekly. During the taper, the parents should watch carefully for return of irritability or other symptoms.

If any deterioration is noted, return to the lowest effective dose (full 10/kg dose is sometimes required) until the child is back to normal for four weeks. Then again try to taper by decreasing the dose by one-quarter at weekly increments.

If repeated tapers fail, usually in the children with longer histories, the azithromycin is continued and tapered again in a slower, more gradual taper.

Prophylaxis

If there are recurrences, or if the symptoms are very distressing, I recommend prophylaxis.

Prophylactic antibiotics (as delineated by the American Heart Association for prevention of Rheumatic Fever) can be given for 6 to 12 months after stopping the daily azithromycin. If the symptoms were severe, or if IVIG was required, I continue prophylaxis throughout childhood, as in rheumatic fever.

Vitamin D, probiotics and Omega-3

Adequate Vitamin D levels have been found to have a protective effect against autoimmune disorders. The new recommendations are for 400 IU for young children and 800 IU for older children (over 10 years).

During the entire course of therapy, *bacterial probiotics* like Lactobacillus GG (Culturelle) should be given daily at a different time of day from the administration of Zythromax. Alternatively, for convenience, Florastor, a yeast-based probiotic, can be used daily, since it can be administered at the same time as the antibiotic.

Supplementation with *fish oil Omega-3* — 500 to 1000 mg/day of the EPA component is recommended by many psychiatrists for patients with anxiety and/or depression. The dose should be geared to the EPA component, since it alone crosses the blood-brain barrier and has been shown to be beneficial to the brain.

Cognitive behavioral therapy

Cognitive behavioral therapy (CBT) has been shown to be a powerful tool in treating anxiety patients. If the child has an anxious baseline nature, this therapy is also recommended.

Treatment failure

If treatment fails initially, or if it fails after initial success, other therapies have been tried successfully by other clinicians. Augmentin in very high doses (2000 mg/day given for 1 to 2 years) has been found to work by some clinicians.

IVIG, a treatment aimed at the abnormal immune response, has been found to be successful in many PANDAS children that did not resolve with other treatment.

Informational web sites

www.pandasnetwork.org — a reliable parents support and information site

www.webpediatrics.org — Dr. M. Kovacevic talks about the IVIG treatment

CHAPTER 49

PANDAS: A Case of Mistaken Molecular Identity

An Interview with Dr. Susan Schulman

Yossi*, an eleven-year-old boy, had been in bed for over half a year. Unable (or was it unwilling?) to move from his supine position, Yossi could not walk on his own, and he was spoon-fed daily by his perplexed parents. Extensive medical tests and examinations had declared the boy to be in perfect physical health. What, then, was reducing a formerly energetic child to this immobile and barely functioning state? Conversion hysteria, an anxiety-related mental disorder, was the official diagnosis by the psychiatrists who evaluated him. The anti-anxiety medications prescribed for the disorder, however, failed to alleviate his symptoms. Yossi remained in bed.

When Yossi's grandmother arrived for a visit from abroad, she was understandably alarmed by his condition. Reports from Yossi's parents describing his deterioration had failed to prepare her for the shock of seeing him lying totally immobile. Where was the lively and impish youngster she'd spent time with just a year ago?

After several days of observing his daily routine of alternately sleeping and accepting meager spoonfuls of food from his parents, his grandmother made him an offer: If he could manage to sit up in a wheelchair, she'd take him home with her. Yossi exerted tremendous effort to cooperate with the physical therapist his parents had hired to keep his limbs from atrophying, and over the course of a week, he managed to raise his head and assume a weak sitting position. His grandmother kept her side of the deal and, to his delight, brought him with her to New York.

Around the same time, Dr. Susan Schulman, a Brooklyn pediatrician, published an article in *Hamodia* alerting parents to the existence of a recently discovered disease. PANDAS, or Pediatric Autoimmune Neuropsychiatric Disorder Associated with Strep, was discovered in 1998 by Dr. Susan Swedo and her team at NIMH (National Institute of Mental Health). They coined the term for the disorder that resulted from strep infections, leading to alarming symptoms that overlapped with those Yossi exhibited. His grandmother, chancing upon the article, felt nearly certain she had discovered the source of her grandson's condition. Without further ado, she scheduled an appointment with Dr. Schulman.

"When I met Yossi, he was completely debilitated," remembers Dr. Schulman. "He couldn't do anything. I evaluated him and discovered that there was a history of strep infections before the problem began. I tried to ascertain whether the possibility of abuse or other trauma may have triggered this type of response, and determined that, to the best of my knowledge, it had not. Although he was lacking one of the most well-known components of a classic PANDAS diagnosis, OCD (obsessive-compulsive disorder), I felt fairly confident that he did indeed have the disease. I proceeded to prescribe azythromycin, which is both an antibiotic and anti-inflammatory medication with immune-modulating benefits."

The medication's effects were dramatic. He began improving almost immediately. Over the next few months, Yossi's normal functions returned. His grandmother registered him in school. It took over a year to treat him and then wean him off the medication. Ultimately, he returned home completely rehabilitated, back to his former active and exuberant self.

To this day, almost a decade after her grandson's harrowing experience with PANDAS, Yossi's grandmother remains haunted by the thought of what might have been if she had not been alerted by Dr. Schulman's article to the possibility of the disease.

Dr. Schulman, who has diagnosed and treated countless cases of PANDAS since Yossi's encounter with the disease, remains determined to alert parents and pediatric medical practitioners to the existence of the disease that can manifest in a number of ways, causing sudden negative changes in personality and behavior in the children it affects.

Dr. Schulman describes a little girl who was brought to her office for exhibiting some strange behavior: She'd react very strongly if her Shabbos dresses touched her "weekday" clothing. If that happened, she'd scream that they were "treif." She describes a boy who insisted on kissing the mezuzah hundreds of times a day. There was the child who drooled excessively, refusing to swallow in the presence of people he deemed unclean. The boy who insisted on walking sideways, lest he bump into another pedestrian. These children all exhibited symptoms of OCD — symptoms that vanished once they underwent treatment for PANDAS.

And then there was Yossi, the eleven-year-old child who entered her office completely immobile and emerged a year later as an energetic and vibrant young boy.

It's stories like these that prompt Dr. Schulman to continue her quest to inform parents and medical practitioners, alerting them to the possibility that their child's sudden negative moods, strange behavior, motor or vocal tics, or loss of cognitive function may be attributed to the body's immune reaction to a bacterial infection.

"I want parents to consider the possibility," she says. "They need to think of PANDAS when their child suddenly morphs into someone they no longer recognize."

HERE ARE SOME FAQS TO HELP RAISE AWARENESS OF THIS DISEASE

How and why is PANDAS triggered by strep?

Strep triggers an immune reaction in the body, the same way all infections cause immune reactions in healthy people. The particular strain of strep that causes PANDAS results in a normal antibody reaction, which in some children becomes exaggerated. Children with PANDAS often have higher than normal antibody levels. In these children there can also be an abnormal immune response. Instead of attacking the germ, some of their antibodies will attack the basal ganglia, the region of the brain that controls mood and some motor activity. Why does this happen?

Dr. Susan Swedo, who, along with her team at NIMH discovered PANDAS in 1998, has found that this strain of strep has a protein code that mimics the patterns in this area of the brain, confusing the antibodies. Basically, it's a case of mistaken identity, or what Dr. Swedo refers to as "molecular mimicry." Once the antibodies attack the brain, there's an inflammatory reaction that can cause depression, irritability, anxiety, regressive behavior, anger, tantrums, OCD, or repetitive activities such as tics and vocal tics — the symptoms vary with each child.

What are the symptoms of PANDAS?

The diagnosis of PANDAS should be considered when the parents ask themselves,

"What happened to the delightful kid we know? Where did he go? Will we ever get him back?" OCD is usually considered the most indicative symptom, although that's a very dramatic manifestation of PANDAS, and not necessarily present. OCD and tics are usually the symptoms focused on by research teams and studies. In my experience, however, other symptoms are just as common — usually in milder forms of PANDAS. These symptoms include any form of anxiety such as phobias, fears, worries, OCD, panic, and extreme irritability. Some kids are hypersensitive — they just never feel comfortable. Cognitive dysfunction, like forgetting how to read or do math can be a manifestation of PANDAS; the child may suddenly lose skills he or she has acquired. I once had a seven-year-old patient who forgot her nekudos from one day to the next. Sleep disorders are also common, as is bedwetting or the urge to run to the bathroom constantly.

What would cause you to suspect PANDAS in a patient?

If a parent comes in and tells me her child is suddenly not acting like himself, and the child is physically healthy and there is no underlying trauma to cause the change in his behavior, I will suspect PANDAS. PANDAS exaggerates the baseline negatives in the child's personality — an anxious child will become *very* anxious, for example.

Is there an overlap between PANDAS and ADHD or autism? Some parents of children with these conditions believe there is a correlation.

ADHD and autism are inborn. Children with either of these can have PANDAS flare-ups, but treating it won't eliminate their baseline conditions. I do see that an unusual percentage of the PANDAS population is autistic. This could be because children with autism will exhibit more exaggerated behaviors, or that parents are quicker to notice and report changes in children with autism. While it's true that PANDAS can cause difficulty concentrating, this would manifest itself as a sudden change in a child who was formerly attentive, or a sudden and dramatically decreased attention span in a child with ADHD.

How is PANDAS diagnosed?

I usually look for a high level of antibodies in blood test results, but the blood test is not necessarily indicative. A history of strep may help point in that direction as well. PANDAS is an autoimmune and neuropsychiatric disease, which is attributed to an abnormal immune response in the body and neural and behavioral irregularity. The patient's medical history is an important part of the diagnostic process, and it is thoroughly examined, and all other causes of his symptoms are ruled out, before suspecting PANDAS.

Without conclusive diagnostic assessment, isn't there room for misdiagnosis? How can you administer antibiotic treatment for a disease that is not conclusively present?

I'm normally very careful about prescribing antibiotics, and prescribing one to a child who has no fever or positive test results goes against my grain as a medical practitioner. PANDAS causes real suffering, and the primary treatment for it is an antibiotic. Because this disease is so disruptive, it is worth attempting to treat it if any other underlying causes have been ruled out. I usually give it about three to four weeks on a trial course, depending on how long the patient has been sick before seeking my help, and if there is no improvement at all, it is obvious that we have to look for other explanations.

How is PANDAS treated?

One of the reasons PANDAS is controversial is because its treatment course is not clearly identified. Immunosuppression in the form of cortisone, for example, will quell the symptoms as long as it's given; however, as soon as it's stopped the disease will immediately flare up again. Amoxil is not a good choice, because while it can protect from strep it can't block the antibodies. Augmentin and azithromycin both work well by fighting strep and acting as anti-inflammatory agents. In my opinion, azithromycin is most effective against PANDAS.

Tanya Murphy, a pediatric psychiatrist at University of South Florida, began a study on the effectiveness of azithromycin in PANDAS patients. She hasn't yet published the results; I'm not sure if she's completed the study. However, she's very well respected in the field and her study will lend much credibility to this method of PANDAS treatment.

There is another treatment that is very effective, which works by rebooting the immune system. This is the intravenous immune globulin (IVIG) treatment, which is administered once over a two-day period. It is very effective, but also very expensive — prohibitively so. It costs $1,000 for every ten pounds of body weight, so a 50-pound child's treatment will cost $5,000. And most insurance won't cover that cost. A study was conducted at Yale University to measure the effectiveness of IVIG in children believed to have PANDAS. They haven't yet published their results, but I believe it will prove that the treatment is very effective. Yale is in the process of setting up an

IVIG treatment center.

Treatment can also include SSRIs (a particular type of antidepressant) and cognitive behavioral therapy (as for OCD or Tourette's). Do you treat solely with antibiotics?

Frequently, antibiotics are all that's required. If resolution of symptoms is not complete following antibiotic treatment, the use of these drugs and cognitive behavioral therapy can be useful. If they are used prior to antibiotic treatment, however, the drugs will usually not be effective and they can cause some very bad side effects. CBT (cognitive behavioral therapy) is also more effective in the treated child.

How long is the average course of treatment with antibiotics?

I can't say for certain; each case is different. I will say that it is a slow process, and one of trial and error. Patients do very well, but reducing the medication can be tricky. If you take a patient off too quickly, symptoms will return. Each case must be considered carefully and monitored closely, adjusting dosage as the patient begins to recover.

How prevalent is the disease? Have you diagnosed many cases?

Recently, I've been seeing more and more cases. Because I have special interest in the disease and people in the medical field are aware of that, they will refer patients to me. I believe that Jewish kids are more prone to PANDAS, based on the incidences we've observed in large Jewish communities in North America, Europe and Israel. Could there be a Jewish genetic predisposition? Maybe. I believe that could be the case.

Could an adult have PANDAS?

A lot of people ask me that question. PANDAS, by definition, has its onset in childhood. I don't believe we can expect the onset of PANDAS during adulthood. But say we have an adult with OCD that suddenly manifested itself back when he was ten years old. It is possible to speculate that it resulted from untreated PANDAS.

What can parents to do prevent the onset of PANDAS?

There is really nothing you can do to prevent it. Retesting your child for strep following a course of medication will not prevent PANDAS. PANDAS can result from any exposure to strep, treated or untreated. It is the reaction of the body to a particular strain of strep. Antibody reactions are a part of the natural immune system. With PANDAS it's an abnormal immune reaction that causes the problem.

I'd like to point out that years ago rheumatic fever was a fairly common autoimmune disease. That disease resulted when anti-strep antibodies attacked the joints or the heart because of mistaken identity-molecular mimicry. Dr. Swedo believes that PANDAS is essentially the same type of disease, except the antibodies attack the brain instead of the heart or joints; it's the reaction to a different strain of strep.

The American Heart Association recommends prophylaxis, or prevention of disease recurrence, with a long-term course of low-dose antibiotics in any patient who has had rheumatic fever. Dr. Swedo recommends the same precaution with severe cases of PANDAS. In my experience, I've done the same for severe cases.

SECTION

EIGHT

Infections

CHAPTER 50

Fever in Children

Why we worry about fever

When a child awakens feeling ill, hot, and flushed, his parents often experience a stab of fear. "He has a fever! Hurry! Get the Tylenol!"

Fever phobia

"Fever phobia" has been around for a long time. Everyone knows that when a child's body temperature is elevated and the heat is felt on the skin, he is ill. The febrile illness causes anxiety, since it could prove to be serious. Although the child is usually only mildly ill with a self-limited viral illness or an easily treated bacterial illness such as strep throat, there is a small possibility that he could, G-d forbid, have a life-threatening bacterial illness such as meningitis, pneumonia, or septicemia.

Fever can cause symptoms

Although it is really a sign of another problem, the fever itself can cause headaches,

Key Points

- Fever is not dangerous.
- Fever is only a sign that there is an illness in progress.
- Fever can cause headaches, nausea, and poor appetite.
- Fever can be left untreated if it is not causing too much discomfort.
- Extra fluids are needed during fever.
- In this day and age, fever is usually not caused by a life-threatening illness.
- Antipyretics can be given to reduce fever and its discomforts.

nausea, vomiting, malaise, and drowsiness. Occasionally, in young children, fever can cause convulsions.

Fever is not dangerous

Until recently it was feared that the fever itself was dangerous to the child's brain. Antipyretics such as aspirin, acetaminophen, and ibuprofen were given to all patients with fever. Emergency rooms had sinks designed to bathe the child to reduce high fevers.

Recently there has been research into the physiological phenomenon of fever, and as a result, pediatricians have become less concerned about fever. Here is a brief explanation of the current medical view of fever in a child.

What is fever?

Fever is an elevation of body temperature above the normal baseline temperature. **It is a sign of illness, not an illness in itself.** Fever occurs when the brain receives signals triggered by an inflammatory reaction.

To produce fever, the brain stimulates an increased metabolic rate by increasing heart rate, increasing respiration, and decreasing skin circulation to decrease heat loss through the skin. (This is why people often feel chilled when they are developing fever.)

Normal rectal temperature is 97°F to 100°F. (It varies during the course of the day and night.)

"Having fever" is defined as follows:

100.4°F in an infant less than 30 days of age.

100.7°F in an infant 1–3 months of age.

101°F in any child over 3 months of age.

Moderate fever is up to 102.5°F. High fever is above 102.5°F and up to 105°F.

105.4°F and above is unusual. When it occurs, a doctor should be contacted.

Reasons to allow a fever to take its own course

1. Since the advent of antibiotics and modern vaccines, many common life-threatening illnesses have become preventable or treatable. For example, since the HIB vaccine was initiated, the incidence of bacterial meningitis in the pediatric population has dropped by **95 percent.** Since the initiation of the Prevnar pneumococcal vaccine recently, the number of children admitted to the hospital for severe pneumonia has dropped by 90 percent.

As it is, most bacterial illnesses can be successfully treated at home with antibiotics. There seems to be less concern that the fever represents a life-threatening illness. (In the early days of my practice, any child with high fever and vomiting had a possible case of HIB meningitis. I had 7 to 10 such patients a year! Since the vaccine came into use, *baruch Hashem,* I have had none!)

2. The fever itself does not seem to cause direct harm to most healthy patients. **There is basically no danger just from the heat of the fever.**

3. In some studies, the **actual illnesses subsided faster when the fever was not reduced** by medications or bathing. Fever is a part of the immune response.

4. Most febrile seizures in patients brought to emergency rooms were found to be due to the HHV7 virus, the one that causes Roseola. It is thought that the virus itself causes the seizures, not the actual fever. The seizures often occur when the fever is rising for the first time, not during the subsequent days of fever.

These facts are all reassuring. Maybe we do not have to treat fever at all. If the child feels well enough to function, we do not need to treat it. There are, however, many instances where treating the fever is appropriate.

REASONS TO TRY TO CONTROL FEVER

1. Fluid loss

When a child has fever, **he requires extra fluid intake** to make up for the water loss from sweating and evaporation. If the fever or the illness is resulting in poor intake of fluids by causing nausea or lack of appetite, dehydration might ensue, which causes even more illness and physiological derangement. When this happens, the administration of acetaminophen or ibuprofen is indicated just to get the child to be more interested in drinking and eating.

2. Aches and pains

There are frequently genuine discomforts associated with fever, such as headache and body aches. If the child is feeling miserable, it usually helps to give antipyretics, which also are good pain controllers. When the fever is down, the child feels better. Many people would rather have a sick but comfortable child remain ill for an extra day than to have an utterly miserable child who recovers one day sooner.

The young infant with fever

Any fever (100.4°F or above) that occurs in an infant less than one month of age is considered an emergency. Treating the fever itself is not important; it is the cause of the fever that requires attention. These neonates are susceptible to serious infections due to immaturity of the immune system. If merely unbundling the child does not take away the fever, the doctor should be contacted.

A temperature of 100.7°F or higher in an infant 1 to 3 months old should be evaluated. It is, however, only considered an emergency if the infant is unable to maintain fluid intake or if he appears ill.

When a child over 3 months is ill with fever

The first assessment must be made by the parents. Is the child feeling very ill, or is he being cute? A smiling playful child is not seriously ill. If the child seems to be very ill, medical care must be sought.

If the child is coping with the illness, maintaining adequate fluid intake, and acting alert, he can be observed for a couple of days to see how he will do. If he gets progressively sicker, has more symptoms (like a worsening cough) or has a decreased intake that is worrisome, medical care should be sought. If the fever persists more than 2 to 3 days, it is probably a good idea to have him checked.

If there are specific symptoms, such as abdominal pain, cough, swollen lymph nodes, redness of a certain area of skin, diarrhea with blood and mucous, sore throat, ear pain or other signs of infection, the doctor should be consulted.

TREATMENTS OF FEVER

1. Bathing – a reasonable treatment of fever

A bath in tepid water for about 20 minutes will often help reduce fever. Sponging with tepid water and allowing the water to evaporate off the skin is actually quicker than the bath. (Never put alcohol in the water. The fumes are dangerous)

2. Antipyretics – fever reducers

Acetaminophen (Tylenol): 10–15 milligrams per kilogram of body weight (**100mg–150mg per 22 pounds of body weight**) every 4 to 6 hours. It is important to look at the dosage in milligrams for each teaspoon or dropper on the bottle.

Infant & Children's liquid 1 tsp. (5 ml) = 180 mg

Chewables = 80 mg per chewable tablet

Suppositories come in varied dosages.

Ibuprofen (Motrin or Advil): 10 milligrams per kilogram of body weight (100 mg. for

22 pounds of body weight) every 6 hours.

    Drops = 50 mg in 1.25cc

    Children's liquid = 100 mg per tsp.(5cc)

Caution: To avoid liver toxicity

Acetomenophen should be limited to no more than four doses in 24 hours. To avoid toxicity, ibuprophen should be limited to no more than four doses in 24 hours. It is acceptable to alternate them.

Common sense

When a child has fever, it is important to stop and think. A parent's fear can be alleviated just by looking at the child and assessing his clinical condition. Most of the time, simple observation, time, and extra fluid are all that is needed. If the child's illness appears more serious, a physician should be consulted.

If a fever lasts more than two days, a physician should be consulted.

There is no reason to keep a feverish child indoors. The outside air gives the child and the caregiver a refreshing sense of well-being.

With a little bit of understanding and common sense, parents can feel more confident dealing with a febrile child. Most pediatricians today are trying to implement this approach to eliminate "fever phobia."

CHAPTER 51

Understanding Antibiotics

Key Points

- Antibiotics have saved millions of lives.

- Some illnesses, such a bacterial pneumonia, meningitis, cellulitis, kidney infections, and Beta Strep inections must be treated with antibiotics.

- Pediatricians treating ear infections, even non-serious ones, have prescribed millions of doses of antibiotics.

- The bacteria that cause this illness have become dangerously resistant to antibiotics.

- A new, more restricted approach to usage of antibiotics has helped to reduce the number of resistant strains.

Although antibiotics have been used for over 50 years, we are now just beginning to understand the impact of their use. Since everyone is affected by antibiotics, it is important that we all understand them.

The toll of infection

In the 1800s, the average life expectancy in the United States was only about 40 years. The most dangerous times were the first year of life, and the elderly years. Infants often succumbed to infections such as pneumonia and septicemia (blood poisoning) in their first few months, due to an immature immune system. The elderly often died of these infections because of an aging immune system.

Soldiers wounded in battle were also vulnerable. When these bacteria caused wound infections, they were usually fatal. Because of the fear of infections spreading into the blood, injured limbs were often amputated.

Scientists focus on infections

In the 1890s, science advanced when Louis Pasteur revealed the concept that microbes cause infections. This resulted in pasteurization of milk to prevent tuberculosis. At around the same time, Dr. Ignaz Semmelweiss discovered that handwashing reduced the rate of infections after childbirth.

Researchers discovered the actual germs for different infections and studied them by growing them on petri dishes. It was found that staphylococcus caused skin, bone, and joint infections; Streptococcus pneumonia (also called Pneumococcus) caused severe pneumonias, ear infections, mastoiditis and meningitis; and Beta Strep caused throat infections, which could lead to rheumatic fever.

Haemophilus Influenza (H. flu) was responsible for 90 percent of childhood meningitis. Despite the knowledge that was gained, people often died of infection. Unfortunately, there was no treatment for these diseases.

Sanitation plays a role

At around the turn of the century, cholera, typhoid fever and typhus epidemics – which often killed millions – were contained by the institution of sanitation practices. The introduction of flush toilets, sewers, waste-processing systems, and clean drinking water greatly improved the health of the community, so that by the early 1900s, average life expectancy had increased to 55 years.

Penicillin: The first antibiotic

In the early 20th century, a scientist named Fleming noted that a certain mold was killing bacteria in his petri dishes. When this observation was investigated, he isolated the responsible component and discovered penicillin. By the 1940s, it was being mass-produced, and it saved many soldiers' lives during World War II. By the 1950s, an oral form was developed, and the drug was prescribed by doctors to millions of patients.

Newer antibiotics

As modifications of the penicillin molecule were developed to treat a wider and wider spectrum of bacteria, it appeared that medical science would soon gain control of all bacterial infections. Erythromycin, tetracycline, and cephalosporins – new and different types of antibiotics – were invented. The fatality rate for pneumonia and other infections decreased, and the average life expectancy increased to 65 years.

Antibiotics were given freely

Antibiotics are effective only in bacterial illnesses. They do not have any benefit in illnesses caused by viruses, such as colds, influenza, and intestinal viruses. Despite this fact, for over 40 years, many primary-care physicians freely prescribed antibiotics to everyone who was ill with fever, often even to people with viral illnesses.

During this time, everyone was blissfully unaware that the bacteria were growing stronger and more resistant to control. Each time an infection was treated, a few germs escaped because they had a mechanism to counter the effect of the drug. With all of the susceptible germs killed off, there was room for these hearty survivors to grow and multiply.

Stronger germs, stronger drugs

No one was particularly worried, since new antibiotics were constantly being developed to control the newer and stronger germs. In the setting of hospitals, the bacteria that survived exposure to the most advanced intravenous antibiotics became true "super-bugs."

In the 1990s, a very resistant strain of Pneumococcus appeared unexpectedly in South America and quickly spread to the United States. For the first time, the medical community stopped and took notice. This dangerous, untreatable germ was spreading in the healthy community. We trembled in fear of returning to the helplessness of the 1930s.

A miscalculation

Looking back at the previous four decades, it became evident that our philosophy of treatment had caused a serious miscalculation. The problem was created by the treatment of a common childhood infection-*otitis media*, or infection of the middle ear. Millions of patients were given antibiotics for this infection. Although otitis media rarely caused serious complications, it was treated routinely with antibiotics. When a pediatrician saw an infected ear, the standard of practice was to prescribe an antibiotic to control the infection. The treatment hastened the resolution of the infection and averted rare but serious complications, such as mastoiditis and meningitis.

The germs are getting stronger and smarter

There are three major organisms that cause most ear infections: H. flu, M.

catarrhalis, and Pneumococcus. In the 1980s, one germ, H. flu, became resistant to ampicillin, so new, anti-resistance antibiotics had to be prescribed. M. Catarrhalis, which began as a benign throat germ, became a pathogen that started causing ear infections and also developed resistance. Pneumococcus, a particularly dangerous organism, was ignored, since it had remained susceptible to penicillin throughout the 1980s. It became routine practice to prescribe the more powerful antibiotics for all ear infections. As the years passed, the escalating war against resistant ear infections caused millions of doses of broad-spectrum antibiotics to be used by pediatricians everywhere.

Negative effects of broad-spectrum antibiotics

These antibiotics are so powerful and broad in their spectrum that they routinely eradicate many of the germs that normally inhabit the healthy throat and digestive system, known as "normal flora." As these benign, protective organisms are cleared out, yeast has more room to grow, and diarrhea often develops from the lack of helpful bacteria in the digestive tract. More importantly, newer germs, which have developed means of protecting themselves from the strongest antibiotics, take up residence. Even healthy people become colonized with these resistant germs, and the germs live quietly in their healthy host until some weakening of the immune system allows them to invade. When this happens, the treatment becomes difficult.

A new approach to otitis media

As a result of the growing threat of resistant Pneumococcus, a call went out to pediatricians in 2003 to reconsider the use of antibiotics in ear infections. Studies had shown that 80 percent of children over one year of age would be able to fight off their ear infections in a few days without the use of antibiotics. Doctors were urged to follow a new protocol: If the infection does not appear severe, simply give pain control, and if the child improves, just observe. If a day or two goes by with no improvement, very high doses of older antibiotics should be prescribed. This seems to be the best way of eradicating an infection completely, without leaving over any resistant organisms and without killing the "normal flora."

There is one exception: The child with a recurrent ear infection who has been treated recently with antibiotics should not be merely observed, since these rebound infections tend to be more difficult to overcome naturally.

To help overcome the threat of resistant Pneumococcus, a new childhood vaccine,

Prevnar, was released. It induces immunity to the thirteen most resistant strains of Pneumococcus.

Some infections must be treated

There are still several types of bacterial infections that must **always** be treated to avert disastrous complications. Throat infections caused by group A Beta hemolytic Strep still require treatment to avoid the complications of rheumatic fever. Bacterial pneumonia, kidney infections, cellulitis, bone and joint infections, meningitis, and other life-threatening infections must be treated with appropriate antibiotics.

Fortunately, the result of the change in prescribing habits for ear infections has been very encouraging. Millions of antibiotic doses were avoided. There is some evidence that fewer new, resistant strains of bacteria appeared in the United States in the last few years.

We physicians have been taught a real lesson. As intelligent as we think we are, since we began this war, **the lowly bacteria has outsmarted us continuously.** This experience is very humbling to all of us, because we now know that even doing what seems correct can cause enormous harm.

Final thought

With the many recent advances in medical care, the average life expectancy in the United States has increased to over 75 years.

We know that we, as physicians, are only the messengers of Hashem, Who sends healing to our patients through us. We must never assume that we fully understand the mysteries of nature. Only the Creator has real knowledge. He sometimes allows us to glimpse a tiny bit of it.

Experience has taught us to be rational and respectful when we attempt to make use of this wonderful, life-preserving gift.

CHAPTER 52

Understanding Probiotics

We often hear about products found in health food stores that are sold to enhance health. Recently, *probiotics* have drawn the attention of both the medical and the complimentary medical establishment.

Probiotics are living germs

Probiotics are not vitamins. They are real germs that have been freeze-dried and are able to come to life when they are rehydrated.

The word *probiotic* was recently invented to describe a product that is the exact opposite of an antibiotic. Whereas antibiotics kill bacteria, probiotics are living bacteria that are given to the patient.

Normal flora

Why would anyone want to give living bacteria to a patient? The answer lies in the biological phenomenon known as "normal flora." Until birth, the unborn infant lives in a sterile environment. Immediately after birth, the infant is colonized by millions of

Key Points

- Normal flora: We all need a healthy population of germs in and on our bodies.

- Antibiotics can kill off normal germs along with the ones that cause illness.

- Probiotics are freeze dried healthy germs that come to life when they are rehydrated.

- Probiotic germs and yeasts have been shown to help maintain good health.

- Probiotics help restore normal flora during and after antibiotic use.

bacteria. These germs take up residence on the skin, in the mucous membranes of the respiratory tract, in the stomach, and in the bowels. These germs are known as *flora*. The harmless ones are called "normal flora." Harmful germs that invade and cause disease are called "pathogenic flora."

Until recently no one paid much attention to the normal flora. It is only in the last few years that medical science has noted that the harmless flora are actually needed for the proper function of the body. A strong, healthy population of good bacteria helps defend against invasion by harmful ones. In the case of the digestive system, the bacteria living in the gut help to digest food, help deny access to pathogenic bacteria, and even help protect from over-growth of harmful yeasts. We now know that antibiotics frequently kill off these good germs while attacking the bad ones. Probiotics are very good for replacing the normal flora during and after antibiotic usage.

Probiotics

Probiotics provide a supplemental source for the acquisition of good bacteria. Using these germs has shown benefits in preventing and treating diarrhea, preventing food allergies and intolerances, and preventing infections in the respiratory and gastrointestinal tracts. In Scandinavia, studies have shown that adding probiotics to infant formulas can be beneficial. In Europe, certain probiotics have been proven to greatly reduce the severity of viral diarrhea and even reduce the infectivity. American formula companies are starting to add probiotics to infant formulas.

Acidophilus

The most commonly used probiotic bacteria is *lactobacillus acidophilus*. This is the germ that is found in yogurt. It is responsible for the fermentation of milk into yogurt. People have known for centuries that it is beneficial. Although many people still use yogurt as their main source of acidophilus, it is probably not sufficient. Most commercial yogurts lose their acidophilus during the processing. Some companies even add the germ back during packaging and label the product "live or active cultures." The colony counts that are achieved this way are mostly too low to be beneficial.

Unfortunately, acidophilus is really one of the weakest probiotic bacteria. This is because most of the germs that are ingested are killed immediately by the acids in the stomach. Only a small percentage survive long enough to pass into the intestine where they do the most good. For this reason, it is recommended to take large amounts several times a day.

Lactobacillus GG

There has been a lot of research done to improve the survival and effectiveness of acidophilus. One product, now available here in the U.S., is *lactobacillus GG*, which is sold as Culturelle. This is an acid-resistant probiotic that requires only one dose a day and delivers huge amounts of effective germs where they can do their best work. (See Chapter 5, GERD and Colic in Infants)

Using probiotics during a course of antibiotics

I usually recommend that anyone taking antibiotics should take Culturelle once a day until a few days after they are finished taking the medication. I always remind people to give the Culturelle at a different time of day than the antibiotic. If they are taken together, the antibiotic kills the probiotic germ in the stomach before it has a chance to help. If there is a severe milk allergy, labels should be checked to make sure the probiotic does not have traces of milk protein.

Other uses

Other uses for probiotics include treating diarrheas, both infectious and nonspecific, and even eczema caused by food allergy. Probiotics have been shown to lessen the symptoms of infant colic. Infant formulas are now being marketed in the United States with probiotics added in processing.

Beneficial yeasts

Beneficial yeasts are also part of the "normal flora." In addition to Culturelle, it is sometimes useful to take a probiotic yeast, which can help prevent candida and other pathogenic yeasts from colonizing. They can also be used to treat diarrheas. The one most commonly used for children is *saccharomyces boulardii iyo,* which is sold as FlorAstor for Kids.

Now that studies have shown how beneficial they can be, probiotics are being recommended by mainstream medical authorities. This is a real example of how "old wives' tales" turn out to be based on real science.

■ ■ ■

CHAPTER 53

Hydration and Dehydration

Key Points

- Water balance is critically important to all living beings.
- Dehydration occurs when water losses exceed water input.
- Dehydration causes a child to look weak and ill, have pasty saliva, lack tears, and have sparse urine output.
- Staying ahead of water needs prevents dehydration, especially when there is excess heat.

All living things are mostly water. About 90 percent of our body weight is water. We need water to survive. Putting fluids into the body is known as *hydration*. We lose water from three mechanisms in our physiology: respiration (the fog on the mirror when we breathe on it); insensible (evaporative) water loss from sweat; and elimination via urination or defecation. **Dehydration, lack of adequate body water, occurs when the losses are greater than the input.**

On the whole, we usually maintain our normal water balance by eating and drinking. All fruits and vegetables, all protein foods, and all cooked starches are mostly water in their composition. All liquids we drink are water. In normal circumstances we replace the water lost from sweat, respiration, and elimination so the body stays healthy and well hydrated.

Dehydration

There are several problems that can arise that can cause more fluid to leave the body than enters it. When this happens, *dehydration* is the result. Those factors are:

- Heat problems, including fever, exertion, or extreme heat, which causes excessive sweating
- Vomiting, which causes the inability to keep fluids that are taken in
- Diarrhea, which causes excessive loss of water from the bowels
- Diabetes mellitus (see p. 154), which causes excessive urination

Thirst

Thirst is our body's natural signal that reminds us to drink. In a normal, healthy person, there is almost never a problem with dehydration if adequate fluids are available. There is really no need to drink more than we are thirsty for. It is important to note that healthy babies (who cannot yet talk) must be offered fluids on a regular basis, especially in hot weather. Infants under 4 months should be offered mother's milk or formula, not water or juice, since they need nutrition, and drinking is their only source. Water is a great drink selection for all children above 9 months. Juice is really just sugar water, so it should be used sparingly on a day-to-day basis.

SIGNS OF ADEQUATE HYDRATION AND DEHYDRATION

Good hydration

How can we tell if the child is adequately hydrated? A well-hydrated child is **alert,** has a **shiny, wet tongue,** cries with an **appropriate amount of tears,** and **urinates regularly.** The urine is light in color.

Dehydration

If there is a deficit of fluid, the urine output decreases dramatically, and the child gets lethargic and irritable. The **tongue gets pasty and the saliva gets stringy, the eyes look dull and sunken,** and there are **no tears** when crying. The **urine,** when it is present, **becomes dark yellow to orange and has a strong odor.** These changes occur gradually as the condition worsens. (One exception: In children with diabetes, paradoxically, the urine output remains high while the child develops all of the signs of dehydration.)

Older children will complain of *headaches, nausea* and *weakness* when they are in the early stages of dehydration.

PREVENTING DEHYDRATION

Heat problems

During high fever, or in very hot weather and during exertion, the fluid loss is mainly from sweat, and it is important to give extra fluids. When there is high fever, the body can be cooled by tepid bathing, or by giving antipyretics such as acetaminophen and ibuprofen. Reducing the body temperature to normal or near normal will decrease the loss of fluids.

During very hot weather, especially **during exertion** in hot weather, the most important precaution is to **drink often** and **replace salt as well as fluid.** Sweat, which is needed to keep the body from overheating, is made up of salt and water. In the circumstance of hot weather and exertion, replacing only water can lead to a salt deficiency, which can cause serious imbalances in the body's chemistry.

I usually recommend that children be given lots of water and small amounts of pretzels, pickles, or other salty foods. There are electrolyte drinks that are sold, like Powerade, which have some salt in them, but there is not enough salt to make them worth all the junk in them. Ordinary tap water, which can be conveniently carried in sports bottles, is the most refreshing drink and the best hydrator.

Simply sprinkling water on the children, or letting them get wet in a pool, will help to cool them off and prevent excess sweating.

Vomiting

There are many illnesses that a child can contract that lead to vomiting. Vomiting can cause dehydration by preventing the entry of fluids into the body.

Overcoming vomiting in a child with viral gastroenteritis can be very challenging. One useful trick is to give very small amounts of fluids at a time. We usually advise parents to start with 1 half-ounce of a clear liquid every 15 minutes for 1 hour, and if it is tolerated without vomiting, increase the amount by one-half ounce every 15 to 20 minutes. If the child vomits, wait 30 minutes and try the last volume that was tolerated.

It is advisable to have some sugar in the clear liquids, to take away the ketones that form during starvation. Ketones can add to the feeling of illness and increase the nausea. Even sugar or lollipops can help this part of the problem.

Infants do well with mother's milk as the fluid, but not with formula. For non-nursing infants and children under 18 months, we usually use the rehydration solution, Pedialyte. This clear liquid, which also comes in ice pops, has the replacement sugar, salt, and fluid needed to maintain the body chemistry.

Older children can drink any clear drink or nibble on regular ice pops. The artificial orange ones seem to allay nausea best. White grape juice is less acidic than apple juice, so it is better tolerated. Clear chicken broth, the age-old remedy, actually works fine.

If the vomiting does not abate and the child shows signs of dehydration, a physician should be contacted. Intravenous hydration may be needed.

Diarrhea

When there is diarrhea present, the loss of water can usually be replaced by oral intake. Once vomiting has stopped, the fluids can be given in any quantity the child will take. At this point the child should be given a full solid-food diet, including milk and milk products. This will increase the number of bowel movements initially, but it will ultimately stop the diarrhea most efficiently.

Probiotics such as Lactobacillus GG (Culturelle) and Sacharomyces boularii iyo (Florastor) are very useful in stopping diarrhea. (See Chapter 34, Probiotics)

If the diarrhea is severe and watery, or contains mucous and blood, or if the child shows signs of dehydration, a physician should be contacted.

Diabetes mellitus

This is very rare in children, but when it occurs, the child has excessive thirst, urination, and weight loss, and appears dehydrated despite the large urine output. If this is suspected, a physician should be contacted.

Final thought

Maintaining hydration is a very important job. It is very helpful to monitor children during the course of a potentially dehydrating illness, so that hydration can be increased whenever signs of dehydration are noted. As in many other situations, prevention is the best cure, so staying ahead of the fluid requirements on a hot day saves us a lot of problems.

■ ■ ■

CHAPTER 54

Flu

Key Points

- Flu is a viral illness that goes through the community every winter.

- Flu is highly contagious to all age groups.

- Flu is preventable by immunization given every year.

- Everyone above age 6 months is eligible for flu shots (except for egg-allergic people).

- Flu shots and nasal flu vaccine are about 90 percent protective.

- There are antiviral drugs that work when given in the first 2 days of the flu.

- Prevention is the best cure!

Every year, sometime between October and February, a flu epidemic occurs in our community. We hear a lot of scary stories about the flu. There are new recommendations about who should get flu shots. Many people are confused and are asking for more information. Here is a list of questions and answers about this virus.

What is the flu?

The flu is an illness caused by a highly contagious respiratory virus, which sweeps through the community yearly in the fall and winter months. The actual virus, the influenza virus, comes in two types: influenza A and B. The illnesses caused by A and B are clinically indistinguishable. Most of our epidemics are caused by influenza A, but influenza B can come along at any time during the flu season.

What is the actual illness caused by the influenza virus?

Although many illnesses are labeled "flu," the real flu has certain characteristics that distinguish it from other viral illnesses. It usually does not cause gastrointestinal symptoms. It is strictly a respiratory virus. The typical symptoms are: headache, fever, watery eyes, runny nose, choking cough, and generalized body aches. The fever and body aches of the "flu" last longer than the symptoms of a typical cold, with many people needing to stay home for a full week before they can resume normal activity.

How is the flu spread from person to person?

The flu is extremely contagious. Once the patient has the headache, or starts feeling ill, the virus is in all of his respiratory secretions, and the smallest cough or sneeze can spread it to anyone else in the room. The virus gets on the patient's hands whenever he (or she) rubs his eyes or nose or covers his mouth to cough. Then anything he touches, like a doorknob or a toy, has millions of viruses spread onto it. The chance of a person getting the flu after exposure to a sick person ("the attack rate") is close to 90 percent. Family contacts tend to get sicker than school contacts, because they have a heavier exposure.

How long does it take to get sick after an exposure?

The incubation period for the flu is very short. Most people will be ill in one to two days, although it sometimes takes up to a week. This is why we often see an absentee rate of 60 to 80 percent in a school setting. Whenever we hear of 10 kids being out at the same time we know it is probably the flu.

Why do adults get the flu so easily?

Adults and older children who rarely get sick are often susceptible to the flu even if they have had it before. The virus has a tendency to frequently change the proteins in its outer coat, which makes it new to our immune systems. Immunity from a previous flu virus does not protect us from the new strains, which appear almost every year.

Why is there so much concern over the flu?

Flu viruses have varying virulence. Most strains are not deadly. There are, however, some strains that are particularly vicious and can cause lung damage and multi-organ failure leading to death. The Von Economo Influenza epidemic, which killed millions of people in 1917, was such a strain.

Unfortunately, pediatric and adult deaths occur every year in otherwise healthy children and adults who contract the ordinary A or B strains that pass through the community.

What is the "bird flu?"

Avian Flu, which has recently been identified in chickens in Asia, is deadly to humans. Millions of chickens have been destroyed to stop the spread of this virus.

What are the consequences of the flu?

Most influenza strains cause moderate illness in healthy people, but there are certain conditions that make the flu a bigger danger. The elderly, infants under two years and people with chronic illness such as diabetes, asthma, emphysema, and cancer are all more threatened by the flu.

Even in healthy people, the flu causes damage to the lining of the nose, sinuses, throat, Eustachian tubes, bronchial tubes, and lungs. This is why over 50 percent of flu patients will return to their physician within one month with a bacterial illness, such as pharyngitis, sinusitis, bronchitis, ear infections, or pneumonia. It is not unusual for a child to have a continuous series of infections the entire winter after a bout of the flu.

How is the flu treated?

Not with antibiotics. Antibiotics do not have any effect on any viral illness. If a patient is treated with antibiotics during the actual viral illness and an infection does arise after the flu, it will probably be a resistant one that is difficult to treat. There are antiviral drugs that specifically treat the flu virus. A physician must prescribe them in the first two days of the illness. These drugs can stop the virus from replicating and decrease the symptoms and the duration of the illness. If more than two days have passed, they are not effective.

Do over-the-counter remedies help?

The flu "remedies" that are sold in every pharmacy do not treat the illness, but they are aimed at treating certain symptoms. Antihistamines (diphenhydramine) dry up secretions. Decongestants (pseudoephedrine) shrink the nasal membranes to open the nasal passages. Ibuprophen and acetaminophen relieve aches and fever. Cough medicines contain guiafenesin, which thins secretions, and dextromethorphan, which suppresses the urge to cough. These drugs are only minimally effective in relieving the symptoms, and they do have some side effects. When it comes to flu, prevention is the cure!

How is the flu prevented?

Every year an injectable flu vaccine is produced for the coming season to induce immunity to the three most likely strains, usually two A's and one B. The vaccine is given by injection starting in October, and induces immunity in about two weeks. This protection lasts the whole season. The most common side effect is a sore arm, but some people will get a mild fever and malaise a day or two after the injection. This is never dangerous and is not a reason to avoid the vaccine.

A new vaccine, Flumist, is available for people who are healthy and between the ages 2 and 65 years old. Flumist is a live vaccine, administered in a nasal spray by a nurse or physician. Flumist is highly effective, and many insurance companies are paying for it, since the price has gone down. Both vaccines are 90 percent protective. People with severe egg allergies are not permitted to receive either vaccine.

Who should be immunized?

The vaccines are safe and effective; and everyone is vulnerable to the flu. Most adults get it from school children. It would be rational to vaccinate all the kids and adults in the community. There are, however, certain people who have top priority for getting flu shots. These are: expectant mothers; people over 65 years of age; everyone living in the same house with or taking care of a baby under 6 months; diabetics; asthmatics; chronic lung disease patients; immuno-compromised people and their household contacts; and anyone with a chronic illness.

The current recommendation is to immunize every child from age 6 months to age 18. If this is followed, there will be very few cases of flu in the community. The immunized children will not bring the flu to their classmates and to their families.

Expectant mothers are strongly advised to get flu vaccines. There is a double benefit. It protects the mother, and the infant will be born with protective immunity.

Any family that has experienced the nightmare of having the flu go through the entire household would gladly tell you how important it is to prevent the flu in children.

CHAPTER 55

Colds and Other Runny Noses

Key Points

- Children commonly get several colds a year.
- Most cold medications are ineffective and cause side effects.
- Saline and humidification help a little.
- Green runny noses should clear up in about two weeks.
- Chronic runny noses should be checked by a physician for a possible treatable cause.

As adults, we have only occasional colds that make our lives miserable for several days. Our kids, however, have about 10 colds a year once they are in a group setting such as day care or school. The reason for this discrepancy is that there are many different viruses that can cause colds. We catch most of them in early childhood so we are immune as adults.

RSV

One of the common cold viruses, known as RSV, often causes a more serious infection in **premature infants and infants with medical conditions** such as heart disease who are less than 1 year of age. This condition, *bronchiolitis*, causes wheezing and difficulty breathing in these babies. Most infants recover in a few days, but some require hospitalization for oxygen and respiratory support. Bronchiolitis also predisposes some children to recurrent wheezing. To avoid this problem in premature infants and those with other medical conditions such as heart disease, a monthly injection, Synagis, is given during the 6 months between November and

April, when RSV is common. Synagis provides protection from RSV.

A cold virus attacks

When a cold virus first enters the body, it usually invades through the throat, so often the **first symptom is a burning sore throat.** Soon the viruses proliferate and spread upwards to the nose and on into the sinuses, causing swelling and congestion, sneezing and excess mucous production. Within a few days the virus travels down into the respiratory tract, causing coughing and choking. The river of mucous from the nose flows outwards through the nostrils when the cold sufferer is standing or sitting up. When the person lies down, it flows backwards into the throat, causing even more coughing and choking.

At this time, the virus also travels up the *Eustachian tube* to the middle ear (See diagram on p. 172). The viral inflammation produces swelling and blockage of the Eustachian tube and an accumulation of fluid in the middle ear space. If this blockage is not relieved at the end of the cold, ear infections often ensue.

The mucous produced in the beginning of a cold is clear. After a few days it thickens and turns green and yellow. After a few more days it turns clear again and the cold subsides. Most colds last about one week.

Cold remedies

There are many products on the market to alleviate the uncomfortable symptoms of a cold. Most of them are useless. Here is a list of them:

Decongestants — these products all do the same thing. They shrink the swollen blood vessels in inflamed areas of the nose and sinuses. This causes a reduction in swelling, which allows more room for the air to get through. Also, decongested tissue produces less mucous, so there is a drying effect.

Nasal drops and sprays, like neosynephrine, which lasts 4 hours, and oxymetazoline, which lasts 12 hours, deliver the decongestant directly into the nose. They are amazingly effective, but they can only be used for a few times before they cause a rebound swelling when the effect wears off. This rebound can cause the user to become dependent on the drug. We recommend using the oxymetazoline only at night, and only on one side each night.

Pseudoephedrine (Sudafed), a popular decongestant, is taken orally, so the drug affects the whole body. Although it does offer some relief, it can cause rapid heartbeat, elevated blood pressure, and sleeplessness. The "daytime," "non drowsy" label usually indicates pseudoephedrine. Paradoxically, some people actually get sleepy from it. Because this drug can be used in the manufacture of a deadly street drug, *methamphetamine,* it is now kept behind the counter in most drug stores, but it does not require a prescription.

Antihistamines — These drugs block histamine, which is the natural chemical released by the nasal cells during a viral invasion. It causes redness and swelling of mucous membranes, itching and burning. Histamine is also responsible for the symptoms of allergy. (See Chapter 41, Allergy in Children)

Benadryl, one of the original antihistamines, can relieve the swelling and the mucous production. It does usually work, but it almost always causes drowsiness. People taking it should not drive a car or operate equipment. It can make a child fall asleep in school. For this reason, it is found in almost all of the nighttime cold medications. Many people think it only helps by making the patient so sleepy that he forgets he has a cold and gets a good night's sleep. Some medications combine the two types of medications with the thought that one would keep the patient awake and cancel out the drowsy effect of the other.

Claritin, or loratadine, is a newer antihistamine, which does not cause drowsiness. It works well on allergy symptoms, but it does not work at all on the symptoms of a cold. The D in Claritin D is pseudoephedrine. Since it is an effective decongestant, many people think it helps them.

Expectorants — These medications, like the guafenicin in Robitussin, are supposed to liquefy the thick mucous and make it easier to cough up. They do not work at all in the dosage recommended. One of the best expectorants is a hot cup of tea or chicken soup.

Cough suppressants — These medications, like DM — dextromethorphan — are supposed to work on the cough centers in the brain and quiet the urge to cough. They do not work at all in the recommended doses.

Are they effective?

In many double-blind studies, cold medicines are not found to be better than placebos. The American Academy of Pediatrics is trying to get **combination cold medications** off the market, since they can cause serious side-effects in overdose and they really do not relieve symptoms most of the time. **At this time there is a warning on the labels to not use them in children under two years of age.**

Antipyretics — Acetomenophen (Tylenol) and ibuprophen (Motrin or Advil) are good for reducing pain and fever. They **have no effect on the usual cold symptoms** of nasal congestion or cough or runny nose.

Saline sprays — These saltwater nasal sprays and drops are good for irrigating the nose to clear out the mucous temporarily. When the sinuses are congested the saline sprays are helpful in clearing the sinus secretions to keep them from stagnating and developing into sinusitis after the cold clears.

Humidifiers — These machines put moisture back into dry winter air. This moisture is soothing to congested noses and makes mouth breathing more tolerable. They can produce either hot or cold mists. They must be cleaned meticulously to prevent mold.

Vitamin C tablets and zinc lozenges — These have been touted to relieve cold symptoms. The problem is that the doses needed to produce results are too high for children. Orange juice and other vitamin C fruits are very good sources of natural vitamin C which are not harmful. Zinc lozenges can cause really bad stomach upset.

Echinacea — This herbal supplement was thought to boost the body's immune response to the cold virus. Detailed studies have revealed that it cannot be documented to alleviate symptoms at all. It was shown that it can actually cause suppression of immunity. It should be avoided.

Buckwheat honey — This dark honey was shown to be more effective than cough medicine in relieving the night cough of a cold. The dose is 1 teaspoon at bedtime.

How colds spread

Everyone knows that droplets released into the air by a sneeze or cough contain viruses that can cause colds. **What is not known is that most of the contagion is from the hands that rub the nose or cover the cough.** Viruses on the hands of a cold sufferer are easily transmitted to doorknobs, toys, and other objects, which are then picked up by other hands, which deliver them to their own face and mouth. The challenge is to try to keep the hands and objects that the cold sufferer touches clean.

One important precaution is to wash your own hands after wiping a kid's nose, and try to teach the child not to share snacks with other kids. When there is a newborn in the house, the children should not touch the baby's hands, since the baby will put his hands in his mouth and catch the cold. It is also a good idea to teach everyone to cover their mouths with their elbow when they cough with no tissue available. This puts the virus into the sleeve instead of on to the hands.

Persistent runny noses

If the thick colored secretions persist **longer than two weeks,** there might be a *sinus* or *adenoid* infection present. Saline irrigation can drain the infection out. If this does not help the problem, a physician should be consulted. Small children sometimes have chronically-infected adenoids that cause persistent thick nasal secretions. If treatment with antibiotics does not resolve the problem, adenoidectomy often provides relief.

It is very important to know that if a child has a **persistent green runny nose on only one side,** especially if there is a **bad smell** associated with it, there may be a **foreign body** lodged in the nose. These can be beads, balloons, beans, or other small objects. If this is suspected a physician should be consulted.

Allergic rhinitis — allergy nose: If a clear runny nose does not clear up in one month, there may be an allergy that is causing it. In young children, this is usually a food allergy to a common component of the diet. In older children, seasonal allergies might be the source.

Final thought

Most colds and runny noses are not life-threatening, but they do affect the quality of a child's life. If a persistent chronic rhinitis occurs, a physician should be consulted. If the cause is treatable the child will feel much better.

■ ■ ■

CHAPTER 56

Understanding Coughs in Children

When a child is coughing, something is not right. The cough may be a sign of serious illness, minor illness, or just a nuisance. If a cough lasts more than a few days, it is probably best to have him checked by his physician.

Here is a basic explanation of coughs in childhood.

Key Points

- The cough reflex is actually a protective mechanism
- The origin of the cough can be in the upper airway or lower airway
- Upper airway coughs are usually caused by virus or allergy
- Lower airway disease can be more serious and often needs medical attention

The cough reflex

Coughs are triggered by a neurologic reflex — the cough reflex. This protective mechanism is stimulated by an irritation of the airway, causing the child to forcibly expel air. If the irritation is caused by a foreign body, or mucous from a viral infection, or an allergic response, the child will cough repeatedly until the sensation is removed — usually by clearing the offending substance (like a popcorn shell) out of the airway. Unfortunately, the irritation sometimes persists so the cough reflex is triggered repeatedly.

Where the coughs originate

Coughs can originate from different regions of the airway. Treatment of the cough often requires locating the area that is causing the cough.

The sinuses, the nasal passages, and the adenoids

The sinuses are air spaces found inside the forehead and facial regions. They are lined by mucous membranes, which produce a thin blanket of clear mucous that is drained through tiny tunnels that empty into the nose. Like any other area with mucous membranes, the sinuses can become inflamed by allergies and viruses, and occasionally develop bacterial infections. This inflammation can cause excess mucous, which can be thick and full of pus.

The dripping of mucous and pus from the sinuses can reach the back of the nose and proceed to drip into the back of the throat. The choking sensation and the irritation from this drip can cause a cough that sounds harsh and junky.

Upper-airway cough

When the membranes of the nasal passages are inflamed, they also produce excess mucous that drips backwards into the throat, especially when the patient is lying down. The resulting cough is often called a *post-nasal drip,* or *upper airway cough.*

Often these coughs and runny noses are self-limiting; They go away by themselves when the cold virus is over. Irrigating the nose with saline solution several times a day washes away the offending mucous and helps alleviate the cough. Drinking hot drinks and taking steamy showers, and taking a teaspoon of buckwheat honey, can also thin the mucous and allow it to be cleared out. Good irrigation like this can help to prevent real infections of the sinuses.

If seasonal allergy is the cause, antihistamines and allergy nasal sprays can help. If a true chronic sinusitis develops, it is sometimes necessary to treat it with antibiotics to relieve the persistent cough. When this is the cause of the cough, the cough can change in character to a dry, hacking sound.

The adenoids are pads of lymphatic tissue that are found in the area where the nose meets the back of the throat. If they become chronically infected, they can be the source of chronic, thick nasal discharge. This can cause a post-nasal drip cough. If this is chronic, antibiotics are sometimes needed to clear the problem.

The upper trachea

The *trachea* is the windpipe that conducts the air downwards. It is protected in the back of the throat by a flap, the *epiglottis,* which covers the opening whenever any food or liquid is being swallowed. It opens to allow breathing.

Infection of this flap, known as *epiglotitis*, was once a very serious threat. Since the HIB vaccine has nearly eliminated the germ that caused this terrible infection, the incidence of epiglotitis is very rare.

The cough reflex protects the trachea by triggering a cough whenever something gets into the airway. The hard cough propels the irritant up and out into the mouth.

Viruses and allergies — and sometimes foreign bodies like popcorn shells — can cause a harsh, dry, rough, non-mucousy cough. The tracheal cough can sound like a foghorn. If this type of cough persists, inhaled steroids can be given to quiet the inflammation. If a foreign body is suspected, the patient should consult a physician.

Reflux cough

It has recently been shown that *reflux of acid material* from the stomach can irritate the upper airway, causing a persistent cough. Although reflux usually causes a burning sensation in the esophagus (heartburn), often it is totally silent. This means that it is not noticed by the patient. If a doctor determines that reflux is the source of the cough, antacids and reflux precautions sometimes stop the cough.

The larynx – croup and laryngitis

The *larynx* is found in the middle area of the trachea. It is the voice box.

When the area just below the larynx gets inflamed the cough can sound like a seal barking. This is called *croup*. Croup is usually caused by a cold virus. It is sometimes accompanied by difficulty breathing and a harsh and noisy *inbreath* called *stridor*. Croup can come in sudden attacks during the night, even 2 to 3 days before a cold has been noted. Treatment can consist of breathing cold night air or air from an open freezer. Some people advocate using steam. Even mild croup will often benefit from a single large dose of oral cortisone. If the child has difficulty breathing, Hatzolah should be called to take the child to the emergency room.

If the larynx itself is inflamed, this condition is called *laryngitis*. Some children become hoarse and voiceless with croup. The parents should sleep with the croupy voiceless child in case he needs help during the night.

Most colds and other viruses cause only upper-respiratory problems. This is what we call URI (upper-respiratory infection). When the inflammation goes lower, the condition is know as lower respiratory tract inflammation (LRTI).

THE LOWER RESPIRATORY TRACT

The bronchial tree

The trachea divides into two large *bronchial tubes* — the right and the left mainstem bronchi. The bronchi branch, and both of these branches branch again and again, with each level of branches getting smaller and narrower. The bronchial tree is lined with mucous membrane, but it also has a muscle layer that can enlarge or narrow the inside of the tube.

Bronchitis

When an infection gets into the bronchial tube, the cough is usually mucousy, but sometimes it is dry and not productive. The person coughs repeatedly to try to bring up the sputum. Bronchial coughs have a deep quality and are very persistent. They do not necessarily get worse while lying down. Hot drinks, lots of other fluids, and steamy showers or baths can help clear the airway. Bronchial infections, known as *bronchitis*, can be caused by viruses or occasionally by bacteria. Most of the time bronchitis clears itself, but if there is a burning pain on coughing, or if the cough gets more frequent or more uncomfortable as time goes by, antibiotics are sometimes needed. Bronchitis rarely causes fever.

Wheezing

When the bronchial tubes are full of mucous, with their linings swollen inside, and if the muscles around the tube have constricted the airway, air gets trapped in the region beyond. This causes a difficulty in breathing out. This problem can frequently produce a high-pitched whistling noise know as wheezing. Wheezing can cause real difficulty breathing. This is seen on the child's chest when the ribs stick out with each breath and the abdomen seems to push each breath out. The child will often be breathing faster than his usual rate. The wheezing child usually coughs a lot but the cough does not clear the wheeze.

Wheezing in children is usually caused by hyperreactive airways. This condition can recur with each cold. Inhaled medicines that reduce inflammation and medication that dilates the bronchial muscles can give dramatic relief. If these do not easily relieve the problem, oral steroids can be very useful. *True difficulty breathing is an emergency.* If it does not respond to medication, the child should be seen immediately by a physician.

Bronchiolitis

The very smallest bronchial tubes, the *bronchioles* (the ones that are actually attached to the lung tissue) do not have a muscle layer. When these tubes get inflamed, the infant wheezes and coughs. Unlike the larger airways, the wheezing is not relieved by inhaled medication. This condition is called *bronchiolitis*. Most of the time a common cold virus like RSV (Respiratory Syncicial Virus) is the cause. Most cases of bronchiolitis are in the first year of life. The younger the infant is, the more likely he is to wheeze. Bronchiolitis resolves without treatment in a few days, but some infants need to be hospitalized for supportive care.

Hyperreactive airway problems are more common in children who had bronchiolitis when they were infants.

The lungs

At the far end of the bronchial tree, just beyond each bronchiole, lies an air sack that fills with air each time a breath is taken. The sack, called an alveolus, is the actual lung tissue. In these sacks, the oxygen that is in the air is transferred to the bloodstream, and carbon dioxide is transferred out of the bloodstream into the air sack. The carbon dioxide is breathed out, and new oxygen-rich air is breathed in with each breath.

Pneumonia

When the lung tissue itself gets infected the condition is called *pneumonia*. Pneumonia frequently causes a fever and a dry hacking cough. Not all pneumonias cause a cough. The most severe infection can just manifest as a pale, very ill child with high fever and vomiting. Some pneumonias are viral and will resolve on their own, but pneumonias accompanied by high fever and toxicity usually require treatment with antibiotics. Pneumonias in the lower lobe of the lung can also cause abdominal pain. If pneumonia is suspected, a physician should be consulted.

Final thought

A child who coughs is usually not really ill. We can see by his color, appetite, and mood that nothing serious is going on. Most coughs clear with time. If lower airway disease is suspected, or if there is difficulty breathing that does not respond to medication, a physician should be consulted.

CHAPTER 57

Ear Problems in Children

Key Points

- Middle Ear problems — otitis media and serous otitis media — are often associated with runny noses.

- Dysfunction of the Eustachian tube and enlarged adenoids can cause middle ear disease.

- Fluid in the middle ear space can muffle hearing.

- The inner ear has the delicate hearing and balance mechanism, the cochlea.

- When the cochlea or the auditory nerve cause the hearing loss, the condition is called *nerve deafness*.

- Hearing aids are glasses for the ears. If they are needed they should be used!

- Cochlear implants can often allow deaf people to hear.

During infancy and childhood, many problems can arise with the ears. Some, like ear tags and malformed outer ears, are purely cosmetic. Some are painful but usually not serious, like swimmer's ear or otitis media. Some are painless but very serious, like congenital deafness. The following is an overview of the problems that can arise in children's ears.

The outer ear

When a baby is born, the ears are variable in appearance. Sometimes the left one looks like the father's and the right like the mother's! The *pinna* (the "cup" of the outer ear, which is made of cartilage and skin), can be big or small, flat or protruding. The normal variability is astounding.

Some babies are born with malformed outer ears. Most of these are only cosmetic abnormalities, but if the ear does not have an opening to the ear canal, or if

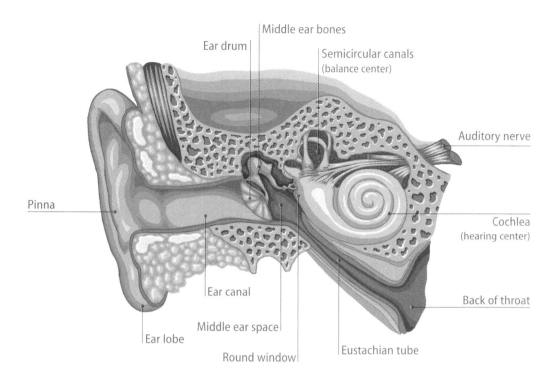

it is very small or rudimentary, there may be serious underlying hearing problems.

Many babies are born with *ear tags* near the *tragus* (the little bump of cartilage in front of the opening). These little extra pieces of skin can be easily removed by a surgeon. Since the kidneys form in the unborn baby at the same time as the ears, many doctors perform kidney sonograms on babies with ear tags, to make sure the kidneys are formed normally. Only a very small percentage of these sonograms are abnormal.

Another common congenital defect is **a tiny hole in the skin in front of the tragus.** This is called a *puncta*. The puncta is actually the opening of a tiny channel. In most cases it never causes a problem, but occasionally a creamy discharge comes out. If this causes an infection with swelling and redness, a physician must be consulted.

The *ear lobe* is the soft lower extension of the pinna. The most common problems seen with the ear lobes are *eczema* and *contact reactions to earrings*. Eczema can usually be treated with moisturizers or 1% hydrocortisone cream.

If the earrings are causing problems, it is usually due to sensitivity to nickel. Nickel is mixed with gold and silver to make those precious metals less brittle. Sometimes, switching to earring posts and backs made of stainless steel or 18-karat gold (which has less nickel) can help.

The ear canal

The *ear canal* is the tunnel from the opening in the outer ear that ends at the eardrum. There is a **natural wax** that forms in the ear canal. In most people it falls out by itself and causes no problem. If there is a lot of hair in the canal, which holds on to the wax, or if the wax becomes dry, it can accumulate and cause a blockage.

It is very important not to stick anything into the ear to remove wax. **Cotton swabs are very dangerous,** and they only push the wax further down. Peroxide-based eardrops such as Debrox or olive oil instilled into the ear with a dropper will soften the wax and help it fall out. Sometimes irrigation with an ear syringe and warm water is necessary.

After swimming, the ear canal sometimes feels blocked by water that has settled inside. A few drops of diluted rubbing alcohol will immediately cause the bubble that is holding the water to disintegrate, and the water will fall out. Many people use diluted vinegar for this purpose. If the water is not drained out, a skin infection called *swimmer's ear* can develop. This condition needs prescription eardrops and a physician must be consulted.

If severe pain in the ear canal occurs, the ear canal should be examined for a possible skin infection like cellulitis. Another very painful condition is a viral infection of the skin like *herpes simplex* or *shingles*. These can be treated with antiviral medication.

The eardrum

The *eardrum* is a thin, translucent window that separates the ear canal from the middle and inner ear spaces. It really looks like the covering on a drum. The bones of the middle ear can be seen through the eardrum. When sound waves enter the ear canal, the eardrum vibrates and conducts the sound to the *stapes bone* that is sitting on its inner surface.

The middle ear

The part of the ear that is immediately behind the eardrum is called the *middle ear.* The stapes bone conducts the sound waves to the two connecting bones inside the middle ear, and then on to the *round window,* which separates the middle ear space from the inner ear. In order for this process to function normally, there must be air behind the eardrum, filling the middle ear space. The air gets in via a tunnel, which connects the middle ear to the throat. This tunnel is called the *Eustachian tube.*

Most of the ear problems in the first three years of life occur in the middle ear. This is the part of the ear where fluid accumulates (a condition called serous otitis media), which can cause dampening of the hearing and infections (known as otitis media). The word "otitis" means inflammation of the ear, and the word "media" means middle.

The Eustachian tube

The most important factor in the healthy function of the middle ear is the Eustachian tube. When this tunnel is working, air goes up from the throat into the middle ear space, and any fluid that forms in the space drains down into the throat. When the tube is clogged, no air can get in, and fluid accumulates. The clogged tube does not allow the fluid, which forms naturally, to drain.

The result of this clogging is a middle ear that doesn't conduct sound waves efficiently. **The hearing can be reduced dramatically by this problem.** This is usually temporary hearing loss, since once the fluid is gone, the hearing returns to normal.

The fluid in the middle ear is usually sterile, but often germs get in and find a very good place to grow. When these germs increase in numbers, an infection develops. The trapped *pus* caused by the infection causes pain and difficulty eating and sleeping. This is otitis media. Even severely painful infections usually do not cause fever, since the space that is infected is very small. If an infection creates a hole (called a perforation) in the eardrum, the pus then drains out into the ear canal. One condition that causes Eustachian tube problems is a change in atmospheric pressure, such as the one experienced during landing in an airplane. In this condition, the Eustachian tubes can close down, causing painful pressure of the ears.

The other causes for the clogging and dysfunction of the Eustachian tube are the same as those that cause nasal congestion, since both areas are lined with similar mucous membranes. Cold viruses, and food or seasonal allergies that cause nasal congestion, are the usual culprits. In fact, it is very rare to see an ear infection in a child who has not had any nasal congestion.

It has recently been shown that *gastro-esophageal reflux* can be a cause for Eustachian tube dysfunction.

The adenoids

The adenoids, which are lymphoid tissue similar to the tonsils, sit very close to the opening of the Eustachian tube, behind the nasal passage in the upper throat. When adenoids are infected or chronically swollen, they can be the source of infection and dysfunction of the Eustachian tubes and the middle ear. Surgical removal of the adenoids is sometimes needed to resolve chronic ear problems.

Management of otitis media and serous otitis media

When infection develops in the middle ear space, the physician should be consulted. In children over one year of age, with early and not severe infections, it is usually good to wait and just treat the pain for 2 to 3 days, since 80 percent will recover on their own. If the condition worsens or does not resolve, antibiotics are prescribed. In infants under one year, in severe infections, or in a child who has needed antibiotics within the previous few weeks, antibiotics are usually prescribed.

As the infection clears, the fluid that caused it often clears up as well. It is a good idea to re-check the ear to make sure that the fluid is gone. Persistent fluid in the ears (serous otitis) indicates continued Eustachian tube dysfunction. Chronic fluid that doesn't drain for months at a time can become very thick, like glue, and the hearing can remain muffled. When this happens, or when infections keep recurring in the fluid, an Ear, Nose, and Throat surgeon (ENT) should be consulted.

The ENT surgeon can drain the ear during a surgical procedure and, at the same time, place ventilating tubes in the eardrum that maintain an air passage and drainage channel between the middle ear and the ear canal. These tubes bypass the problem by doing the job of the Eustachian tube. By the time they fall out, about one year later, the Eustachian tube function usually has returned to normal.

Most Eustachian tube problems occur in the first 3 years of life. This is because the Eustachian tubes in a small child are tilted in a vulnerable position. This corrects as the child grows. If a chronic runny nose is part of the problem, investigating the possibility of allergy may help resolve the problem.

The inner ear

The *inner ear* is the part of the ear that is closest to the brain. It is located just beyond the middle ear space on the other side of the round window. When a sound wave is conducted through the middle ear bones, it is transmitted through the round window and on to the real hearing mechanism of the ear. Inside this space there is a spiral, snail-shaped organ called the *cochlea*. The cochlea is a delicate organ that contains the nerve endings that pick up the sound waves and transmit them via a large nerve (the auditory nerve) to the hearing center of the brain. The balance center of the body is also found in the cochlea, in the structure known as the *semcircular canals*.

Dysfunction of the cochlea causes hearing loss and/or dizziness. Unlike the middle ear, this area does not fill up with fluid and does not get bacterial infections. Viral infections can sometimes affect the cochlea, usually causing a circular dizziness called *vertigo*. **The main symptom of cochlear dysfunction is hearing loss.**

Nerve deafness

Hearing loss caused by cochlear dysfunction or dysfunction of the nerve connecting the ear to the brain is called *nerve deafness*. This is sometimes present at birth and sometimes acquired during childhood or adulthood. When this happens, the person's hearing reception becomes unclear. Sometimes only certain sounds are not perceived, like very low tones, or very high, squeaky sounds, or very soft sounds like whispers. The more types and intensities of sound that are missed, the more severe the hearing problem is. Sometimes the hearing loss is progressive, starting off as mild and progressing to profound.

Hearing augmentation – "glasses for the ears"

To help a person hear more efficiently, augmentation devices are used. The type of assistance needed depends on the severity of the problem.

FM systems are radio devices that consist of a microphone mounted on the teacher's lapel and a receiver in the child's ears. This makes the teacher's voice louder and blocks out the classroom noises that might interfere.

Hearing aids filter and amplify sounds and transmit them to the ear's hearing mechanism. Modern hearing aids are tiny and not cosmetically obvious. There is no reason to avoid using them.

When a child who cannot hear well goes to school, it is very much like a child with nearsightedness who goes to school without glasses. He can manage to get around, but he cannot see clearly and cannot read the board. No one would prefer that he not wear his glasses. He cannot function well without them.

The same is true of a child who needs hearing aids. Not having them will consign him to fuzzy, indistinct hearing. This will cause frustration and poor performance. In very young children who have not yet learned to talk, it can cause terrible speech problems.

Cochlear implants

If the hearing is profoundly impaired, a new device called a *cochlear implant* can be surgically implanted into the area behind one ear. **This computerized modern miracle can give hearing to the deaf child.** Since the implant destroys the natural hearing mechanism on that side, it is only used when the hearing is so poor that this will not matter.

Since the invention of cochlear implants, the number of completely deaf people has dropped dramatically. Older implants had infection vulnerability, but the newer models are much safer in this regard.

Now that we understand all of the things that must work normally to have normal ear function, we have a profound appreciation for the Creator of this intricate mechanism.

Final thought

This overview of ear problems in children only touches upon the types of problems that children can encounter with their ears. As with any medical issues in children, a child's pediatrician should be consulted whenever problems arise.

CHAPTER 58

Understanding Group A Beta Hemolytic Strep (GABS)

We all know that "Strep" infections are very common in childhood. The bacteria *Group A Beta Hemolytic Strep* causes several types of illness. Here is an overview of the problems caused by Strep.

Diagnosing Strep

There are two diagnostic tests that can be performed in the doctor's office: Throat culture-and Rapid Strep tests. For the throat culture, the throat is swabbed with a long, sterile swab and the material obtained is placed on a blood agar plate. The plate is put in an incubator and observed after 24 and 48 hours. If there is growth of group A beta hemolytic strep colonies on the plate it is read as positive. If there are no strep colonies it is read as negative. In the rapid test, the material is tested for the presence of Group A beta hemolytic strep antigen. This test is completed in 10 minutes. If the rapid test is positive it is considered accurate. If it is negative, a throat culture should be done since it is more reliable, and it might show growth that was

Key Points

- Streptococcal pharyngitis (strep throat) is a common childhood infection

- Treatment with antibiotics can prevent later autoimmune complications such as rheumatic fever.

- Strep can be detected by throat swabs for rapid testing or culture.

- The presence of anti-strep antibodies in the blood does not mean there is an active infection, but it does indicate recent infection or exposure.

missed by the rapid test.

The illnesses caused by Strep are divided into two categories: *actual infections,* and *illnesses caused by the patient's immune response to the strep bacteria.*

INFECTIONS CAUSED BY STREP

Tonsillitis or pharyngitis — Strep throat

When Strep invades the tissues of the tonsils and throat, a typical illness occurs. In older children the typical symptoms are pain on swallowing, fever, malaise, headache and nausea. The lymph nodes in the region of the upper neck are swollen and tender. The tonsils are swollen and red, sometimes with pus evident on the surface. Joint pains in the knees and elbows are not uncommon.

In children under one year the infection often causes a runny nose and cough in addition to the sore throat

Scarlet fever

Certain strains of strep throat cause a red rash all over the body which has the texture of fine sandpaper. The area around the mouth is usually not involved. Peeling of the hands and feet is often noted after the illness subsides.

The treatment for these ordinary Strep infections is oral antibiotics. When antibiotics are given, the illness subsides and most of the suppurative complications, such as abcesses, are avoided.

Suppurative complications of strep throat

A more severe invasion by Strep can cause *lymph node abscess* in the neck, *retropharyngeal abscess* in the back wall of the throat or an abscess in the tissues next to the tonsil — *peritonsillar abscess.* These conditions often require surgical drainage and injectable or IV antibiotics. These rare complications can cause high fever, drooling, stiff neck, and sometimes respiratory compromise.

Strep Otitis (ear infection)

When Strep invades the middle ear space it can cause a very severe infection that often ruptures the ear drum within a day. Only about 15 percent of ear infections are caused by Strep. Occasionally the rapidly worsening ear infection can spread to the mastoid bone causing *mastoiditis.*

Strep Otitis is treated by oral antibiotics, but the dose is always high to allow the antibiotic to penetrate into the middle ear space and to cover for the other germs that might be causing the infection. Mastoiditis is treated with injectable or IV antibiotics and sometimes requires surgical drainage.

Strep sinusitis

Strep can invade the sinuses and cause headache, sinus pressure, cough and sometimes fever. This infection is rarely identified as Strep, since sinus cultures are rarely done. Bacterial sinusitis is treated with high-dose oral antibiotics and saline or medicated nasal sprays.

Strep Vulvitis

When strep invades the female genital tract it causes a thick yellow discharge with redness and irritation. The pus can be cultured and if Strep is identified it is treated with oral antibiotics. This infection does not usually cause fever.

Perianal Strep

When strep invades the tissues around the anus, a raw red ring of irritation forms. This painful condition rarely causes fever. It often presents in young children as toilet refusal or bath refusal. It is treated by mupiricin ointment.

Strep skin infections

When Strep invades the outer layers of the skin it causes *Impetigo*. This infection looks like an open, weeping sore with a golden crust. Impetigo can spread on the skin and can be spread to others. It usually starts in a scratch or bite that has broken the skin. Impetigo can be treated by the topical antibiotic mupiricin in the form of cream or ointment. If there are many lesions, or if they are in different areas of the skin, it is treated by oral antibiotics.

Strep Cellulitis

This infection is in the deeper layers of the skin. It is very red and painful, and often comes with high fever. Cellulitis is treated by antibiotics. Oral antibiotics are usually adequate, but very severe cases need injectable or intravenous doses.

Severe invasive strep infection — also called "man eating strep"

In the last several years there have been reports of deep skin infections that invade the muscles and the connective tissues in the area deeper than the skin infection.

These are life-threatening infections that can cause severe damage and scarring. These infections are rare and tend to be fulminating. They invade rapidly and cause high fever and extreme illness. The treatment often requires high dose antibiotics and surgery to drain the infection as quickly as possible.

Auto immune illnesses caused by Strep

If left *untreated,* the typical Strep throat would usually subside in about a week to ten days. The reason that these infections are always treated with antibiotics is that there is a rare immune reaction to the infection that can lead to severe complications. This is known as *Rheumatic Fever.* This complication does not usually occur if the infection is treated within ten days of its onset. Since Rheumatic Fever does not occur under two years of age, some physicians do not treat strep in children this young unless they are very ill.

When the immune system fights an infection, proteins known as *antibodies* are formed. These antibodies attack the invading germs to destroy them and prevent them from replicating. In some patients the immune response is misdirected and the antibodies attack their own tissues. The antibodies that fight strep can cause several illnesses.

Blood tests for antibodies

There are two antibodies that are measured to indicate an immune response to strep. The *ASLO* is one that rises during an infection or at the time of exposure and stays elevated for about three months. The *Anti DNASE B* antibody rises after the infection and can stay elevated for many months. The presence of the antibodies merely shows an immune response. The antibodies only cause illness very rarely. When they do cause problems, the illness is called *autoimmune.* This means that the person is producing immune antibodies that attack their own body's tissues.

Rheumatic Fever

In the condition known as *Rheumatic Fever,* anti strep antibodies can attack any or all of the following: the *heart valves,* the *joints,* the *nervous system,* and the *skin.* The *heart valves* can become thickened and full of calcium, causing them to malfunction. The damaged valves can cause severe derangements in cardiac function. This damage often requires open-heart surgery to correct.

The *joint pains* in Rheumatic Fever can be very intense. They migrate from joint to joint during the acute episode.

Sydenhams chorea, the neurological disorder of Rheumatic Fever, causes unrelenting restless movements, a balance disorder, and psychiatric symptoms such as OCD.

Erythema Marginatum, a fleeting rash, and *Rheumatic Nodules* are the skin manifestations of Rheumatic Fever.

Of all of the complications of Rheumatic Fever, the heart damage is the one that causes permanent damage. The other symptoms subside over a period of weeks.

Treatment of Strep infections within 10 days of the onset of symptoms can prevent the development of Rheumatic Fever.

Acute Post-streptococcal Glomerlulonephritis

Anti strep antibodies can attack the *kidneys* and cause cola-colored blood in the urine, high blood pressure and other signs of kidney dysfunction. The high blood pressure can sometimes cause neurological complications such as stroke or seizures. *Acute glomerulonephritis* is self limiting. It goes away in a few weeks and rarely causes kidney damage. The blood pressure must be monitored and treated until the condition subsides.

Acute Glomerulonephritis is rare. *It is not preventable with identification and treatment of strep.* The process is set in motion before the sore throat is evident.

Post-streptococcal arthritis

When the anti strep antibodies attack the joints , without migration of the pain and without other signs of rheumatic fever, the condition is known as post-strep arthritis. The joints can be slightly swollen, and the child complains of pain and often limps. This condition is usually mild. The treatment consists of ibuprofen or naproxen and watchful waiting. It usually clears within a few weeks.

PANDAS

Pediatric Autoimmune Neuropsychiatric Disorder Associated with Strep was described earlier in the book. The anti-Strep antibodies attack the basal ganglia of the brain causing tics, Obsessive Compulsive Disorder, and other psychiatric symptoms. The child has an abrupt onset of irritability and a mood disorder and/or tic disorder. There is usually a dramatic negative change in personality.

The treatment of this condition is controversial. Most pediatricians use antibiotics such as Augmentin or Zithromax. It is not yet clear whether treating a strep throat or preventing strep throats can prevent of this condition.

(I have written a more complete discussion of PANDAS in *Understanding Your*

Child's Health, Chapter 42 page 198)

Treatment of Strep infections

The Strep germ itself is sensitive to many antibiotics, including plain penicillin. Most doctors prefer to treat Strep throats with oral amoxicillin, which is better absorbed than penicillin. Ten days of this type medication is needed. The patient is not contagious after the first 24 to 48 hours on medication.

If there is penicillin allergy, cephalosporins such as cefalexin or cefodroxil are effective.

If there is allergy to both types of antibiotic then erythromycin, or biaxin or azithromycin can be used.

Recurrent infections

Some children experience many Strep infections a year. These can be due to incomplete treatment, repeated exposure to Strep at home or in school, or deep-seated infection that flares up as soon as the antibiotic is stopped.

Some physicians recommend removal of the tonsils if there are more than seven episodes in one year. I have found that tonsillectomy is rarely needed. The following year is usually not as bad.

Strep carriers

Some children always have positive throat cultures or Rapid Strep tests, even when they are not sick at all. These people are called Strep carriers. They have Strep on the surface of their tonsils but it does not invade and cause illness. There is a lot of confusion about what to do with Strep carriers. They are somewhat contagious. They do not seem to be prone to rheumatic fever or other complications. If they do come down with fever and sore throat it is not clear whether the infection is viral or the Strep itself.

Most physicians treat them only if they develop a Strep-like illness. The carrier state usually clears on its own in a few months. There are strong antibiotic treatment protocols that can eliminate the carrier state. These would be used if the family seems to be constantly infected by the carrier child.

Why no vaccine?

There have been many years of research into the possibility of a vaccine that would prevent Strep. Since the antibodies that would be produced by the vaccine are the same antibodies which can occasionally produce autoimmune problems, no vaccine that is reliable and safe has been developed yet.

Strep phobia

Many parents, especially in families which are known to have had Rheumatic Fever, are very worried about Strep. They will bring in the children with almost any symptom — sore throat, belly ache, limb pain, headache, fever or malaise – for throat cultures or Rapid Strep tests. Most of these children are not really sick and do not need to be tested. Experts feel that this approach will identify too many healthy carriers and result in over- use of antibiotics. However, in large families, in day care centers, and in crowded schools there is a high rate of actual Strep infections, especially during the school year. For this reason, many physicians are more liberal in allowing their patients to have throat cultures and Rapid Strep tests when they are requested.

Final thought

Strep throats have been a part of childhood for many years. The vast majority of patients do fine no matter what we do for them. At this point in time, the experts recommend that we only test and plan to treat sick children who have typical Strep symptoms. This is probably the wisest approach except in families where autoimmune conditions have occurred.

CHAPTER 59

Lice, Worms, and Scabies
Unpleasant, *but not tragic*, infestations in children

Key Points

- Head lice can be found in any children, even those who live in the cleanest homes.

- Pinworms occur in one out of five healthy children and only cause symptoms in a small percentage of them.

- Scabies is caused by a small bug that burrows under the skin. Symptoms only occur when the child becomes allergic to them.

- These annoying infestations are treatable and not serious.

We live in a modern, clean environment, and we do not expect to have insects and worms plaguing the lives of our children. The fact is, however, that head lice, pinworms, and scabies are common in school children in every community. As clean as we are, these bugs are everywhere! Here is an overview of infestations and how to treat them.

Head lice

Head lice are so common that nearly one in four schoolchildren is infested every year. These tiny, fast-moving insects prefer clean hair and are a common problem, even in very clean home and school environments. The lice can scoot very quickly from head to head and can be spread by sharing hats, combs, brushes, headbands, and ribbons. They can also spread by sharing pillows and headrests. They feed on the scalp by sucking blood through tiny bites that itch like mosquito bites.

The adult female louse lays approximately ten eggs a day for about one month before she dies. These eggs are glued to the hair shaft near the scalp. The eggs and their casings are called *nits*. The nits stay glued to the hair shaft after the tiny insect hatches. They turn white and are easier to see after hatching. The new insect, known as a nymph, grows to full maturity in ten days and starts laying eggs.

Treatments

Many treatments have been tried to remove head lice infestations. For many years it was common to put Vaseline, mayonnaise, butter, and other thick, greasy substances in the hair in an effort to smother the lice. This method was very messy and it was not effective, since it is almost impossible to smother lice.

Tea tree oil, olive oil, and other oil-based treatments have also been used with variable results.

Chemical pesticides, such as Qwell, Nix, and Rid, which actually kill the lice and eggs, were the treatment of choice until about ten years ago. Since that time, many of the lice have become resistant to almost all of the pesticides. These extremely strong lice first appeared in the Middle East, particularly Israel. It is not surprising that the first place in the United States to experience these superbugs was Brooklyn.

In the past ten years, there have also been reports of toxic effects of Lindane (Qwell) on children, so the safety of these drugs is in question.

Today, only one lice-killing drug is still considered effective and safe – Malathion (Ovide). This drug was removed from the market years ago because it smelled so terrible that no one would use it. Ovide was recently released in a better-smelling formulation. It must be left on the hair overnight.

In the last few years, another method, "wet combing," has been found to be effective in treating head lice. The hair is saturated with conditioner that has a silicone base. The conditioner loosens the grip of the glue that attaches the nits to the hair shaft. The lice and eggs are combed out in a careful and systematic fashion with a specially designed lice comb that has a V-shaped notch between each tooth. This method does not kill the lice at all, so care must be taken when disposing of the combed-out material. This task is tedious, especially in long hair. A whole new industry has developed, with people who will perform lice removal for a fee. Lice ladies and lice salons have appeared in every community.

Since the lice problem is ubiquitous – in every school, camp, and dormitory – it is wise to check children's hair periodically and remove any lice or nits that have appeared.

Pinworms

Pinworms are small white worms that live in the human intestine. They do not cause illness. Many healthy people live their whole lives with pinworms and never even notice them. The problem with pinworms is that they can cause a lot of discomfort. The most common symptom is itching around the anal opening, or in the genital tract in girls. The adult female worms come out at night to lay their eggs in these warm, moist areas.

The worms can also be a source of vague abdominal pain that is not associated with any real gastrointestinal problem. It can also cause genital discomfort in boys.

Pinworms are very contagious. The eggs that are laid around the anus can be picked up under the fingernails if the person scratches the itchy area. These tiny microscopic eggs are shed into the child's pajamas and underwear and onto the bed linens. Just shaking out the bed linen of an infested child can put thousands of eggs into the air and dust in the room. Wherever they land, they can be picked up by fingers. Nail biting, thumb sucking, and just eating with the tiny invisible eggs on the fingers can spread the infection.

Prevention of pinworms includes these basic measures: keeping fingernails short, stopping hand-to-mouth habits, washing hands thoroughly before eating, vacuuming playrooms, and washing pajamas, underwear, and bed linens in hot water.

Treatment

Pinworms are so contagious in the home setting that many doctors treat the whole family if they treat one child. The treatments consist of anti-parasitic medications, mebendazole (Vermox), albendazole, or pyrantell (Pin-X). These drugs are given once and then again in two weeks. It takes about two days to note relief of the itching after taking the medication. The treatments can be given repeatedly if re-infestation occurs.

There have been many herbal and folk remedies used over the centuries for pinworms. There are no clinical trials published on their usage, so it is hard to know what really works. Fresh garlic seems to work as a preventive treatment. The garlic cloves can be crushed in a garlic press, and a small amount of the juice can be added to food. The child should eat enough of this essence that his breath smells of garlic after the food is eaten. Garlic toast with the garlic added to the butter is usually accepted well by the child. Since the worms seem to be intolerant of the garlic, it would be a good idea to give the fresh garlic at least two to three times a week in a family which is experiencing the problem.

A study done in a very wealthy school district in Texas showed that one out of five healthy (and wealthy) school children has pinworms, and only one out of ten of the infested children has any symptoms from the infestation. This means that pinworms are really everywhere, so there is no point in worrying about them. Most infested kids are between the ages of three and ten. As they get older, they give up their hand-to-mouth habits, so the pinworm problem is less common in older children.

Scabies

Mites, which are tiny insects, burrow under the skin and cause a reactive rash known as *scabies*. The insect is so tiny that it cannot be seen without a microscope. The scabies rash consists of tiny, red, raised dots that are found in straight lines, about 1/4 to 1/2 inch apart from each other. The pattern of these lines can be straight or curved. The lines look like a "connect the dots" design.

The lines of dots can appear anywhere in young children – hands, legs, trunk, even the face. In older kids and adults, they usually appear in the backs of the hands and track up the arms. They can also be found on the trunk, or anywhere else as the rash spreads. The most common complaint is that the rash is intensely itchy at night.

The scabies rash takes four to six weeks to develop after the mite gets into the skin. The rash is really an allergic reaction to the bug, its eggs, and its waste products. The mite burrows under the skin, laying eggs and making waste as it moves on. The skin over these materials becomes irritated after the immune system begins producing antibodies against the mites.

Mites are contagious. They can be spread by skin-to-skin contact and by clothing, bedding, towels, and other materials. Once scabies is diagnosed, the pajamas, clothing, towels, and bedding should be washed in hot water and dried in hot dryers.

Treatment

There have been some natural scabies remedies suggested. Tea tree oil added to the bath water might work, but it has to be a 15-minute bath every night for three weeks. Other remedies are equally tedious and time-consuming.

Standard medical treatment of scabies consists of one application of an anti-parasitic medication lotion, permethrin (Elimite). A second application one week later is also suggested. This lotion is applied to the entire skin surface and left on overnight. Permethrin actually kills the mites and cures the problem. The rash, however, can still be present for up to one month after treatment. It may persist until the body eliminates all of the byproducts of the dead mites from under the skin. Anti-itch medications and lotions can be used. Sometimes the doctor will advise the use of cortisone creams on the areas that are persistently itchy.

Some doctors treat the whole family if scabies appears in one child. I usually just warn the contacts that if they develop an itchy rash that lasts for more than one week, they should be seen by a doctor.

Scabies is an inconvenience and can be really uncomfortable, but it rarely causes serious problems. Skin that has been severely scratched can develop *impetigo*, a crusted pustular infection, when germs invade. This condition needs medical attention.

Final thought

When a problem such as lice, worms, or scabies turns up in the family, it is not a tragedy, and it is not a reason to clean the entire house as if Pesach is coming!! Cool, logical assessment will point to the necessary tasks, such as washing linens and clothing. Remember, whatever the child picked up can be picked up again in school, no matter how clean your house is. You cannot be in complete control. Just deal with it as it comes along, and know that "this too shall pass."

CHAPTER 60

The Urinary Tract

The Kidneys

The kidneys are *vital organs* - we need our kidneys to live.

(The word renal is a synonym for kidney, the word nephron is the functional unit in the kidney)

As blood pumps through the kidneys from the renal artery it is cleansed and regulated. The nephrons in the kidneys-provide a filtering system that *removes wastes* from the blood stream, *maintains water balance* and helps *maintain acid and sugar balance*. Kidneys are also critical in *controlling blood pressure*. The by-product of this system is *urine*. Once it is produced, the urine must be eliminated from the body.

The *renal pelvis* or *collecting system* is the area in the kidney where the urine is collected before being channeled down to the *ureters*.

The *ureters* are the long tube like structures that conduct the urine from the kidneys to the *bladder*. The lower ends of the ureters channel through the bladder wall and empty into the bladder.

Key Points

- UTIs occur equally in boys and girls for the first few weeks of life.
- UTIs occur mostly in girls after early infancy.
- Upper UTIs cause high fever and serious illness.
- LowerUTIs cause bladder discomfort and problems with bladder control.

The *bladder* is the hollow expandable receptacle, which is made of layers of muscle. The bladder collects urine from both ureters and holds it until ready to release it. The releasing process is called *voiding*. The bladder's sphinchter muscle is allowed to open and the bladder muscles contract to eject the urine through the *urethra.*

The *urethra* is the tube like structure which connects the bladder to the outside.

Congenital defects

There are some defects of the urinary tract that are present from birth. These can sometimes be detected before birth during ultrasound evaluation. One kidney may be in a dropped position, or one of them could be missing. Sometimes one of the kidneys may be enlarged due to poor drainage. These defects are often not serious. One kidney is adequate to maintain good health. Most of these children grow up healthy and fine.

Urinary tract infections — UTIs

There are two tests that are done on the urine.

The first — the *urine analysis* – can be done by a dip stick screening or microscopic analysis, both of which can give immediate results.

The second — *urine culture* — actually has to incubate at least 1 to 3 days to reveal the bacteria.

Upper and lower

The urinary tract can be infected in either the lower or upper region. Infections of the *bladder and urethra* are called lower urinary tract infections. Infections in the *kidneys and ureters* are called upper urinary tract infections. These infections have different symptoms and different treatments,

Lower UTIs

Bladder infections present with symptoms of poor bladder control, urinary frequency, urgency, bladder pain, and pain on urination.

This pain is often more intense at the end of urination. The infected urine is often cloudy and foul smelling. The *urine analysis* usually shows the presence of blood, pus and bacteria, and the cultures reveal the actual bacteria within two days. Lower UTIs rarely cause fever. They are more common in girls than in boys.

Upper UTIs

Kidney infections in children and adolescents usually present with high fever, nausea, vomiting, abdominal pain and back pain. Because the kidney itself is infected, the Upper UTI can be extremely dangerous. The bacteria causing the infection can get into the bloodstream and cause life-threatening septicemia. If the infection is not treated quickly, and completely it can leave scars in the kidney. In a child, the scars can cause the kidney not to grow properly. This can result in high blood pressure and decreased kidney function as the child grows up.

Upper UTIs in infants

In the first few weeks of life, the newborn infant is vulnerable to infection. The newborn who develops a fever, or a weak cry, poor suck, or excessive sleepiness needs to be evaluated for infection. Since UTIs are the most common infection in this age group, a urine test must be obtained by catheter. The insertion of the catheter (which is not dangerous or painful) ensures that the urine is taken directly from the bladder without contamination. In very young infants, the urine might not appear to be infected on the urine analysis, but the culture reveals a growth of bacteria indicating infection. The incidence of this infection is the same in boys and in girls.

Treatment of UTIs

Since UTIs are bacterial infections the treatment consists of sulfa medications or antibiotics. In upper UTIs the first doses are usually given by intravenous or intramuscular injection. Lower UTIs can be treated by oral medication.

The cultured bacteria can be tested to indicate which medications will be most effective. This test, called *sensitivity,* takes one day longer than the culture.

Flushing the urinary tract with a high intake of fluids is recommended in UTIs. Cranberry extract has been shown to be helpful in preventing the bacteria from clinging to the bladder.

Constipation can increase the risk of bladder problems, so this condition should be treated to improve urinary health. Also, any child who holds back urine should be trained to empty promptly and properly.

Follow up testing

After recovering from an upper UTI, it is important for the child to have two tests done.

The *Renal Sonogram* gives a complete picture of the structure of the urinary tract. It will show the position and size of the kidneys and it will reveal major structural abnormalities that may have led to the infection.

The *VCUG* test is done by filling the bladder with contrast material and then taking an image during voiding. This will show if the urine is ejected completely from the bladder. If any urine backs up the ureters towards the kidney, the diagnosis of *bladder reflux* is made. About 15 percent of the children tested actually have this condition.

Bladder reflux

Bladder reflux is graded as grade I, II, III, IV, or V, according to the extent of the reflux. This condition can lead to recurrent upper UTIs. The children who have grades I or II or sometimes III bladder reflux often outgrow it by about 4 years of age.. In high grade reflux – grades IV to V – surgery or an endoscopic procedure is often needed to correct it.

In any reflux patient the child's urine should be tested whenever there is fever or undiagnosed systemic illness. For years, most of these children were placed on low-dose antibiotic prophylaxis to prevent infection. This practice has been questioned lately, so there is a controversy among doctors whether or not to use prophylaxis. Most doctors still use it in very young infants.

Hydronephrosis

Hydronephrosis is dilitation of the collecting system and/or the ureter, caused by a blockage of the drainage somewhere in the urinary tract. Kidney stones can sometimes be a cause. Congenital anomalies can pinch off the outflow from the kidney. These sometimes require surgery. This problem is usually not severe. If a narrowing is mild it is often outgrown with time.

Rare conditions

There are many rare conditions which can occur in children, such as large cysts, stones, tumors, and functional abnormalities like renal tubular acidosis, nephrosis and nephritis. There are two types of specialists that treat kidney and urinary tract issues in children.

The *pediatric nephrologist* is a medical specialist who treats kidney function disorders and high blood pressure in children.

The *pediatric urologist* is a surgeon who treats structural problems, including congenital defects and bladder reflux in children. Bladder control problems are often treated by PAs or Nurse Practitioners in the pediatric urologist's office.

Final Thought

In past generations infections of the kidneys often led to kidney damage and even death. We are truly fortunate to live in a time when these infections can be easily treated. It is important to remember that any child who has had a kidney infection needs careful follow-up and rapid treatment of recurrences.

CHAPTER 61

Understanding MRSA

Key Points

- MRSA is a germ that grows on healthy people's skin.

- MRSA first developed in hospital patients and recently started appearing in the healthy population.

- MRSA is very resistant to most antibiotics, tends to be invasive, and can cause serious infections.

- There is no real prevention, but "diluted-bleach baths" can help reduce the problem in families with MRSA infections

As time goes by, we are often faced with new infectious diseases that were previously not seen.

One major source of new diseases is the development of resistant organisms. These are germs that have developed resistance to antibiotics after years of repeated exposure to these drugs. One such infection, MRSA has recently moved from the hospital setting to the community.

MRSA: Where did it come from?

The germ *Staph Aureus* has long been known to cause skin infections. Until recently these were relatively easy to treat. Unfortunately, a very invasive and powerful strain of Staph Aureus has developed recently.

For years these very strong bacteria were only found in patients in hospitals. The germs gradually developed resistance to multiple antibiotics, including Methicillin, a drug that was developed specifically to cure tougher Staph infections. Many powerful antibiotics were given in high doses to the sick, hospitalized patients.

In the last few years we have begun seeing infections with MRSA all over our community in healthy patients who had not been in the hospital.

This germ is not just resistant. It is very invasive, meaning it is much more likely to cause severe infection than its less-resistant cousins that used to live on our skin.

Multidrug (and Methicillin) Resistant Staph Aureus (MRSA) is an organism that can live on healthy skin in healthy people without ever causing a problem. When the skin is broken, it can invade and create a severe infection. This infection appears as cellulitis — a painful redness which enlarges rapidly. MRSA can also infect the deeper layers of the skin, causing abscess formation. An abscess is a firm, painful mass which is actually a pocket of pus under pressure inside the skin. Many people with MRSA infections have fever and are generally ill.

Treatment

The treatment for these serious infections includes taking antibiotics and drainage of the abscesses. The problem is that this germ is very likely to develop resistance to any antibiotic that is used to treat it. Constant surveillance by specialists helps determine which antibiotic will be effective at any given time.

MRSA has arrived in our world. It is now living on the skin of most healthy people in our community. It is now part of our normal skin flora. We are "colonized."

Family hygiene

There is no real way to prevent infection by MRSA once colonization has occurred. It seems that some families are more prone to clinical infection .When more than one person in the family has had an MRSA infection it is a good idea to try to decrease the actual numbers of germs living on everyone's the skin. This can be done by giving a weekly "bleach bath." Add 1/4 cup of bleach to a full bath and soak for 10 minutes. The bleach is not bad for the skin when diluted this way. It actually softens the skin. The tub will smell like a swimming pool.

Recognizing and treating MRSA-type infections

When any area of skin becomes very tender, red and warm, MRSA should be suspected. If the infection is small and on the surface of the skin, the topical antibiotic mupirocin can be applied 3 times a day. If the redness spreads, or if fever develops, or if a red line or streak appears, originating from the infection, a physician should be consulted. If a hard red pimple forms that is very tender to the touch, moist heat —

including baths or compresses — should be applied to try to allow a "point" to form, which can be drained. If it drains out and the area gets smaller, no antibiotics are usually needed. If it does not drain, and a firm and tender area continues to enlarge and deepen, a physician should be consulted.

Complications

MRSA infections can worsen very quickly. Once an infection is suspected, moist heat should be applied and the area should be monitored carefully.

Although most MRSA infections resolve with treatment, it is possible for the germ to invade the bloodstream and settle in a bone, a joint, or even in the brain, causing serious illness. If high fever develops or if there is illness with limping, bone pain, or joint swelling, a physician should be consulted. These more serious infections often require hospitalization and intravenous antibiotics.

Final thought

Although we are doing our best to control MRSA when it causes infections, we are humbled by one serious fact. Modern science thought it could eliminate infection by producing stronger antibiotics. We have learned from MRSA that the germs are smarter than we are. They are survivors.

New approaches will have to be developed to avoid the development of super bugs like MRSA. In the future, we will probably have to have a completely different method. Maybe we will be able to produce protective "good " germs which will limit the colonization of the bad ones. Meanwhile we must try very hard not to overuse antibiotics. We now see it is up to us to limit the development of these resistant organisms.

Injuries and Trauma

CHAPTER 62

Head Injuries

Throughout a child's life there are many opportunities to receive a bump on the head. Most of these injuries are minor, but it is important to know when to worry. The following is an overview of head injuries in children.

Prevention of serious head injury: helmets

There is one type of head injury that is potentially serious and could be prevented. That is falling off a bike and hitting the pavement with the head. Since this type of injury has a fall from a height, and an impact on a very hard surface, the chance of real damage is great. The best way to prevent this problem is to *always wear a helmet* when riding a bike. Helmets, when properly fitted and worn can be extremely effective in preventing brain damage. The concept of wearing helmets should be consistently linked to riding a bike or skating so that the child puts one on automatically whenever he gets on his bike or *any rolling equipment*. Just like using seatbelts and car seats in the car, this habit is a real lifesaver.

Key Points

- Helmets prevent serious head injury in rolling sports.
- In children bumps on the forehead and back of head cause less injury than bumps on the side of the head.
- Loss of consciousness and vomiting can be signs of serious head trauma.
- Repeated head trauma soon after an incident can lead to more serious injury.

Minor head trauma

Infants and toddlers often bump their heads as they explore and exercise with high levels of energy and low levels of caution. If the injury is caused by a minor fall or bump and only causes small bruises, and if the child recovers immediately after the initial crying, there is no need for concern.

Mechanism of traumatic brain injury

Injury to the brain occurs when the impact to the skull causes the brain to bump into the inside of the skull. In general, a hard object flying or falling and striking the head is much less likely to cause injury than the head itself moving and striking a hard object like the floor.

The seriousness of the injury depends on the actual conditions of the fall or head bump. Certainly, being struck by a car or bike, or falling from a high place, puts the child at higher risk. The height of the fall is important. Falls from over 5 feet high are more likely to be serious. The surface that the head strikes is also an important factor. Concrete, asphalt, marble, stone and ceramic are more likely to cause injury than linoleum, wood, and carpeting.

The location of the injury on the head is also important. Bruises lumps and bumps can be seen after a bump on the head. If the bruise is on the forehead there is usually very little concern.

Shaken Baby Syndrome

An infant's brain can be seriously injured when a caregiver shakes the baby hard repeatedly, causing the brain to be bumped inside the skull with each shake. There is no external sign of trauma, but there are often blood spots in the baby's eyes when an opthalmoscopic examination is performed. The baby can appear dazed or not alert. The development might be delayed. *This injury is a sign of child abuse.*

SKULL FRACTURES

Basic signs of skull fractures

Signs of skull fracture at the base of the skull:
- "raccoon eyes"
- blue bruise behind ear
- fluid running out of one side of nose

- blue blood behind the eardrum (seen through an otoscope)

Signs of fractures of the skull bones:
- the bruise is on the side of the head, particularly above the ear
- the bruise is very large
- jello-like lumps

Most normal head bruises are hard and the size and shape of a small nut or olive. If there is an enlarging *soft jello-like area* in the scalp over the side of the head, there might be a skull fracture. This type of lump might take several hours or even days to be noticed, since it grows slowly.

Children with fractures *who do not have signs of brain injury* are rarely seriously injured, but they need to be seen in an emergency room if a fracture is suspected. Occasionally the fracture is indented and can cause pressure on the brain. This injury might require surgery.

Most skull fractures do not need treatment unless they are associated with signs of serious head injury.

Non-serious head injury

Basic criteria:
- child is acting normally
- no loss of consciousness
- no cognitive impairment (like memory loss or confusion)
- mechanism of injury was not serious (height of fall, surface, etc.)
- the bruises are only on the forehead
- no signs of fracture
- no vomiting

When these criteria are met, the injury is considered *not serious*. Vomiting immediately after the fall is normal, *but if there are repeated episodes of vomiting, a more serious problem is suspected. The child should be taken to the emergency room for closer evaluation.*

Concussion — mild traumatic brain injury

When the brain actually experiences physical trauma from the injury, the condition is called a *concussion*. This means that the brain itself has been shaken up and is experiencing some dysfunction from the injury.

Signs of concussion:
- loss of consciousness
- loss of memory of the event
- confusion, disorientation
- not responsive to questioning or commands
- headache
- vomiting

If a toddler cries and has a breath-holding spell at the time of the fall, the child might faint and lose consciousness from the spell. This loss of consciousness is *not* considered a symptom of brain injury if the breath-holding is witnessed by a responsible observer.

The treatment for concussion without signs of fracture is just observation. The child should regain his normal functions within a few minutes of the injury. If the child is sleepy it is okay to allow him to sleep, and there is no need to waken periodically.

Serious traumatic brain injury

If serious injury is suspected, a CT scan is done to look for bleeding in the brain.

The signs of serious head injury:
- vomiting
- headache not responding to acetomenophen
- *continued* altered mental status
- signs of fracture

If the CT scan reveals blood in the brain, careful assessment is done to see if emergency surgery is needed. *The two categories of bleeding are subdural bleeding and epidural bleeding.* Many times the *subdural* bleeding is minor and the patient can be just observed. If the bleeding is *epidural,* surgery is often required urgently.

Follow-up of head trauma

When a child has experienced a minor brain injury or concussion, there can be several weeks of headaches on and off. If these headaches are severe, or if they are increasing in frequency and intensity, a neurologist should be consulted. Irritability for the first week after a concussion is common, but if the child does not recover his personality quickly, a neurologist should be consulted.

Second-impact syndrome

The big issue we have to deal with is the chance of a concussion being followed by another trauma to the head before it the brain is properly healed. Even thought the child feels fine, it takes a few weeks for the brain to recover from the injury. *During that time the brain is vulnerable to more serious injury if it is injured again*. It is advisable to restrict the child's play to quiet activities for at least two weeks after the injury. Swimming is okay if there is careful restriction to running around in the pool area. No running and jumping. No playing on slides and swings. No climbing. Sports activity should be curtailed. This might seem a bit overcautious, but it is the right thing to do.

In contact sports like football and basketball, the restrictions should be extended to at least one month.

As in all injuries, prevention is better than cure. Bike helmets worn for all rolling sports, seat belts and car seats, basic street safety training, and common sense can prevent many serious head injuries. Although most head injuries are not serious, repeated vomiting and any change in the child's cognitive function should be considered a cause for immediate attention.

■ ■ ■

CHAPTER 63

Injuries to the Muscles and Bones

Key Points

- Sprains are not very painful initially but become swollen and painful after a day or two.
- Fractures are very intensely painful initially, and they become discolored and swollen immediately.
- Dislocations like Nursemaid's Elbow need immediate attention.

Children are very active and they frequently experience injuries to the bones and joints. Parents and caregivers are often unsure how serious the injury is and whether it needs medical attention. The following is an overview of bone and joint injuries, and guidelines on how to assess these injuries.

Sprains and strains

When a child injures an area around a joint, such as a finger or ankle, the injury is usually a *sprain*. The ligaments can be over-stretched and sometimes small tears occur. This injury often only hurts a little or very briefly when it happens and the child will go on playing or running with minimal complaint. Later, as the tissues swell up, the injury becomes black and blue and the region becomes swollen.

Limping and favoring the joint is common for the first few days after a sprain. Elevating a sprain and applying cold compresses the first day is somewhat helpful, but most kids do not cooperate with this treatment. Sprains heal on their own.

Ankle sprains that cause a lot of swelling and pain should be given medical attention. Sometimes an ace bandage or ankle brace is needed and, occasionally crutches are prescribed until the healing is in a more advanced stage.

Sprained fingers can be splinted by taping two fingers together or by the application of a supportive splint. If the finger looks deformed or if it cannot move normally, a doctor should be consulted within three days.

Fractures

A fracture is actually a break in the bone itself. Some fractures are only cracks in the surface, some go through only part of the bone, and some actually break the bone into two separate parts.

When a fracture occurs, the pain is usually very intense. The impact can be so painful that the child can scream or even faint from the pain. This pain does not pass quickly, so it is hard to console the child. The pain often causes the child to be unable to sleep, even with pain medications.

The area over the fracture often swells up immediately and turns black and blue quickly. All fractures are very tender, so any pressure applied to the area causes severe pain.

Treatment

The treatment for non-displaced fractures is usually *immobilization*. The bones will heal themselves if the edges are close together. This process usually takes a few weeks. The purpose of *casts and splints* is to keep the bones in a good position for healing. They also prevent further injury while the bones heal.

Another device, the *external fixator,* or *x fix,* is sometimes placed during surgical repair of more-serious fractures. This is a brace that is screwed into the bone, brought out through the skin and attached to a metal external brace. The *x fix* usually secures the bones during healing and no cast is needed. There is a risk of infection with this device, and it must be kept clean as directed.

During the first few days after a fracture, pain control is very important. The doctor might even prescribe narcotics like codeine or morphine until the acute pain subsides.

Clavicle fractures

The most commonly fractured bone in the body is the collar bone, or clavicle. This is the bone that reaches from the notch at the base of the neck, across the front of the shoulder, to the just before the top of the arm. This bone is often injured by a fall off a bed, chair or couch when the child lands on his side. The injury is not always visible, but it can be suspected when the child cries *when he is picked up under his arms* ("shrugging the shoulder") or *when the arm is lifted above the shoulder* when pulling off or putting on a shirt. A baby will often refuse to crawl because of the pain. Gently pressing on the clavicle inch by inch can often locate the fracture by feeling for swelling or a crunchy sensation, or by causing the child to cry or wince when the fracture is touched.

Most clavicle fractures heal without treatment. If a fracture is suspected, a doctor should be consulted. Sometimes a clavicle strap can make the child more comfortable, and sometimes strong pain killers are needed for the first few days and nights.

Rib fractures

Rib fractures are not common in children. They occur in real trauma such as car accidents. Unexplained fractures of the posterior ribs can be a sign of child abuse.

ARM-BONE FRACTURES

Humerus fractures

The *humerus* is the long bone in the upper arm. It rarely fractures unless there has been a serious impact injury, like a car accident. Occasionally a trivial injury will cause a fracture of the humerus. This is usually due to an unsuspected congenital bone cyst defect which is fragile and prone to fracture. The cyst usually disappears during the healing of the fracture.

Elbow fractures

When a traumatic *elbow injury* is very painful and swollen, *medical attention should be sought immediately.* Although many elbow injuries are not serious, there is a critically important nerve that passes over a groove in the elbow joint that can be injured if the fracture entraps it. This nerve affects the function of the hand. For this reason, elbow injuries require immediate evaluation in an emergency center or orthopedic office.

Wrist fractures

Wrist fractures are also very common during childhood. This injury occurs when the child falls forward and he breaks his fall by landing on his hands. The injury, called a *Colles fracture,* happens when the wrist bones buckle under the force of the impact.

These fractures often only require splinting to prevent further injury until healing is complete. If the wrist bones are actually displaced, they might need emergency orthopedic intervention.

Finger fractures and dislocations

Most finger injuries are sprains. The finger can be swollen but usually is not distorted in shape. The finger can be splinted by taping it to the adjacent finger or by applying a pop-stick or finger splint. If the finger swelling and pain is not much improved in two to three days, medical attention should be sought.

When a finger injury results in a distortion of the shape of the finger, especially at a joint, medical attention should be sought to evaluate for fracture or dislocation.

LEG BONE FRACTURES

Femur fractures

The thigh bone, also called the *femur,* is a very strong bone. It only fractures when there is a strong impact such as in a car accident or a fall from a height. In infants the most common mechanism of injury for a femur fracture is having an adult fall while carrying the baby. The adult falls on top of the baby, causing a heavy weight to be added to the baby's impact. The infant with a fracture of the femur might hold his leg in a flexed position and cry whenever he is moved.

This is a very serious injury which requires immediate orthopedic attention. Often surgery is required and body casts are sometimes required for proper healing.

Tibia fractures

The *tibia* is the larger bone in the lower leg, sometimes called the shin bone. It is attached to a thinner bone, the *fibula.* Fractures of these bones are common when a child falls hard on a twisted leg. These fractures are very painful and they usually require casting.

Knee injuries

The knee joint is mostly ligaments and cartilage, so fractures are unusual. If a knee is injured and swelling occurs, medical help should be sought within 24 to 48 hours.

These injuries usually heal on their own, but splints might be needed. If cartilage and/or ligaments are torn, surgery is sometimes required.

Toe and foot fractures

Toe and foot bones can be fractured when they hit, or are hit by, a hard object. The pain is very intense when these bones are broken. Most of these fractures are not treated by casting, but special boots are sometimes prescribed for walking to relieve pressure on the fracture while walking. If a fracture is suspected a doctor should be consulted within 24 to 48 hours.

DISLOCATIONS

"Nursemaid's Elbow"

When a child under 3 suddenly stops using one arm, often after a pulling injury, a condition known as "Nursemaid's Elbow" should be suspected. A simple maneuver can be performed by a doctor or other experienced person to restore the elbow to normal function. This is not a sprain, it is slight dislocation (called a *subluxation*) of a ligament that fits in a groove in the elbow.

Dislocated shoulder

This injury usually occurs during sports activity. The pain and disability are noted immediately. The shoulder will appear uneven, with a boney bulge where the head of the humerus is evident. Dislocated shoulders should be seen immediately by an orthopedist or in an emergency center. After repositioning the shoulder, the arm is immobilized for several weeks. The shoulder may need surgery at a later date to prevent further injury.

Hip dislocation in newborns

This condition is *never* related to trauma. *Congenital dysplasia of the hip* is a congenital condition in which socket of the hip joint is not properly formed. The baby can be born with a hip dislocation or a tendency for the hip to dislocate. This diagnosis is confirmed by hip sonogram. The treatment of CDH is a strap or harness which maintains the baby's leg in a hip-flexed position until the socket matures at around 4 months of age.

Final thoughts

Many children experience injuries to the bones and joints from the natural activity of childhood. In general, injuries that are *very painful, swollen* and *disclolored at the time of the injury* are more likely to be fractures. Injuries that are only painful the next day are more likely to be sprains. Ice packs and elevation are good for all injuries, but they are difficult to administer to children. The most important task is to give pain relief and objectively assess the injury. Medical help should be sought within 24 to 48 hours if a small bone fracture or dislocation is suspected. Suspected fracture of the femur, elbow, and tibia require immediate attention.

CHAPTER 64

Skin Injuries: Bruises, Scrapes, Cuts and Lacerations

Key Points

- Skin injuries can be burns, cuts or abrasions.

- Injured skin is prone to infection so wounds must be properly cleaned

- First-degree burns (redness only) need no medical attention

- Second-degree burns (blistered or loss of skin) need treatment by a physician or burn unit, depending on the size of the burn

- Third-degree burns need hospital (burn unit) management

Injuries like bruises and cuts are a normal part of childhood. Most injuries are minor and are easily handled by the caregiver. The following is an overview of the topic of injuries to the child's skin. It provides guidelines on how to assess an injury and decide how it should be treated.

Bruises

A bruise, or hematoma, is an accumulation of blood that has escaped from small blood vessels and leaked into the tissues under the skin. Most bruises are not at all serious. Bruising usually occurs when there is blunt trauma from falling or hitting a hard object. Most bruises are noted over boney areas like the shins or knees or foreheads. Most active kids have bruises on their shins. Most babies who are starting to stand or walk have bruises on the forehead, arms and legs. When there is significant bruising on the softer parts of the body like the shoulder or back or upper arms, or when the bruise is very large, like the size if the palm of the hand, medical attention should be sought.

In most cases, quickly putting pressure on the bruise with a cold, hard object like an ice pack stops the bruise from getting larger. The fact is that most kids do not cooperate with this maneuver, so it is rarely used effectively. Since bruises eventually get reabsorbed by the body it doesn't really matter if they are a little larger.

The body's process of reabsorbing the bruise entails breaking down the blood that is lying under the skin. This process actually changes the color of the bruise, and the age of the bruise can be estimated by the color.

1 to 2 days — blue/black

3 to 5 days — green

5 to 10 days — yellow and fading to skin color

Bruising on the forehead over the eyebrow can cause a "black eye" a few days after the injury as the blood under the skin migrates down the forehead into the region around the eye. This looks bad but is completely normal.

Scrapes — abrasions

When the outer layer of skin is scraped off, the wound is called an *abrasion*. Abrasions usually heal without scarring. The open skin of an abrasion should be washed with soap and water and triple antibiotic cream or ointment applied for one day to prevent infection. Abrasions are really burns caused by friction. Rarely, the abrasion is so deep that it is considered a second-degree burn. If there is total removal of skin from the wound, it should be treated as an abrasion but medical attention should be sought within 24 to 48 hours.

Covering a skin wound with a gauze bandage is okay to prevent contamination, but bandages should be removed at least daily and they should not be applied too tightly. Wounds heal better with air.

Puncture wounds

When a sharp object punctures the skin, the skin usually closes immediately, leaving a small hole. These wounds do not bleed much, and besides cleaning the little hole with soap and water, there is no treatment. The wound area has to be watched for a day or two to see if an infection has developed under the skin. Tetanus can be contracted from such a wound if the sharp object was outdoors and dirty. For this reason it is important to give DPT shots for protection.

One very specific wound can get very badly infected very quickly. This is the "sneaker foot" injury. That is, the sharp object penetrated the bottom of the foot *through the bottom of a sneaker.* This injury should be watched carefully, and special antibiotics must be given if an infection arises.

Burns

Most burns are caused by fire, hot objects or hot liquids. Some are caused by caustic chemicals like oven cleaners. All burns should be treated as soon as possible by cooling in cool water. Chemical burns should be rinsed continuously while emergency help is sought.

Burns are rated according to which layers of skin are damaged. *First-degree burns* are superficial and only cause redness at the time of the burn.

These burns, like sunburn are not really treatable. After a few days, the skin that was burned peels off but the under layer is intact so there is no danger of infection. Cooling the burn with cool water helps if it is applied quickly. If the burn is cooled immediately, the injury can be prevented from damaging deeper layers of the skin.

Second-degree burns destroy the outer layers of skin, which results in a blister or an area of open, raw skin. Blisters can be left intact. The water in them is sterile and infection cannot set in while the blister is unopened. These burns should be washed twice a day and antibiotic cream or silvadene should be applied. Burns that are open and larger than a quarter should be seen by a doctor within 24 to 48 hours. Any bandage applied should be porous-like gauze with a layer of non-stick telfa on the wound. Second-degree burns that are larger than the palm of the hand should be seen immediately by a physician.

Third-degree burns cause damage to all the layers of the skin, leaving the deep layers of fat and muscle exposed under the charred layers. These wounds are serious and must be seen by a physician or emergency room immediately. Third-degree burns will heal if they are not too large, but some require skin grafting. The risk of serious infection is much greater in these wounds.

Cuts — lacerations

Scratches are superficial cuts in the skin that look like red lines on the skin. These are easily managed by normal cleaning with soap and water and application of triple-antibiotic ointment once at the time of injury.

Lacerations are cuts in the skin which leave a gap between the edges of the wound.

There are two reasons to close a wound; First, to prevent infection, and second to improve the appearance of the scar. When the edges are brought together properly, the healing process is quick since the scar has to close only a very narrow gap. This closure prevents germs from entering the wound and leaves a thinner scar.

When a laceration occurs it is important to clean the wound and apply pressure with a clean cloth or gauze to stop the bleeding. The wider the gap, the wider the scar that will form when it heals. *If the wound edges lay together there is usually no need for repair.* Cleaning the wound with soap and water and covering it with triple-antibiotic ointment with a band aid is usually adequate. *If the wound is actually gaping so that the edges do not lie together, it is advisable to have a medical professional close the gap by either steri strips or glue or stitches.* Deep wounds need to be closed in layers with sutures by a physician.

Steri-strips

Steri-strips are tape-bandage strips that bridge the wound to pull the edges together. They are used for minor lacerations and sometimes to close the wound temporarily to prevent infection.

Skin glue

Skin glue is an alternative to sutures. The glue holds the wound's edges together while the healing process takes place. It is quick and painless and does not need a follow-up visit for removal of sutures. The resultant scar is often the same as it would be with sutures, but some doctors prefer sutures for a more acceptable cosmetic result. In my practice about 80 percent of lacerations are closed by skin glue. The medical professional who evaluates the wound will recommend which closure will be appropriate.

Sutures

Sutures or stitches are wound closures that are accomplished by sewing the edges together with a curved needle and specially designed thread. This procedure requires local anesthesia and restraint of the patient. Some suture materials dissolve by themselves, but most need to be removed by the physician several days later after the wound heals.

Facial lacerations

If the wound is in an area that would leave a noticeable scar, the quality of the closure is more important since the cosmetic appearance of the scarring must be minimized. These wounds usually need a plastic surgeon to treat them. Generally, facial lacerations that are not gaping widely that are horizontal (across the face) heal well with glue or steri-strips, but most lacerations that are vertical (up and down) require more careful closure. If the wound is in a non-cosmetic area such as under the chin line, plastic surgery is rarely required.

Lacerations of the lip usually heal without repair and without scarring, but if the laceration crosses the outer border of the lip line, a careful plastic surgery repair will be needed to prevent "notching" of the lip when it heals.

Lacerations inside the mouth heal well without treatment, as long as the bleeding is easily controlled.

Scalp lacerations bleed a lot. Pressure should be applied to the wound until the bleeding stops then the wound should be inspected. Sometimes only a tiny laceration is found, which will close on its own. However, often glue or stitches are required.

Every parent and caretaker should know basic first aid. It is important to stop the bleeding when a laceration occurs. This is done by applying pressure with a clean cloth, or gauze. Once the bleeding has stopped, the wound should be inspected and cleaned with soap and water. If the edges are not laying together, a medical professional should be consulted. Although many people feel that wound closure is an emergency, if the bleeding is stopped and the wound is clean and covered it is usually acceptable to wait up to 24 hours to repair.

CHAPTER 65

Understanding Medical Imaging

Key Points

- Medical imaging has come a long way from plain film x-rays.

- Sonography and MRIs do not expose the patient to radiation.

- Xrays, nuclear scans and CT scans expose the patient to radiation. They should be used only when necessary.

- Since the lifetime dose of radiation is cumulative, it is important to limit the amount of radiation exposure during child hood.

- Dental x-rays and mammograms have extremely small doses of radiation, so they can be done routinely.

Among the miracles of modern medicine, the development of medical imaging is one of the most amazing. When x-rays were first used in the early 1900s, doctors were miraculously able to see the bones inside the body. X-rays created a whole new way of evaluating patients. Bone x-rays showed fractures to help alignment. Soon chest x-rays became possible. This technique allowed doctors to view the patterns in the lungs that defined pneumonia, tuberculosis, and heart failure. X-rays of the rest of the body soon followed.

It was many years after the invention of x-ray that it became known that exposure to ionizing radiation can cause cancer. The early radiologists often developed skin cancer. Many died of leukemia and other cancers. We now know that the dose of radiation is cumulative and must be limited to protect long term health.

In the 1970s with the invention of computers, a dizzying array of new and much more informative imaging techniques were developed. As computers became faster and able to handle larger amounts of information, these new imaging modalities have become more and more available. Here is an overview of the different imaging methods used in children today. I have divided the topics into two groups — those that use radiation and those that do not.

IMAGING THAT USES RADIATION

X-rays

"Plain films" x-rays use ionizing radiation which is beamed through the patient onto a photographic plate or a digital receiver. The images are two-dimensional like a photograph. Since the amount of radiation a person receives is cumulative over a lifetime, it is important that the most modern machinery is used, which delivers the least radiation and the most focused beam.

To protect the unexposed parts of the body, lead aprons and shields are used to block any unnecessary exposure.

The most common x-rays are chest x-rays, abdominal x-rays, and x-rays of bones. "Plain films" are still a basic and important diagnostic tool. Sometimes *contrast* material is used to enhance the image of the x-ray, such as in an upper-GI x-ray. One of the most common uses of contrast in children is the test called a *VCUG, Voiding Cysto Urethrogram*. Contrast material is put into the bladder and then imaged during voiding. This important x-ray can show if the urine is refluxing into the ureters instead of coming out completely during urination.

Some x-rays such as mammograms and dental x-rays use extremely low doses of radiation that do not contribute to the lifetime dose more than normal background radiation that is experienced just living in the world.

Computed tomography — CT scans

The CT scan uses ionizing radiation like x-rays, but it takes many pictures in a few seconds. These images are interpreted by the machine's computers, which produce images in slices. The CT scans look like slices through the body done by a magical, painless knife. Each slice shows the organs and tissues in the plane of the image. With this method the brain, spine, chest, abdomen — almost everything in the body — can be imaged. Sometimes contrast material is injected to show the blood flow or other features in the area. CT scans are quick and available in emergency rooms.

They are often used to look for bleeding and fractures in a head injury or stroke. The only consideration is that the radiation dosage with CT scans is high. Even though the scan only takes a few short minutes, the amount of radiation is much higher than an x-ray.

Nuclear scans

For a nuclear scan, radioactive material is injected into the blood and taken up by the tissue to be examined. After a period of time the patient is scanned by a radiation-detecting device that localizes the place in the body where the radioisotope is concentrated and an image is made. Thyroid glands are often scanned in this way. The other use of nuclear scans in children is to look for hidden infections in the body. The dose of radiation is not high in most types of nuclear scans.

Positron emission tomography — PET scans

A tiny amount of radioactive material is injected into a vein and then detected by a scanner similar to other nuclear scans. But the PET scan is much more sophisticated. It provides a very detailed image of the actual energy-consuming activity in the area being scanned. It is used for evaluation of tumor tissue before and after treatment. *Brain PET scans* have enabled the imaging of which area of the brain is actually being used during thoughts and actions. This new information has enhanced our understanding of mental illness and degenerative brain diseases.

What radiation does to the body.

Radiation is all around us. Everyone is constantly bombarded with tiny amounts of radiation from the earth and, especially, the sun. This is called background radiation. The highest dose of radiation occurs naturally when a person is flying in an airplane, since the person is closer to the sun. Little by little we naturally accumulate all the radiation we receive over a lifetime. When the total amount of radiation becomes very high, it can accumulate to high levels in the body and can cause an increase in the incidence of cancer and other chronic problems. It is for this reason that it is advisable to limit the total dosage of radiation a child receives. Most imaging is done only occasionally and, with newer equipment the total dose is not dangerously high. The rule is to save the x-rays for when they are really needed, then use them as recommended by the physician.

IMAGING THAT DOES NOT USE RADIATION

Sonograms

Sonography is an imaging technique that uses ultra-high frequency sound waves to create the image. The sound waves are emitted by a transducer that sends the waves bouncing off the target. The rebound waves differ in various tissues .The computer uses these differences to produce a picture.

Sonography is used to image only soft tissue — not bone. It is used in obstetrics to image the fetus as it develops. It is used in the abdomen to look for cysts, tumors, ovarian problems, gall bladder, liver, spleen, and even appendicitis. It is used to examine the urinary tract, the thyroid gland, and many other structures. The test is painless. The sonography technician applies a jelly to the skin and moves the transducer around on the skin to obtain a clear picture. This modality is the only imaging that is totally dependent on the skill of the technician to get accurate images.

Echocardiograms

This is sonography of the heart. Echocardiography allows the imaging of the structure and function of the beating heart. It is used in all ages from prenatal to adults.

Doppler

This technique uses sound waves and specialized detectors to image blood flowing through a blood vessel. It is often used to assess veins to look for inflammation or clots. It is also used in echocardiography to observe the flow of blood through the heart and large blood vessels.

Magnetic resonance imaging – MRI

This imaging technique uses magnetic fields to produce detailed views in slices similar to the CT scan. The difference is that soft tissues are much better defined. Imaging the brain, central nervous system, internal organs, muscles and any soft tissue is most clearly shown on an MRI. The disadvantage of an MRI is that the imaging takes a much longer time — up to 30 to 40 minutes, depending on the size of the area.

The patient is put in a tunnel-like device and must lie still to get a proper image. There are a few open MRIs available for claustrophobic patients, but the images are not always of good quality.

To do an MRI on a baby or young child, an anesthesiologist is brought in to anesthetize the child and carefully monitor his vital signs during the time it takes to get the image.

MRIs are much more expensive than CT scans. They must be justified to the insurance company and approved prior to obtaining the test.

There are new MRIs being developed that can image a beating heart.

Final Thought

Imaging technology is rapidly advancing. It is now possible due to new computers to take a sonographic, CT, MRI or PETscan image and create a three-dimensional (3-D) picture of the part of the body that was scanned. The image can be rotated to see it from any angle. This is already being used every day in obstetrical sonograms.

Medical imaging has come a long way since the invention of the x-ray. We always look forward to see what will come next!

■ ■ ■

- *Autism's False Prophets: Bad Science, Risky Medicine, and the Search for a Cure*, by Paul A. Offit, MD (2008) — a complete and understandable explanation of the issues of autism and immunizations. It is very reassuring and much more authoritative than the things being written in the media.

- *Caring for Your Baby and Young Child: Birth to Age 5*, American Academy of Pediatrics, by Steven P. Shelov, MD, MS, FAAP (2004) — a basic information guide.

- *How to Talk So Kids Will Listen and Listen So Kids Will Talk (How to Help Your Child)*, by Adele Faber and Elaine Mazlish (1999) — a nice approach to communicating properly with your children.

- *Let's Stay Safe*, by Project Yes (2011), published by Artscroll/Mesorah Publications, Ltd. — a wonderful illustrated children's book that deals with child safety and personal safety.

- *Siblings Without Rivalry: How to Help Your Children Live Together So You Can Live Too*, by Adele Faber and Elaine Mazlish (2004) — a guide to dealing with jealous brothers and sisters.

- *Solve Your Child's Sleep Problem*, by Dr. Richard Ferber (1985) — describes a gentle, gradual method for weaning a baby or child off of settling methods that are not independent.

- *The Difficult Child: Expanded and Revised Edition*, by Stanley Turecki and Leslie Tonner (2000) — an excellent book to help parents understand and deal with a normal child who is difficult for everyone to live with.

- *The Explosive Child: A New Approach for Understanding and Parenting Easily Frustrated, Chronically Inflexible Children*, by Ross W. Greene (2005) — a practical approach for parents of a child who is prone to tantrums and rigid behavior.

- *The Secrets of a Baby Whisperer*, by Tracy Hogg (2005) — a guide to understanding what the baby needs and how the baby fits into the family life.

- *What To Do When You Worry Too Much; A Kid's Guide to Overcoming Anxiety*, by Dawn Huebner, Ph.D. (2005) — .

- *Your Baby's First Year*, by Steven Shelov (1998) — a medical guide.